C000037119

HARDPRESS.NET
HOME OF HARD-TO-FIND BOOKS

Memorials of Methodism in New Jersey
by John Atkinson

Copyright © 2019 by HardPress

Address:
HardPress
8345 NW 66TH ST #2561
MIAMI FL 33166-2626
USA
Email: info@hardpress.net

Memorials of Methodism in New Jersey

John Atkinson

THE N... YORK
PUBLIC LIBRARY

ASTOR, LENOX ...
T... ... ...

(ATHUSIN)

NEW YORK
PUBLIC LIBRARY

ASTOR, LENOX AND
TILDEN FOUNDATIONS

ENGRAVED BY P. B. WELCH FROM AN ORIGINAL DRAWING.

JAMES STIRLING.

MEMORIALS

OF

METHODISM IN NEW JERSEY,

FROM THE FOUNDATION OF THE FIRST SOCIETY IN THE STATE IN
1770, TO THE COMPLETION OF THE FIRST TWENTY
YEARS OF ITS HISTORY.

CONTAINING

SKETCHES OF THE MINISTERIAL LABORERS, DIS-
TINGUISHED LAYMEN, AND PROMINENT
SOCIETIES OF THAT PERIOD.

By Rev. JOHN ATKINSON,

OF THE NEWARK ANNUAL CONFERENCE.

SECOND EDITION.

PHILADELPHIA:
PERKINPINE & HIGGINS,
No. 56 NORTH FOURTH STREET.
1860.

289374

Entered according to the Act of Congress, in the year 1860, by

PERKINPINE & HIGGINS,

in the Clerk's Office of the District Court for the Eastern District of
Pennsylvania.

WILLIAM W. HARDING, STEREOTYPER.   C. SHERMAN & SON, PRINTERS.

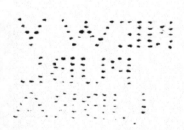

PREFACE.

THIS work consists of such important facts and incidents connected with the rise and progress of Methodism in New Jersey, within the first twenty years of its history, as could be obtained at this late day, and of sketches of most of the ministers who labored in the State during that period, and of several of the more prominent and influential laymen. I cannot claim to have gathered all, or even a considerable portion, of the facts illustrative of the work and of the laborers during those early years; but I have attempted to do what could be done towards rescuing such as were still within reach, but which were rapidly passing down the current of time into oblivion's unfathomable depths. The ministers of that period have all passed away, and with them have perished many important reminiscences of their labors and of the early trials and triumphs of the Church. But very few of the laity who lived and prayed in those chivalric times yet linger behind their associates who have gone to heaven, and, consequently, the material for such a work was meagre. But I have gleaned from nearly every available source such facts as would tend to

3

DUP. EXCH. 30 AUG 1904

throw light upon those early years of our history, and I have succeeded in rescuing many which otherwise would, in all probability, have soon been irrecoverably lost. I deeply regret that this effort was not made sooner. Had it been attempted twenty-five years ago, preachers who were prominent in the struggles of that day might have been consulted, and their recollections would have greatly enriched such a work, and been of incalculable worth to the Church. But for this, alas! it is now too late; yet wisdom dictates that we should make haste to gather what still remains to remind us of the labors, sacrifices, and successes of our fathers. The period immediately following that embraced in this volume is within the recollection of some yet living, and no time should be lost in gathering such reminiscences from them as may be of service in a subsequent work, by whomsoever it may be prepared. Fifty years hence such data will be invaluable.

As the period about which I have written is so remote, I have had to rely mainly upon printed documents for authority. The books and periodicals from which the larger portion of the material for this volume has been derived are, to a considerable extent, entirely beyond the reach of the general reader; many of the more important of them having long been out of print, and could not be purchased for any price whatsoever. In addition to this I have gathered from original sources very important data, which have never appeared in print before. Such as it is, the work is sent forth with the humble hope and the ardent prayer that it may be an instrument of blessing to such as may read it.

I am greatly indebted for important favors in the preparation of the work to Rev. Drs. Whedon and Porter of Newark,

Ex. Gov. Fort, New Egypt, N. J., Revs. H. B. Beegle, F. A.
Morrell, and G. R. Snyder of the New Jersey Conference,
Rev. Dr. Roberts, Baltimore, Rev. John Lee, West Bloomfield,
N. J., Revs. E. W. Adams and J. P. Daily of the Newark
Conference, and others. I would also gratefully acknowledge
my obligations to Rev. S. H. Opdyke, A.M. for kindly ex-
amining most of the work before it was stereotyped, and for
valuable suggestions

CONTENTS.

CHAPTER IV.

CHAPTER V.

CHAPTER VI.

CHAPTER VII.

CHAPTER VIII.

CONTENTS.

CHAPTER I.

CHAPTER II.

CHAPTER III.

7

CHAPTER IV.

CHAPTER V.

CHAPTER VI.

CHAPTER VII.

CHAPTER VIII.

CHAPTER IX.

CHAPTER X.

CHAPTER XI.

CHAPTER XII.

CHAPTER XIII.

CHAPTER XIV.

CHAPTER XV.

CHAPTER XVI.

CHAPTER XVII.

CHAPTER XXI.

MEMORIALS OF

METHODISM IN NEW JERSEY

CHAPTER I.

RISE OF METHODISM IN NEW JERSEY.

WHEN the Wesleyan reformation began to spread over New Jersey, it was exceedingly small and feeble. A Methodist in those days, was a rare phenomenon. The first of this sect, of whom we have any information, was JOHN EARLY, a native of Ireland, where he was born in the year 1738. He immigrated to this country in 1764, and settled in New Jersey. Somewhere between this period and 1770, as near as can be determined by the record,* he embraced the doctrines of the Gospel as presented by Methodism; but whether there was at that time any regular Methodist society in the province cannot be affirmed. However, he lived respected and useful in the communion of the church of his choice for

---

* Christian Advocate and Journal, 1829, p. 160.

about sixty years, when he died at the advanced age of four score and ten.

He resided in Gloucester county, and for forty years filled the offices of class leader and steward on the circuit to which he belonged.   He was a consistent Christian, a faithful friend, an obliging neighbor, a kind husband, and a fond parent—devoted to the interests and welfare of those whom Providence had committed to his care.   His long life of fidelity contributed much, doubtless, to the prosperity of the cause of Christ in the region where he lived; and in the history of Methodism in the State, his example appears like a lone star shining in a clear place in the heavens, and shedding its serene effulgence upon the darkness, clouds, and tempest of a dreary and fearful night.

While he was one of the first in New Jersey to identify himself with the people called Methodists, he also gave, at an early and trying period in the history of the denomination, a son to the itinerant ministry of the Church.   That son, the REV. WILLIAM EARLY, remembering his Creator in the days of his youth, entered upon the arduous life of an itinerant at the age of twenty-one. In 1791, by appointment of the New York Conference, he bore the cross into the wilds of Nova Scotia and New Brunswick.   He prosecuted his mission there about two years, during which time he traveled extensively through those provinces, encountering great difficulties, performing severe labors, and suffering persecution for Christ's sake.   He was arrested and imprisoned, but when released he went on his way rejoicing in God, and preaching to the people the glorious Gospel of Christ.   He traveled in New Brunswick in the winter on foot, bearing his saddle bags upon his back.   When, in 1793, he left that region, he had become so reduced in his pecuniary resources that he could not command enough means to pay his passage from St. Johns to New York, until he sold his saddle bags and a pair of shoes.   Though in his father's house in New Jersey there was "bread enough and to spare," yet as a stranger in a strange land, whither he had gone to carry the bread of life to the perishing, in addition to his other trials he was subjected to the stern pressure of absolute poverty.

He continued to labor within the bounds of the Philadelphia Conference, part of the time as a located minister, but chiefly in the itinerancy, until his death, which occurred on the first day of June 1821.   He was the victim of pulmonary disease, and endured great affliction in his last days.   Several of his brethren occasionally visited him, and generally found him happy in the love of his Saviour.   In the full assurance of faith, rejoicing in hope of the glory hereafter to be revealed, he met death in triumph and departed in peace.   He was a worthy son of New Jersey Methodism, whom she early gave to labor, suffer, and triumph in the missionary and itinerant field. His works follow him, and his record is on high.

But Methodism, in its ecclesiastical form, owes its origin in New Jersey, under God, to the labors of a local preacher, an officer in the British army, Captain THOMAS WEBB. The first Methodist society in the city of New York was formed in the latter part of the year 1766, by Philip Embury, a local preacher who had emigrated from Ireland about six years previously. The infant society was soon joined by the zealous cáptain, who was as brave a soldier of the cross as he was of his king. He soon proceeded to Philadelphia, and lifted the standard of Methodism in that city and formed the first class there in 1767 or 1768.* As New Jersey lies between these two cities, and its upper territory is close adjacent to the former, and its southern to the latter city, it is to be presumed that those earnest pioneers of Methodism would not long prosecute their mission without carrying their message of mercy to its inhabitants.

Accordingly we find Captain Webb preaching justification by faith in the town of Burlington, New Jersey, as early as the year 1770. It is probable, indeed, that he preached in the province at a little earlier

* Christian Advocate and Journal, 1829, p. 120.

period than this, but in that year he was stationed in Burlington on duty, and preached in the market house and in the court house.*   On the 14th of December 1770, he formed a small class, and appointed Joseph Toy, who will shortly receive more particular notice in our narrative, its leader.   Mr. Toy is, probably, entitled to the honor of being the first class-leader in New Jersey. As Captain Webb laid the foundation of Methodism in New Jersey, it is fitting that in tracing its progress to its subsequent commanding position and influence, the memorialist should pause to pay a respectful and grateful tribute to his character.

He was a lieutenant under Gen. Wolfe at the capture of Quebec in 1759, where he received a wound in the arm, and lost his right eye.   He was converted under the ministry of Rev. John Wesley, after enduring severe mental struggles in which he was led to almost despair of the divine mercy.   This happy event occurred at Bath, England, about the year 1765.   He joined the Methodist society, and soon commenced to exercise his gifts as a public speaker.   "The congregation with which he was waiting being disappointed of their preacher, he was called upon to address them, which he did with such acceptance as soon to induct him into the office of a local preacher.   Soon after this event he was appointed Bar-

* Methodist Magazine, 1826, p. 438.

2

rack-master in Albany, in the province of New York, whither he immediately removed with his family. Here, establishing ' a church in his own house,' several of his neighbors desired permission to be present at his family worship, which was granted. To these he soon adopted the practice of addressing a word of exhortation; and thus Albany became one of the first scenes for the display of Wesleyan zeal and devotion, although with no immediate results. Being in New York about this time, he heard of the little society under Mr. Embury, and in the true spirit of ' a soldier of the cross,' he was not ashamed of the great difference between their social position and his own, and sought them out."*

One day, while they were engaged in worship in a room they had rented for that purpose, near the barracks, " the most infamous part of the city," they were surprised by the appearance of a dignified figure in the midst of them, in the uniform of a British officer. At first his presence caused them some alarm, but they soon observed that he knelt in prayer with them, and paid due regard to all the proprieties of the place and the occasion. He at once made himself known to them, and "this event constituted an era in their progress."

He now opened his spiritual mission in New York, and boldly proclaimed the gospel to the people. " The nov-

* Rev. S. W. Coggeshall in Methodist Quarterly Review, Oct., 1855.

elty of a man in regimentals, with his sword and *chapeau* laid at his side, preaching the gospel of peace, immediately attracted crowds to hear."* He united, in an eminent degree, the more noble characteristics of the soldier with the earnest zeal and heroic enthusiasm of the sect to which he belonged. He declared to his auditors "that all their knowledge and religion were not worth a rush, unless their sins were forgiven, and they had the witness of the Spirit with theirs that they were the children of God." This "increased the surprise and amazement of some, while others, more thoughtful and considerate, were led to seek this pearl of great price." He soon went forth into the regions beyond, proclaiming the word, and sowed the seed of Methodism on Long Island and elsewhere.

It is not known with certainty how long, at this time, he remained in this country, but in 1772, Mr. Wesley, in a letter, speaks of him as being in Dublin, Ireland, and says, "He is a man of fire, and the power of God constantly accompanies his word." In 1773, he also speaks of his preaching at the Foundry Chapel in London, and says, "I admire the wisdom of God in still raising up various preachers, according to the various tastes of men. The captain is all life and fire; therefore, though he is not deep or regular, yet many, who would not hear a

* Rev. S. W. Coggeshall in Methodist Quarterly Review, Oct. 1855.

better preacher, flock together to hear him.   And many
are convinced under his preaching, some justified, a few
built up in love."   Ten years later he says, Captain
Webb "lately kindled a flame here," (in the neighborhood of Bath,) "and it is not yet gone out.   Several
persons were still rejoicing in God.   I found his preaching in the street of Winchester had been blessed greatly.
Many were more or less convinced of sin, and several
had found peace with God.   I never saw the house so
crowded with serious and attentive hearers."   In 1785,
he bears similar testimony to his labors and usefulness.

His labors were productive of great good in this
country.   An incident "connected with the very existence" of Methodism in Schenectady, New York, may
be properly mentioned here as an illustration of the
effect produced by his ministry.   "Conversing with an
aged member of our church the other day," writes Rev.
George Coles, in the Christian Advocate of February
10, 1827, "I had the curiosity to ask him *when, where,*
and *how* he was first convinced of sin, &c.   He informed
me that a Mr. Van Patten, a blacksmith, was the means,
in the hands of God, of opening his eyes.   Do you
know, said I, how the blacksmith was awakened?   'Seeing a black man die happy in the Lord,' said he.   Do
you know, said I, how the black man came by his serious
impressions?   'His master was a religious man and

taught him the fear of the Lord.' And where did he [the master] meet with his conviction? said I. 'Hearing Captain Webb preach,' said he. It is also remarkable that this aged friend's mother was awakened under Captain Webb."

In the year 1774, he was again, as we shall see, in New Jersey, and also in Philadelphia. During the session of the Continental Congress of this year, the elder Adams heard him preach, and bears a high tribute to his ability as a public speaker. The testimony of this eminent statesman ought, we think, to go far towards deciding the question concerning the rank his mental qualifications entitled him to hold, as a preacher of the gospel. That testimony is as follows: "In the evening I went to the Methodist meeting and heard Mr. Webb, the old soldier, who first came to America in the character of a Quarter Master, under General Braddock. He is one of the most fluent, eloquent men I ever heard; he reaches the imagination and touches the passions very well, and expresses himself with great propriety."

Captain Webb possessed a clear and happy experience of Divine things; yet it is said "that he always took care to guard weak believers against casting away their confidence, because they could not always realize the same bright testimony of their justification by faith in

Christ with which he had been so highly favored."* He was accustomed to relate his own Christian experience to illustrate and confirm the truths he proclaimed respecting experimental piety.

The death of the old veteran is said to have occurred suddenly. "Having a presentiment of his approaching dissolution, a few days before his death he expressed his wishes to a friend respecting the place and manner of his interment, adding, 'I should prefer a triumphant death; but I may die suddenly. However, I know I am happy in the Lord and shall be with him, and that is sufficient.' A little after 10 o'clock on the 20th of December, 1796, after taking his supper and praying with his family; he went to his bed in apparent good health; but shortly after his breathing became difficult; he arose and sat at the foot of the bed; but, while Mrs. Webb was standing by him, he fell back on the bed, and before any other person could be called, he sunk into the arms of death without any apparent pain, aged 72 years."†

Thus ended the labors and the life of the hero of the first battle of Methodism in New Jersey, and the founder of one of the most commanding and powerful ecclesiastical structures in the State. His name and virtues deserve a chief place in the registry of the cause upon its

* Bang's History of the M. E. Church, Vol. 2.   † *Ibid.*

historical records, and are worthy of being enshrined forever in the hearts of New Jersey Methodists.

JOSEPH TOY, who, as we have seen, was appointed leader of the first class in Burlington, was born in New Jersey, April 24, 1748. His father, who was a descendant of the first settlers of the province, died when he was a child. When young, he was placed in the boarding-school of Mr. Thomas Powell, in Burlington, where he remained until about the twentieth year of his age. While there his mind was much impressed by a sermon delivered by a clergyman of the Protestant Episcopal Church, on the being and omnipresence of God. These impressions were lasting. Impelled to do something by which he might obtain deliverance from the wrath of his Maker, he strictly observed the claims of morality, expecting by his works to render himself acceptable to God. He now heard the gospel from the lips of Captain Webb, in Burlington, and was offended at first at the doctrine which he preached. He was unwilling to relinquish his self-righteousness, and be justified by faith alone. At length, deeply sensible that the justification of which he heard was necessary to his happiness, he sought it with all his heart, and after various painful exercises, he obtained a sense of the Divine favor, and rejoiced therein with joy unspeakable. From this time he felt bound to devote his all to the service and glory of God.

In a year or less from the time he was placed in the charge of the class in Burlington, he removed to Trenton. He there found a man who had been a Methodist in Ireland. With this man and two or three more, he united, and agreeing among themselves, they met together in class. Thus was formed in 1771 the first Methodist society in the city of Trenton, the most prominent member, perhaps, of which, was the result of Captain Webb's ministry.

In the meantime, the feeble band .in Burlington was cared for. The first place in New Jersey in which it appears Asbury preached, was that town. He landed in Philadelphia from a port near Bristol, England, on the 27th of October, 1771. On the 7th of November, he went to Burlington, on his way to New York, "and preached in the Court-house to a large, serious congregation." He felt there, he says, his "heart much opened." He proceeded on his journey to New York, and met with one P. Van Pelt, who had heard him preach in Philadelphia. Mr. Van Pelt resided on Staten Island, and invited him to his house, which invitation he accepted, and preached at his house, and in the evening at the house of one Justice Wright, where he had a large company to listen to the word. To Asbury therefore, is the honor due of first sounding the trump of Methodism on that beautiful and fruitful Island. He remained laboring in New York and vicinity, until the 21st of February, 1772, when, "having a desire to see his friends on Staten Island, he set off, contrary to the persuasion of his friends in" the city. He was received and kindly entertained by Justice Wright and preached at Mr. Van Pelt's "to a few persons with much satisfaction." He was invited to preach in the house of one Mr. D., which he did, Justice Wright sending him "there on the Lord's day with several of his family." He preached twice at that gentleman's house to a large company. "Some," he says, "had not heard a sermon for half a year; such a famine there is of the word in these parts, and a still greater one of the *pure* word." He returned to Justice Wright's in the evening, "and preached to a numerous congregation with comfort." He says, "Surely God sent me to these people at the first, and I trust he will continue to bless them, and pour out his Spirit upon them, and receive them at last to himself." He preached three times more on the Island, and then on his way to New York he took his stand at the Ferry, and preached "to a few people."

After preaching in Amboy, in a large upper room to many hearers, in which he "was much favoured in his own soul," and receiving evidences of respect and kindness from an innkeeper there, he started on the 27th of February for Burlington. He rode a "rough-gaited horse," by whom he was "much shaken," and finding the road very bad, and himself and horse weary, he stopped, at the invitation of a Quaker, at or near Cross-wicks, on whom he called to inquire the way, and lodged in his house. He was treated with much kindness by his host, and the next day rode to Burlington, "very weary." The day following was the Sabbath, and he preached in the court-house to many hearers.

The work was now extending. New Mill,* a small village several miles from Burlington, presented its claims upon his attention and labors, and accordingly he rode over in a wagon with some friends, and "preached in a Baptist meeting-house, and was kindly received." He remained until the next day, when, finding the people were divided among themselves, he preached from the words, "This is his commandment, that we should believe on the name of his Son, Jesus Christ, and love one another." He indulged hope that his labor was not in vain. He returned in the evening to Burlington.

On Wednesday, the 29th of April, we again find him at Burlington; where he "found the people very lively." "Two persons," he says, "have obtained justification under brother W.; and a certain Dr. T——t, a man of

* Afterwards called Pemberton.

dissipation, was touched under brother B.'s sermon last night. I admire the kindness of my friends to such a poor worm as I. O my God, remember them, remember me." The next day he writes, " I humbly hope the word was blest to a large number of people who attended while I preached at the court-house." He departed to Philadelphia, but on Tuesday the 5th of May, he was again in Burlington. He preached to a serious people, but felt troubled in soul that he was not more devoted. "O my God," he exclaims, " my soul groans and longs for this !" On the day following, he writes, " My heart was much humbled ; but the Lord enabled me to preach with power in my soul!" The next day he visited some prisoners, and one of them, who was to be tried for his life, seemed much affected. In the evening he preached " and felt," he says, " my heart much united to this people." The next morning he "set off for Philadelphia," but in five days afterward, we again find him in New Jersey, in the neighborhood of Greenwich, where he speaks of preaching on "Behold I stand at the door and knock," and says, "Oh what a time of power was this to my own soul !" After this, he went to one Mr. T.'s, and many persons assembled at eight o'clock, to whom he preached with life. He speaks also of going " to the new Church," and after preaching with great assistance, lodged at I——c J——s, who conducted him

in the morning to Gloucester, whence he went by water
to Philadelphia. If this new Church belonged to the
Methodists, it is probable that it was about the first which
they erected in the province.

Asbury was one of the first preachers that visited the
little society at Trenton and preached to them. We
find him there proclaiming his message on Wednesday,
the 20th day of May, 1772; and he says, "As the
court was sitting, I was obliged to preach in a school-
house to but few people; and as there were soldiers in
the town, I could hardly procure lodging." The few
Methodists who resided there at the time were not, it is
probable, in circumstances to furnish very superior
entertainment to the preachers.

On Sunday, the 24th of May, Asbury was again in
Greenwich, and preached to about three hundred people
who had assembled from different parts. In the afternoon, at three o'clock, he preached at Gloucester, to
about two hundred people, and then went up the river,
in a boat, to Philadelphia, where he preached at night.
The next day he was unwell, but went to Burlington, and
though he was very sick, he preached in the evening.
The following day he was still unwell; but, ever anxious
to obey the call of duty, he visited a prisoner under sentence of death, and "strove much to fasten conviction
on his heart." On Wednesday he went to New Mills,

where he preached at four o'clock, and again at ten the next morning. On Friday, he was at the execution, and preached under the jail-wall. He attended the prisoner to the place of execution. "When he came forth, he roared like a bull in a net. He looked on every side and shrieked for help." Asbury prayed with him and for him, but he says, "How difficult it is (if I may use the term) to drench a hardened sinner with religion!" He saw him "tied up," and then stepping on a wagon, he "warned the people to flee from the wrath to come, and improve the day of their gracious visitation, no more grieving the Spirit of God, lest a day should come in which they might cry, and God refuse to hear them." He then returned to Philadelphia, where he exhorted in the evening.

On Tuesday, the 2nd of June, Asbury is again in New Jersey, at Haddonfield. The next day he preached at five at Mantua Creek, and had a time of power. After the service was over, about a hundred people went to Mr. F.'s, one and a half miles off, where he also "preached with life." On Thursday he was at Greenwich, weak in body, but had some liberty in preaching to about two hundred willing people; "but at Gloucester," he says, "I preached only to a few dead souls, from this striking passage, ' The word preached did not profit them, not being mixed with faith in them that heard it.' " He observes that in this journey he was kept in peace, "and had more freedom, life, and power than ever he had experienced in the city."

On Sunday, the 7th of June, he preached and held a love-feast in Philadelphia, and "some of our Jersey friends," he says, "spoke of the power of God with freedom." The next day he proceeded with much disagreeable company to Trenton, where many felt the Divine power accompanying the word preached. Two days afterwards, he returned to Philadelphia, after which he visited Bristol, Pennsylvania, and on returning, he soon proceeded to Burlington, and though weak and infirm in body, he preached with liberty. He then bent his course for New Mills, groaning for more life, and desiring to reach greater attainments in holiness. After preaching there twice, he returned to Burlington, whence, after spending a sick night, he proceeded, quite unwell, to Philadelphia. A few days afterward he walked down to Gloucester Point, and then rode to a brother C.'s, and though very weak, weary, and wet, he preached with some degree of power, while it rained very hard, to many people from the text, " As the rain cometh down, and the snow from heaven, and returneth not thither, but watereth the earth, and maketh it bring forth and bud, that it may give seed to the sower and bread to the eater; so shall my word be that goeth forth out of my mouth; it shall not return unto me void, but it shall accomplish that which I please, and it shall prosper in the thing whereto I sent it." At Greenwich, he met a Mr. S., who preached and baptized several people that seemed deeply affected. He went to Gloucester, and called on Esquire P., and presented him a petition for raising one hundred and fifty pounds to discharge the debt on the preaching house in Philadelphia. He promised both to contribute toward the object himself, and propose it to others.

On Monday, the 29th of June, after a Sabbath "of sweet rest to his soul," in which the Lord gave him "power to speak with some affection," Asbury again left Philadelphia for Trenton. His conveyance was by stage, in which there was "some loose and trifling company." After preaching in the evening with some life and energy, he went the next day and preached in the field, and then returned, and enjoyed liberty, while he preached to many people in the court-house. On the following Wednesday, he "went over the ferry and preached to many people, among whom were some fine women who behaved with airs of great indifference." He then returned to Trenton and preached at night, and again the next morning at five, after which he "set off for Philadelphia." On his return, he again fell into "unprofitable company," among whom he says, "I sat still as a man dumb, and as one in whose mouth there was no reproof. They appeared so stupidly ignorant, sceptical, deistical, and atheistical, that I thought if there were no other hell, I should strive with all my might to shun that."

He was again in Burlington on Saturday, the 4th of July. He went there to attend the execution of a murderer, "and declared to a great number of people under the jail wall, 'He healeth the broken in heart!' The poor criminal appeared penitent, behaved with great solidity, and expressed a desire to leave the world." He then returned to Philadelphia, and delivered an exhortation that night, and after spending a peaceful Sabbath, departed again on Monday for Burlington. He remained there three days, labouring among the people, and "many," he says, "seemed much stirred up to seek the kingdom of God." He then returned to Philadelphia, where he remained a few days, and then went to New Jersey again, and preached near Mantua Creek,* at his friend, Mr. T.'s, and though it was the time of harvest, nearly one hundred people assembled; and while he discoursed on the words, " Ye were sometime in darkness, but now are ye light in the Lord," many felt the power

* So I judge from the connection, and from collating this with other passages in the Journal. Sometimes there is indefiniteness in the Journals in regard to localities.

of the truth. He delivered another sermon the same day, and the next went to Greenwich, where he felt much "shut up" while preaching to about a hundred people, on "Fear not, little flock." He then went to Gloucester, which, he says, " is one of the dullest places I have seen in this country." The same night he went to Haddonfield, and the next day preached "to a few attentive hearers, who seemed much affected by the truths of God." One man especially, who had been much devoted to company and liquor, was much concerned on account of his past life; but Asbury entertained fears that his impressions would not be permanent. The man, however, accompanied him to the ferry, whence he proceeded, on Friday, to Philadelphia, where he arrived "time enough for intercession, and found it a good time, both then and at the evening preaching." On the Sabbath, after preaching in the morning, he set out in the afternoon for Trenton, where he did not arrive until noon on Monday, but at night he proclaimed the word with a good degree of animation.

During this short visit of two days, to Trenton, he met the society and gave them tickets. The society showed signs of growth, as it now, though in about the first year of its existence, had nineteen members in its communion. Mr. Asbury denominated them "a serious

3

people," and saw a prospect of much good being accomplished there.

Mr. Toy, to whom we may now properly revert, was still an efficient labourer with the little band in Trenton. They were supplied occasionally with preaching by Bishop Asbury, and the other preachers subsequently stationed in Philadelphia, until the storm of the Revolution burst upon them, when the English preachers fled from the country, and they were left with none to break to them the bread of life. Notwithstanding, however, the greatness of their difficulties and the smallness of their number, they succeeded, by extraordinary exertion, in erecting a small frame house for Divine worship. In this humble temple Mr. Toy held weekly meetings, and the little society held on its way; but in 1776, they were called to suffer an important loss in the removal of Mr. Toy and his family to Maryland.

In his new home he manifested the same spirit of devotion to God and Methodism which had previously characterized him. He opened his house for preaching, and became the leader of a class. In November, 1779, he removed, at the instance of Bishop Asbury, to Abingdon, subsequently the seat of Cokesbury College. Here he instituted prayer meetings, and read Mr. Wesley's sermons to the people, and became the leader of a small class which had been formed there. He was also the instrument of building there a house of worship, which stood for many years, a monument of his devotion and zeal. In July 1787, the Conference was held in Abingdon, and as the facilities for entertaining the preachers were limited, Mr. Toy lodged twelve at his own house.

Not far from this time he became an instructor in Cokesbury College. He was elected to this position on account of his knowledge of Mathematics and English Literature. About 1789 or 1790, he began to preach, and in October 1797, he was ordained a Deacon. In 1801, he entered upon the privations and toils of an itinerant life, and was appointed to Baltimore circuit. He was subjected to discouragement in his work by being tempted to doubt his call to the ministry. He endured painful struggles of mind on this account, but finally obtained a complete victory over his subtle adversary. On one occasion, having preached several times with but little apparent effect, and having lost his horse, he attempted to walk a distance of five miles with his saddle-bags on his arm. The suggestion entered his mind that this had befallen him because he had undertaken a work to which God had not called him. He retired into the woods, oppressed beyond measure, and wrestled in fervent prayer, with God, requesting an evidence of his call to the work if he were truly called. His prayer was heard, and that day several souls were awakened and converted to God.

When the service was concluded, the man of the house informed him that his horse was found and lodged in his stable. From that day he never doubted his Divine vocation to the ministerial office.

He continued to perform the work of an itinerant Methodist preacher for about seventeen years, during which time he showed himself a workman that needed not to be ashamed, rightly dividing the word of truth. He travelled the following circuits respectively, namely, Calvert, 1802; Norfolk, 1803; Severn, 1804; Prince George's, 1805; Montgomery, 1806; Frederick, 1807; Severn, 1808; Great Falls, 1809–10; Calvert, 1811; Severn, 1812; Baltimore circuit, 1813; Great Falls, 1814–15; Harford, 1816–17; Prince George's, 1818. In 1819, he passed into the honored, but unenviable company of his superannuated co-laborers, where he remained, preaching almost every Sabbath, and sometimes twice, never failing to fulfil his engagements, until December 1825.

He fell at his post, with his armor on, and his hand clasping the Spirit's sword which he had wielded so successfully in many a fierce and trying conflict. He was conducted from the pulpit to his death bed, on which he declared his submission to the will of God. He testified that he had a Divine assurance of the peace and love of God, that he had trusted in Him for fifty-five years, and now rested his whole soul upon his promise.   Thus believing and thus sustained, he tranquilly met the inevitable hour, and passed serenely to his reward on high, on the evening of Saturday, the 28th of January, 1826.

Mr. Toy possessed an intellect naturally strong, and a very retentive memory.   In addition to the liberal academical advantages which he enjoyed in his youth at Burlington, his mind was stored by diligent attention to reading.   He was deeply read in the works held in the highest estimation by the Church, and he especially delighted in the Holy Scriptures.   These he studied with unwearied attention, and was thus prepared to bring forth out of the treasury, things both new and old.   He was a first cousin to the late Bishop White, of the Protestant Episcopal Church, and was, says a Methodist authority,* one of the purest men and soundest preachers known to early Methodism.

* Rev. William Hamilton, Baltimore, Md.

CHAPTER II.

PROGRESS OF THE WORK UNTIL THE FIRST CONFERENCE.

AFTER his visit to Trenton, Asbury returned to Philadelphia, but was shortly in New Mills again, preaching the word both evening and morning. He found them a very affectionate people. He then went to Burlington, where he found many friends from Philadelphia, and they had at night a time of power. He departed the next morning for Amboy, which place he reached after a tedious journey through much rain and over bad roads. He took lodging at a tavern, as there was probably no other place for the entertainment of a Methodist preacher. He, however, was kept in peace in his journey and felt great courage in the work of God. He preached to a small congregation at Amboy, but they did not appear to have much relish for the word, and he entertained but a small hope for the place.

He again visited Staten Island, and preached to large congregations at Mr. Van Pelt's and Justice Wright's.

He then proceeded to New York and labored to promote the interests of the work there and in the vicinity. During this time he visited Amboy again and dined with a mixed company of Assemblymen, Churchmen, and Quakers. With characteristic sincerity he proclaimed his message, and, though many of them went to hear him for sport, "they went away very still." On one occasion, when he went to Staten Island, Justice Wright met him and informed him that the court was holding its sessions and engrossed the attention of the people. He then proceeded to the ferry, and lifted up his voice in behalf of the truth, while many people listened attentively to his word. "Hitherto," he exclaims, "hath the Lord helped me!"

On the nineteenth of October he started from New York in a stage across Jersey for Philadelphia. He was annoyed during the journey by the profanity of a young man, who was a fellow passenger. Asbury determined to reprove him when a suitable opportunity offered. At length he found such an opportunity, when none but himself and another person were left in the vehicle with him, when he told him how his conduct had grieved him. He received the admonition quite well, and excused himself by saying he did not think what he was doing. He afterward appeared to exercise more care over his words. They stopped at New Brunswick to dine, and then procceded to Princeton, a place Mr. Asbury had long desired to see, on account of the pious Mr. Davies, who was the late president of the college there. He tarried there during the night, and the next day went to Trenton, but, on arriving there he found that a drunken sailor had locked up the court-house, so he was obliged to preach in a school-house, where he had a comfortable meeting. He also preached at five o'clock the next morning. The day following he went over the river and preached, and then returned and proclaimed the word in the evening at Trenton to an audience in which there were many young people.

The following Sabbath was spent in Burlington, where he was much dejected in spirit, but felt greatly assisted in preaching, and the truth reached the hearts of the people. After preaching at five o'clock the next morning he left for Philadelphia, where he again preached in the evening.

After an absence of nearly six months, in which he traveled and labored in portions of Delaware and Maryland, he again appears in New Jersey, where he preached at different points, and often to large congregations, from Saturday, the seventeenth, till Thursday, the twenty-second of April, 1773. Speaking of this visit, he says; "The Lord was frequently with us in mercy and power; and my heart was greatly enlarged. How I long to be more holy—to live more with God and for God! Troubles encompass me about; but the Lord is my helper. Before my return to Philadelphia I had the pleasure of seeing the foundation laid of a new preaching house, thirty-five feet by thirty."*

While Asbury was traveling to and fro preaching the word publicly, and performing as much labor of this kind as most clergymen, at the present day, would consider sufficient to tax the energies of nearly a half dozen men, he was not unmindful of the more personal work of a pastor.

Hence, while on a tour "through the Jerseys" in May of this year, we find him speaking faithfully and closely to a certain man, who, he says, "has a great regard for us, but seems to be too much taken up with worldly cares." He showed him the deceitfulness of riches in producing a spirit of independence towards God, hard-

---

* Though I have no data, by which to determine, with certainty, the location of this "preaching house," I think it highly probable it was Trenton. The society there must have commenced to build about this time, as they had their house erected and Mr. Toy held service in it some time before he removed to Maryland, which was in 1776, three years after the foundation here mentioned was laid. This opinion is strengthened by the fact that Asbury frequently preached in Trenton, and it is not improbable, therefore, that he was there on that occasion. See p. 46.

ness of heart, and pride in its various forms, while they promise safety and happiness.

The Methodist preachers of that early day, though having authority from the Great Head of the Church, in virtue of their Divine call, to perform all the offices of the ministry, and consequently to administer the Sacraments, had not received Episcopal ordination, and it was not considered proper, therefore, for them to perform this part of religious service. Hence, the preachers themselves, as well as their people, were accustomed to go to the Episcopal Churches to receive the Sacrament of the Lord's Supper, which was sometimes administered by unholy hands. One of the rules for the government of the connection, agreed to by all the preachers present at the first Conference, in 1773, was, that " all the people, among whom we labor, are to be earnestly exhorted to attend the Church and receive the ordinances there."* Accordingly, on Sabbath afternoon, the sixth of June, after preaching in the morning at Burlington, Mr. Asbury went to Church in order to receive the Sacrament. " The parson," he says, " gave us a strange discourse, full of inconsistency and raillery. Leaving him to answer for his own conduct, I took no further notice of it, but preached that night from these words, ' The natural man

---

* Sketch of Rev. Philip Gatch, by Hon. John McLean, LL. D. Judge of the Supreme Court of the United States.

receiveth not the things of the Spirit of God, &c.,' and showed, First, what the things of God are. Secondly, described the natural man. And, Thirdly, showed how they appear to be foolishness to him; and that he cannot know them by the strength of his natural or acquired abilities." The little society in Burlington, he continues, appears to be in a comfortable and prosperous state. He proceeded to Trenton, where many people assembled to hear him preach, though but a short notice had been given of the service. During this visit to Trenton he writes, "My soul has been much assaulted lately by Satan; but, by the grace of God, it is filled with Divine peace. My heart thirsteth for God, even for the living God. I wrote to Mr. Wesley to day, and in the evening addressed my discourse, chiefly, to the young people. May the Lord apply it to their hearts."

We have thus traced, with some degree of particularity, at the risk of wearying the reader with the sameness of the narrative, the movements of Mr. Asbury in the State from the time he first preached within its limits till the session of the first Conference held in America. We have done this because these records are essential to our narrative, and because they cast light upon the infant Methodism of the province, which is furnished from no other source. In these brief memorials which

Asbury has bequeathed us, we catch just and reliable, if not dazzling, glimpses of the early struggles and progress of the cause.

That most remarkable man, Benjamin Abbott, joined the society this year. He was converted the twelfth of October of the previous year. He was a very wicked man until about the fortieth year of his age, being addicted to drinking, fighting, swearing, gambling, and kindred vices, yet he was industrious and provided well for his household. Sometimes, during his life of sin, he was troubled on account of the peril to which he felt his follies exposed him, but his religious concern was of short continuance, and he would rush as greedily as before into sinful employments and indulgences. Sometimes his outraged conscience would be terribly alarmed by awful dreams, which had the effect of producing promises of amendment, but, though he would reform his outward conduct for a season, his vows were as often broken as made, until he was brought under pungent and powerful conviction by a sermon preached by a Methodist. His wife was a serious and praying woman, and a member of the Presbyterian Church, which he sometimes attended, and in the doctrines of which he had been reared; but, though a professor of religion, she did not possess any very just notions of experimental godliness.

One Sabbath her minister was sick, and, being inclined

to attend religious service, she asked permission of her husband to go to a Methodist meeting, which she heard was to be held about ten or twelve miles distant. He consented to her request, and, in company with her eldest son and daughter, she went to the meeting. When she returned he asked her how she liked the preacher. She replied that "he was as great a preacher as ever she had heard in all her life," and persuaded him to go and hear for himself. The next Sabbath he went. The preacher took for his text, "Come unto me all ye that labor and are heavy laden, and I will give you rest." He was much engaged, and the people were greatly affected. This was surprising to Abbott, as he had never seen the like before. The sermon, however, made no impression upon his mind until, in making his application, the preacher said, "It may be that some of you may think that there is neither God nor devil, heaven nor hell, only a guilty conscience; and, indeed, my friends, that is bad enough. But I assure you that there is both heaven and hell, God and devil." He proceeded to argue that fire was contained in everything, and that there was a hell dreadful beyond comprehension, and urged the people to fly to Christ for refuge. He showed the reality of the existence of God by a beautiful illustration of his works, and called upon the people to come unto Him for Christ had died for their redemption.

The service being over, two dreams, which he had dreamed about seven years before, one of which related to hell and the other to heaven, rose vividly before his mind. He thought of his misspent life, "and in a moment," he says, "all my sins that I ever had committed were brought to my view; I saw it was the mercy of God that I was out of hell, and promised to amend my life." He went home distressed in spirit, and oppressed with awful thoughts concerning a future life. His convictions increased, and for several days he suffered severe and almost insupportable mental agony. The doctrine of election troubled him, and he feared he was a reprobate, doomed to suffer forever the wrath of God. In this state of mind he was tempted to commit suicide, and even went so far as to take the first steps towards the commission of the awful deed, when it occurred to his mind, as if uttered by a voice, "This punishment is nothing to hell;" this restrained him and he continued to seek for mercy. On one occasion he went to hear the preacher, who was the means of awakening him. He had an interview with him before the services commenced, and told him the state of his mind, and desired to be baptized, hoping, by that means to gain relief. The preacher asked him if he was a Quaker. He replied he was not, only a poor, wretched, condemned sinner. He then exhorted him to believe in Christ for salvation; and, in reply to his misgivings concerning the willingness of God to save so great a sinner as he felt himself to be, he assured him that he was the very man Christ died for, else he would not have awakened him; that he came to seek the lost and to save the greatest of sinners, and applied to his case the promises of Scripture. They went to the house, where the meeting was to be held, but Abbott remained outside, as he was afraid to go in lest he should cry out as he had done at a meeting a day or two previous, and thus expose himself to ridicule. The preacher, in his prayer, especially dwelt upon the case of "the poor, broken-hearted sinner." He says, "His cries to God, on this occasion, ran through my heart like darts and daggers; after meeting I returned and prayed in my family, and ever after continued that duty. That night I lay alone, expecting to sleep but little, but to pray and weep all night; whenever I fell into a slumber, it appeared to me that I saw hell opened ready to receive me, and I just on the point of dropping in, and devils waiting to seize me. Being thus alarmed, it would arouse me up, crying to the Lord to save me; and thus I passed the whole night in this terrified unhappy condition. Just at the dawning of the day I fell into a dose more like sleep than any I had

and tell the neighbors what the Lord had done for his soul.

He first went to the house of a Baptist; and, as he and his wife were professors of religion, he supposed they would understand the nature of the change he had experienced and rejoice with him; "but, to my great surprise," he says, "when I related my experience and told what God had done for my soul, it appeared as strange to them as if I had claimed possession of Old England, and called it all my own." He then proceeded to a mill, where he thought he would see a number of people, and have an opportunity to exhort them, and tell them what a blessing he had obtained. On his way he exhorted all he met with to turn to God; and, on reaching the mill, he told his experience to the people and urged them to flee from the wrath to come, while "some laughed, and others cried, and some thought" his reason had departed. "Before night," he says, "a report was spread all through the neighborhood that I was raving mad." When he returned home he asked his wife about her conviction and conversion, expecting that, as she was a professor of religion, she was acquainted with the mysteries of the new birth, but he was mistaken. She was led by domestic affliction, a few years after her marriage, to covenant with God to be more religious, and became a praying woman, and united with the Church, but remained destitute of the power of godliness. He told her she had no religion, and was nothing more than a strict Pharisee. This displeased her, and the next day she went to seek advice from her minister, who counseled her to not regard what her husband said, for he expected to be saved by his works. She returned better satisfied in mind, and took a book from the minister for him to read. It was Bellamey's New Divinity, in which he insisted on conversion before conviction, and faith before repentance. He read the book about half through, and finding the author to be a rigid Calvinist, he threw it aside, "determined," he says, "to read no more in it, as my own experience clearly proved to me that the doctrines it contained were false."

The minister sent for Abbott to visit him, which he did; and, after dinner, he requested the family to withdraw from the dining room, when he informed him that he had learned that God had done great things for him. Abbott then related to him an account of his conviction and conversion, to which he paid strict attention until he had finished, when he told him he was under strong delusions of the devil. He handed him a book to read, which he felt he ought not to take, however he resisted the impression and took it. On his way home he was tempted to doubt, and called to mind his various sins, but none of them condemned him. He then recurred to a particular sin which he concluded would condemn him; "but in a moment," he says, "I felt an evidence that that sin was forgiven as though separate from all the rest that ever I had committed; but, recollecting the minister had told me 'I was under strong delusions of the devil,' it was suggested to my mind, it may be he is right. I went a little out of the road, and kneeled down and prayed to God if I was deceived to undeceive me, and the Lord said to me, 'Why do you doubt? Is not Christ all sufficient? Is he not able? Have you not felt his blood applied?' I then sprang upon my feet and cried out, Not all the devils in hell, nor all the Predestinarians on earth should make me doubt; for I knew I was converted. At that instant I was filled with unspeakable raptures of joy."

He pursued his way, leaving it luminous with the light of his holy example, steadfast to the end. He was a true hero, facing mobs and enduring reproach, but never daunted in the work of God. For several years, as a local preacher, he abounded in evangelical labors in West Jersey and elsewhere, and was one of the most powerful and successful instruments employed in spreading Methodism in the southern section of the State. He will appear again and again, a valiant actor in some of the most heroic scenes of our narrative.

CHAPTER III.

THE FIRST CONFERENCE.

ASBURY had now been in the country a little over twenty months, and had traveled and labored extensively in Pennsylvania, New York, and New Jersey. In the latter province especially, he had borne the lamp of truth into many a dark and neglected neighborhood, and through his labors, the work of reform was spreading, the feeble societies were waxing stronger and stronger, and the few faint streaks of light, which had been gilding the horizon for more than two years, were increasing in number and in power, and had already wreathed themselves into a bow of promise, which cast a cheering and grateful radiance over the otherwise portentous future.

When Asbury first arrived at Philadelphia, the entire membership, in that city, did not exceed thirty-eight.*

* So says Rev. Thomas Sargeant in the Christian Advocate,.1829, p. 120 ; but Asbury in his Journal, Vol. III. p. 121, says, " In 1771, [which was the year of his arrival,] there were about 300 Metho-

It is not probable that at that time the number in New Jersey was much greater, if, indeed, it was as great; but at the Conference, which sat in Philadelphia, in the summer of 1773, Philadelphia reported 180 members and New Jersey 200.

Nothing of very great importance occurred at this Conference, except the adoption of certain rules for the government of the connection, the stationing of the preachers, and the debates in relation to the conduct of some of the preachers, "who had manifested a desire to abide in the cities and live like gentlemen." It was also discovered that money had been wasted, improper leaders appointed, and many of the rules broken. The rules adopted by the Conference were the following:

dists in New York, 250 in Philadelphia, and a few in New Jersey." In 1773, according to the minutes, there were only 180 in Philadelphia. Here is a discrepancy between the authorities, either of which, in ordinary cases, would be regarded as perfectly reliable. If there were 250 in 1771, as Asbury says, how is the decrease of 70 in less than two years to be accounted for? But, if, as Mr. Sargeant affirms, there were only about 38 in 1771, we can account for the increase of 142 members in less than two years upon the principles of Methodist progression. It should be remembered that until 1775, New Jersey suffered no decrease from the Revolutionary excitement, but made steady progress in numbers, and at the Conference of 1775, Philadelphia reported 190 members, which was an increase of ten on the number reported in 1773.

1. The old Methodist doctrine and discipline shall be enforced and maintained amongst all our societies in America.

2. Any preacher who acts otherwise cannot be retained amongst us as a fellow laborer in the vineyard.

3. No preacher in our connection shall be permitted to administer the ordinances at this time, except Mr. S., and he under the particular direction of the assistant.

4. No person shall be admitted more than once or twice to our love feasts and society meetings, without becoming a member.

5. No preacher shall be permitted to reprint our books, without the approbation of Mr. Wesley, and the consent of his brethren. And that R. W. shall be allowed to sell what he has, but reprint no more.

6. Every assistant is to send an account of the work of God in his circuit to the general assistant.

There were now ten traveling preachers in the whole American connection, and 1160 members. These were included in the provinces of New Jersey, Maryland, and Virginia, and in New York, and Philadelphia. Beyond these limits Methodism in this country had not pushed its conquests.

JOHN KING and WILLIAM WATTERS were appointed by the Conference to labor in New Jersey, which constituted one circuit. It is not probable that the preachers traveled regularly over the whole province, but rather bestowed their labors upon those points which promised the best results, and in nurturing and building up the few societies which had already been formed. As the way opened and the work spread, they extended the area of their toils.

At that day, the fact that a preacher was appointed at the Conference to a given field is not a certain proof that he labored there. Changes were more frequent than Conferences, and they sought to accommodate the exigencies of the work without much reference to the preferences or convenience of the laborers. Hence, though Watters was appointed this year to New Jersey, it does not appear that he labored there. In a short account of his ministerial labors, written by himself, Mr. Watters says that, in October 1772, he accompanied Mr. Williams, a local preacher, to Virginia, and that he remained there eleven months, and in the following November took an appointment on Kent circuit, Delaware. As he was in Virginia until the fall of 1773, and then went to Kent circuit, it is not probable that he was in New Jersey at all during this year. In the fall of this year Philip Gatch was sent to labor in New Jersey. Gatch was a native of Maryland, and was sent by Mr. Rankin to this field of labor. In Philadelphia he met Mr. King, with whom he crossed into New Jersey.

King preached and held a love feast, and, "on the following morning," says Gatch, "he pursued his journey, leaving me a 'stranger in a strange land.'" It thus appears that King was in the province and preached during the year, but how much labor he performed there it is impossible now to tell.

Mr. King was an Englishman, and came to this country in the latter part of 1769. Soon after his arrival he waited upon Mr. Pillmore, (who and Richard Boardman were the first preachers sent by Mr. Wesley to this country, where they arrived, landing at Gloucester Point, New Jersey, the 24th of October, 1769,) and desired permission to labor in a public capacity, in the society in Philadelphia. Pillmore, not being satisfied with regard to his qualifications, declined giving him authority; but so intent was he on proclaiming the doctrines of free grace to the multitudes there, that he appointed a meeting, on his own responsibility, in the Potter's field. His sermon produced so good an impression, that some of the members of the society, who heard him, desired Mr. Pillmore to encourage him to go forward in the work. "After examination he was permitted to preach a trial sermon; and, as he appeared to be a young man of piety and zeal, and much engaged for God, he received permission from Pillmore to go down to Wilmington, Delaware, where Methodism had already been introduced, and to exhort among a few awakened persons, who were earnestly seeking the Lord."*

He was the first Methodist preacher that publicly proclaimed the gospel in the city of Baltimore. It was in the year 1770. He mounted a blacksmith's block, at the intersection of Front street and the great eastern road, and held up the cross to the gaze of his discordant and wondering auditors. A deputy surveyor of the county, who was one of his hearers, was brought under conviction for sin, and was afterward converted to God. He was the first fruit of Methodism in Baltimore, and "some of his descendants are still living in the city and county, and are influential and pious members of the Methodist Episcopal Church.†

Inspired with the conviction that he was in the line of his duty, and encouraged by the success which had already attended his efforts, he plunged into the very heart of the citadel. He took a table for his pulpit, at the corner of Baltimore and Calvert streets, and shouted his message to the crowd; and, "it being a day of general muster of the volunteers and militia, some young men of the 'higher class,' who considered it manly to get drunk on such occasions, determined to interrupt the

---

* Rev. S. W. Coggeshall in Methodist Quarterly Rev., Oct., 1855.

† Rev. W. Hamilton's article on Early Methodism in Maryland, etc., in Methodist Quarterly Review, July 1856.

services and break up the meeting. In the confusion which followed, the table was overturned and the preacher thrown to the ground." The captain of the company, however, who did not approve of such treatment of a stranger, and perceiving that King was a countryman of his, flew to his rescue and protected him from further molestation. Soon after this an invitation, it is said, was extended to him to preach in St. Paul's Church. It is not known who was the author of this civility, but the sermon gave offence to the rector of the parish, and the preacher was informed "that hereafter the cannon should not be spiked for his benefit." One, who was present on the occasion, said "that Mr. King made the dust fly from the old velvet cushion."

Such was the man who was appointed to superintend the interests of the cause in New Jersey, in 1773. His heroic disposition and burning zeal were eminently suited to the exigencies of the work ; and though it is probable he did not perform much labor in the province this year,* yet the frail bark of New Jersey Methodism was favored with brave and skillful guidance, by which, with the blessing of God, it passed safely along the treacherous current on which it had been launched, and glided into wider and clearer waters, where the favoring

* Judge McLean's Sketch of Gatch, p. 27-8.

breezes and the serener skies betokened a tranquil and triumphant voyage.

At the Conference of 1774, Mr. King was appointed to Norfolk, Virginia, and in 1775, he is again in New Jersey on the Trenton circuit. In 1776 he located, but in 1801 his name again appears in the itinerant lists, and he was appointed to Franklin circuit, and in 1802 to Sussex circuit. In 1803 he again located. He was a man of true piety and usefulness, and so continued until he departed to heaven, at a very advanced age, from the vicinity of Raleigh, North Carolina.

PHILIP GATCH appears to have been the first preacher officially appointed to the province, who for any considerable period performed in it regular ministerial labor. He entered upon the appointment, as we have already seen, in the autumn of 1773, and continued in it until the latter part of May, 1774, when he left it to attend Conference in Philadelphia. As he sustained so early and so important a relation to the cause in New Jersey, it is proper that he should receive more than a passing notice in these Memorials.

He was born on the second of March, 1751. His parents were members of the Episcopal Church; but they were destitute, he says, of experimental religion; yet they paid some attention to its restraints and forms. He was the subject of religious impressions at a very early age, and suffered keenly from his convictions of the evil and demerit of sin. He feared the Lord and greatly desired to serve him, but knew not how, yet he attended to his private religious duties with commendable punctuality. "All was dark and dreary around me," he says, "and there was no one in the neighborhood who possessed religion. Priests and people, in this respect, were alike."

When in his seventeenth year, through the influence of wicked associations, he lost much of his concern for his spiritual welfare; but, by means of afflictive providences, his religious anxieties were reawakened; and, terrified by thoughts of death, judgment, and an eternity of misery, he mourned in secret places, often wishing he had never been born. For years he continued his efforts to find rest to his soul, but without success, until January, 1772, when he was permitted to hear the gospel from a Methodist lay preacher. The word was accompanied to his understanding by the Holy Spirit. "I was stripped," he says, "of all my self-righteousness. It was to me as filthy rags, when the Lord made known to me my condition. I saw myself altogether sinful and helpless, while the dread of hell seized my guilty conscience." He continued to attend Methodist preaching as he had opportunity, though his father forbade him to do so, declaring that his house should not hold two reli-

gions.   At length he attended a prayer meeting.   Feeling that he was too sinful to remain where the worship
of God was being performed, he arose and left the
house; but a friend, in whom he had confidence, followed
him, requesting him to return.   Influenced by respect
for his friend's piety, he yielded to his request, and, under the deepest exercise of mind, bowed himself before
the Lord, saying in his heart, If thou wilt give me power
to call on thy name how thankful will I be!   "Immediately," he says, "I felt the power of God to affect my
body and soul.   It went through my whole system.   I
felt like crying aloud.   God said, by his Spirit, to my
soul, 'My power is present to heal thy soul, if thou wilt
but believe.'   I instantly submitted to the operation of
the Spirit of God, and my poor soul was set at liberty.
I felt as if I had got into a new world.   I was certainly
brought from hell's dark door, and made nigh unto God
by the blood of Jesus.

> "'Tongue cannot express
> The sweet comfort and peace
> Of a soul in its earliest love.'

Ere I was aware I was shouting aloud, and should have
shouted louder if I had had more strength.   I was the
first person known to shout in that part of the country.
The order of God differs from the order of man.   He
knows how to do his own work, and will do it in his own

way, though it often appears strange to us. Indeed, it is a strange work to convert a precious soul. I had no idea of the greatness of the change, till the Lord gave me to experience it. A grateful sense of the mercy and goodness of God to my poor soul overwhelmed me. I tasted and saw that the Lord was good."

He at once became a decided and earnest Christian. His father soon renounced his opposition, and became, with most of the family, a member of the Methodist society, which was now formed in the neighborhood. Gatch soon began to give a word of exhortation in the prayer and class-meetings, and was blessed in so doing. His mind then became exercised on the subject of making his hortatory exercises more public, but he felt such a sense of weakness that to do so appeared impossible. His comforts failed, and he sank into despondency. He tried to stifle his impressions, but they would return with increased force, and again a sense of weakness would sink his feelings lower than ever. He knew not what to do. He read the first chapter of Jeremiah, portions of which seemed to suit his case. He then concluded that if the Lord would sanctify him he would be better prepared to speak his word. He now began to seek for a deeper baptism of the Holy Spirit. He says, "I labored under a sense of want, but not of guilt. I needed strength of soul. God knew that it was necessary for me to tarry in Jerusalem till endued with power from on high. The struggle was severe but short. I spent the most of my time in prayer, but sometimes only with groans that I could not utter. I had neither read nor heard much on the subject, till in the midst of my distress a person put into my hands Mr. Wesley's sermon on Salvation by Faith. The person knew nothing of my exercise of mind.

"I thought if salvation was to be obtained by faith, why not now? I prayed, but the Comforter tarried. I prayed again, and still the answer was delayed. God had his way in the work; my faith was strengthened, and my hope revived. I told my brother that I believed God would bless me that night in family prayer. He knew that my mind was in a great struggle, but did not know the pursuit of my heart. In the evening, while my brother-in-law prayed with the family, a great trembling seized me. After it had subsided, I was called upon to pray. I commenced, and after a few minutes I began to cry to God for my own soul, as if there was not another to be saved or lost. The Spirit of the Lord came down upon me, and the opening heavens shone around me. By faith I saw Jesus at the right hand of the Father. I felt such a weight of glory that I fell with my face to the floor. * * My joy was full. I related to others what God had done for me. This was in July, a little more than two months after I had received the Spirit of justification."

With increased moral strength and greater spiritual enjoyments, his impression that it was his duty to preach the gospel returned. Still he hesitated. He was visited with affliction, and in his extremity, like Jonah, he promised the Lord that if he would spare him he would speak his word " though it should be in ever so broken a manner."

Thinking he would be less embarrassed in his public exercises among strangers than among his relatives and acquaintances, he went into Pennsylvania, and made appointments and held meetings. He continued to exhort and preach, and was greatly blessed in so doing, and had the pleasure of seeing the work prosper, until he was sent to labor in New Jersey.

In entering upon his new and extensive field of labor, which had received but little moral or religious culture, three considerations, he says, rested on his mind with great weight: first, his own weakness; secondly, the help that God alone could afford; and thirdly, the salvation of the souls of the people to whom he was sent.

He realized the presence of the Master with him in his work, and his labors were crowned with a good degree of success. The Methodists were then, he says, very much spoken against. Much devotion, patience,

5

and labor were, therefore, necessary to gain even small accessions; every inch of the ground had to be strenuously contested, and obstacles, such as would have appalled a weaker spirit or a less resolute faith, had to be assailed and overcome. But he was not the man to shrink from difficulties, and during this period of service in New Jersey, fifty-two, he says, united with the Church, most of whom professed religion.

Among those, who at this time joined the society under Mr. Gatch, was the wife of Benjamin Abbott, and three of her children. Mrs. Abbott attended, with her husband, a meeting, one day, where Gatch was to preach. His discourse was of an alarming character, and it reached her heart. After the sermon she called him aside and said, "If what my husband tells me, and what you preach, be true, I have no religion." He went to Abbott and told him his wife was awakened and that he must take her to the place where he was to preach in the afternoon, to which he assented, and they accordingly went. After he had done preaching he called upon Abbott to pray. "This," says the latter, "was a great cross, as I had never prayed in public, except in my family; however, I felt it my duty to comply, and accordingly took up my cross, and the Lord wrought powerfully upon the people; among the rest, my wife was so wrought upon that she cried aloud for mercy. So great was her conviction that for three days, she eat, drank, or slept but little. She now saw she had only been a Pharisee, and was in a lost condition. On the third day, in the afternoon, she went over to John Murphey's, a neigbor of ours, a sensible man, and one well experienced in religion. After some conversation with him, she returned home, and upon her way the Lord broke in upon her soul, and she came home rejoicing in God. During her absence I went from home to visit a sick man, with whom I tarried all night. On my return next morning, she met me at the door with tears of joy; we embraced each other and she cried out, 'Now I know what you told me is true, for the Lord hath pardoned my sins.' We had a blessed meeting ; it was the happiest day we had ever seen together. 'Now,' said she, 'I am willing to be a Methodist, too ;' from that time we went on, hand in hand, helping and building each other up in the Lord. These were the beginning of days to us. Our children also, began to yield obedience to the Lord, and in the course of about three months after my wife's conversion, we had six children converted to God ; two sons and four daughters, the youngest, of whom, was only seven years old." One of the sons, David, afterwards became a useful preacher.

Abbott must have resided, at this time, in Salem

County, and, probably, in Pittsgrove Township. For some months after his conversion, he tells us, there was no Methodist society in the neighborhood where he lived. As Mr. Gatch received his wife and some of his children into society, and as he also called upon him to pray the first time he prayed in public, it is probable that Gatch formed the first class in Pittsgrove and appointed him leader, for he says, after speaking of his first attempts at preaching, "About this time we formed a class in our neighborhood and I was appointed to lead them. We were taken into the circuit and had regular circuit preaching once in two weeks: I continued to preach on Sabbath days and the circuit preachers on week days."* We think it is not very improbable that this class may have formed the nucleus of either the Broadneck, or Murphy's, since called Friendship Church, two of the oldest societies in the County of Salem, and which now constitute the Pittsgrove charge, New Jersey Conference. Nothing, however, on this point can be affirmed positively. We only speak of the probabilities indicated by the facts.

At length the time for Conference arrived, and Mr. Gatch was called to part with the people for whom he had labored. Though he found the cross to be heavy,

* Life of Abbott. p. 35.

while serving the circuit, on account of the low estimate he placed upon his abilities, yet he felt it to be a great trial to part with the friends whose servant in the gospel he had been, for they possessed the unity of the Spirit, and he was united with them in the bonds of peace.

CHAPTER IV.

THE WORK IN 1774.

THE Conference sat in Philadelphia, on Wednesday the 25th of May, 1774. It was, says Asbury, all things considered, a harmonious session, and was attended with great power. The appointments of the preachers were acquiesced in, and it closed on Friday "with a comfortable intercession." At this Conference New Jersey reported 257 members, an increase during the year of fifty-seven. There were only two preachers appointed to labor at a time in New Jersey this year, but there were two circuits, Trenton and Greenwich. William Watters was appointed to Trenton, and Philip Ebert to Greenwich circuit. They were to change with Daniel Ruff and Joseph Yearby, who were sent to travel Chester circuit, in Pennsylvania.

William Watters was the first native Methodist preacher that entered the traveling connection. He was not, however, it is said, the first American preacher that was raised up by Methodism. This honor is assigned to Richard Owings, who was converted under the labors of Robert Strawbridge, in Maryland. But, though Owings was a local preacher before Watters, his name does not appear on the minutes until 1775, after which he again retired into the local ranks, but two or three years before his death he re-entered the itinerancy, in which he closed his life.

Though Watters stands first on the list of native Americans that entered the itinerant field, yet he and Gatch were very nearly assimilated in their history. "They were born the same year. Watters experienced religion first, but they began to exercise in public in the same summer of 1772. While Watters was laboring in Virginia, Gatch was laboring in Pennsylvania and other parts where the openings of Providence directed. Mr. Watters' name being on the minutes for 1773, brought him into the number admitted, and made an assistant May 25, 1774. Gatch was placed in the same relation at the same Conference, which shows that the Conference considered the act of the quarterly meeting at which Mr. Gatch was employed, which Mr. Rankin and Mr. Asbury attended, as regular. Mr. Watters and Mr. Gatch sat, each for the first time, in the same Conference in the same relation. This detail is rendered proper, as these venerable ministers were the first recruits for the itinerancy in America."*

WILLIAM WATTERS was a native of Maryland and was born in the year 1751. He professed conversion and joined the Methodists in the year 1771. He had six brothers older than himself, all of whom, with two sisters, professed religion within a period of nine months, and all joined the society the same year. The names of the brothers were John, Henry, Godfrey, Nicholas, Stephen, and Walter. They were among the first whose hearts and houses were opened to receive the Methodist preachers when they entered Harford County, in Maryland, and several of them early became official members in the Church. Nicholas became a useful preacher, and was admitted on trial by the Conference, in 1776, and continued to labor on different circuits until 1804, when he died in peace and triumph, in the sixty-fifth year of his age. As he approached the dark river he said, "I am not afraid to die, if it be the will of God; I desire to depart and be with Christ; the Church will sustain no loss by my death, for the Lord will supply my place with a man that will be more useful. Thanks be to God I have continued to live and labor faithfully to the end." Among his last utterances was the following couplet:

* Sketch of Gatch.

" Farewell, vain world, I'm going home,
My Saviour smiles and bids me come."

William entered upon the duties of the ministry in the local sphere in 1772, and in 1773, as we have seen, he was appointed by the first Conference to New Jersey, but did not labor on that appointment, but labored during that year in Virginia and Maryland. In 1774 he is appointed to Trenton Circuit, New Jersey. He entered upon his appointment, and was, he says, most kindly received. He labored successfully, his efforts being made a blessing to saints and sinners. "I felt," he says, "freedom of spirit, and preached as if every sermon was my last. I felt myself on the Lord's business, and forgot, comparatively, all other concerns."

While in this circuit, he met, for the first time, with the Life of Thomas Walsh. He was much impressed and affected in reading it. "I saw," he says, "perhaps much plainer than I ever did before, what manner of person a preacher ought to be, and that it was the privilege of all the children of God to love him with all the heart. Oh! how did I long to be delivered out of the hands of all my spiritual enemies. Lord! let me 'die the death of the righteous, and let my last end be like his.' Though I had too much reason to fear that I increased much faster in gifts than in grace, yet did the Lord sustain me in my weakness, and in some measure gave me the desire of my heart, in seeing a gracious prospect of sinners being daily added to the Lord, and to his people; while our brethren sweetly went on, hand in hand, bearing each other's burthens, and striving together for the hope of the gospel."

While he was in New Jersey, "the dreadful cloud," he says, "that had been hanging over us, continued to gather thicker and thicker, so that I was often bowed down before the God of the whole earth, fearing the evils which were coming on our sinful land. I was in Trenton when Hancock and Adams passed through on their way to the first Congress in Philadelphia. They were received with great pomp, and were much caressed by the inhabitants of the town."

After Mr. Watters had been in New Jersey about one fourth of the year, Mr. Rankin, who was, at that time, the Superintendent, thought it best that he should exchange with Daniel Ruff, who was on Chester circuit, in Pennsylvania; promising him, however, that he should return at the end of a quarter. Accordingly he went to Chester, where he was blessed with a revival, but at the end of the quarter he gladly recommended the people to God and to the word of his grace, to return to his kind Trenton friends, who, he says, "received me with as much affection as ever."

Having entered again upon his appropriate field of labor,

he had large congregations at most of the preaching places, and says he enjoyed, in this circuit, many conveniences for improvement. In the latter part of the winter and through the spring he was favored with seeing the work of religion reviving. "Many," he says, "in the upper end of the circuit were greatly wrought on, and our meetings were lively and powerful. The cries of the people for mercy were frequently loud and earnest, so that the voice of the speaker, or any one praying, was frequently drowned. Several, who had long rested in a form of godliness, were brought under pressing concern, and found the Lord; and many of the most serious were greatly quickened. I was often much blessed in my own soul, and my hands lifted up, which were too apt to hang down. Oh! how sweet to labor where the Lord gives his blessing, and 'sets open a door which no man can shut.'"*

He spent nine months of the year in the Trenton circuit, much to his own comfort, and was greatly encour-

---

* A Short Account of the Christian Experience and Ministerial Labors of William Watters. Drawn up by Himself. Alexandria, 1806. This work has long been out of print, and probably very few copies are now in existence. Through the kindness of Rev. Dr. Roberts, of Baltimore, I have been favored with the use of a copy, which bears unmistakable marks of age, but is a precious memorial of the first American Methodist traveling preacher, and his times.

aged to go rejoicing on his way. He attended the Conference in Philadelphia, in 1775, and was appointed to Frederick circuit in Maryland, to labor in connection with Robert Strawbridge, who formed, in that state, one of the first Methodist societies that existed in America. He felt afflicted with this appointment, and for a considerable time after he entered upon it he had great conflicts of soul, "and was often so exceedingly dejected" that he was scarcely capable of performing his work; but in the summer a revival broke out, which spread all round the circuit, and increased during his stay, so that he was led to rejoice that his lot was cast there.

In 1776 he was appointed to Fairfax in Virginia; in 1777 to Brunswick; in 1778 to Fairfax again; in 1779 he was sent to Baltimore; in 1780 to Frederick; in 1781 he was again in Baltimore; in 1782 he was appointed to the Fluvana circuit in Virginia; and in 1783 to Calvert. In 1784 he located. He entered the traveling ministry again in 1801, and was stationed in Alexandria; in 1802 Georgetown and Washington city; in 1803–4 Alexandria; in 1805 Washington. In 1806 he again located. He was a man of "good report" and occupied, as his appointments show, a very responsible and honorable place in the early ministry of American Methodism. He maintained the character of a laborious and successful minister of Christ until his death.

The work advanced in New Jersey during the year 1774, though in not quite the same ratio as it did the previous year. After making allowance for removals, expulsions, and deaths, three hundred members were reported at the close of the year, which was an increase of forty-three. One, and we cannot tell how many more, of the first fruits of the movement was, this year, gathered to the heavenly garner. Bishop Asbury, being in Burlington, says; "Here Mrs. H. gave an account of the triumphant death of her sister, whose heart the Lord touched two years ago under my preaching." And from that time till the present, multitudes, who have been regenerated and sanctified through the agency of Methodism, have been ascending year by year from New Jersey, to the celestial abodes on high. Some of their beautifully affecting and triumphant death scenes we shall have occasion to notice in the future progress of our work.

Captain Webb was again in Burlington, in the latter part of November of this year, in company with Bishop Asbury. When they arrived they "were saluted with the melancholy news that two unhappy men were to be hung on the Monday following; one for bestiality, and the other for abusing several young girls in the most "brutish and shocking manner." They visited them as ministers of Christ, for the purpose of assisting them in preparing for their terrible doom. One of them, who was a Papist, manifested a little attention to their words, but wanted to know if he might not trust for pardon after death. The other was a young man, who appeared stupid and careless in regard to his immortal interests. In the evening Asbury preached, and "showed the people the emptiness of mere externals in religion, and the absolute necessity of the inward power and graces thereof."

On Friday, December 2, Mr. Asbury writes in his Journal, "My soul enjoys great peace; but longs for more of God. We visited the prisoners again; and Captain W. enforced some very alarming truths upon them, though very little fruit of his labor could be seen. Mr. R. came to Burlington to day and desired me to go to Philadelphia. So, after preaching, in the evening, from Prov. xxviii. 13, I set off the next morning for the city; and found the society in the spirit of love."

Abraham Whitworth, who was appointed to Baltimore in 1773, and to Kent in 1774, fled from his circuit on account of immorality, and came into Jersey. Here he poisoned the mind of Ebert, who was on Greenwich circuit, with the fallacies of Universalism, and he was therefore dismissed. In consequence of this the circuit remained for some time destitute of preaching. Mr.

Gatch was appointed to labor on Frederick circuit this year, but he had been on it but a short time when he was sent to Kent circuit to fill the vacancy caused by the treachery of Whitworth. He labored there successfully till a short time before Conference, when he returned, by direction, to New Jersey, to look after the scattered sheep who, by the dismissal of Ebert, had been left without a shepherd.

Having fulfilled his mission, he proceeded to the Conference which was again held in Philadelphia the 19th of May 1775. At this Conference he was appointed to Kent circuit. He remained there until the fall when he went to Baltimore. There he remained for a time, and then exchanged with the preacher on Frederick circuit, so that he had three different appointments in the same year. In the last appointment he was most cruelly persecuted. On one occasion he heard that a man, whose wife had been convicted under another preacher, meant to revenge himself upon him. A company of his friends gathered around him, and when he was assailed by the mob they desired to fight for his protection, but he persuaded them not to use violent means, telling them he could bear it for Christ's sake. Two men held his horse by the bridle, while a third, elevated at a suitable height, applied the tar, commencing at the left cheek. The uproar was very great, some swearing and some crying;

the women especially, who were present, "dealt out their denunciations against the mob in unmeasured terms." The man who applied the tar laid it on liberally, and called out for more, saying that Gatch was true blue. At length one of the company cried out, "It is enough." The last stroke made with the paddle was drawn across the naked eyeball, which caused indescribable pain, and from the effects of which he never entirely recovered. His horse became so frightened that when released he dashed off with such violence that he could not rein him up for some time, and he narrowly escaped being thrown against a tree. "If I ever felt for the souls of men," he says, "I did for theirs. When I got to my appointment, the Spirit of the Lord so overpowered me that I fell prostrate in prayer before him for my enemies. The Lord, no doubt, granted my request, for the man who put on the tar, and several others of them, were afterward converted." The next day a mob lay in wait for him on his way to an appointment, but, by the direction of a friend, he eluded them by taking another route. The mob designed to tie him to a tree and whip him until he promised to preach no more. A very worthy young man, who was an exhorter and class leader was attacked by the persecutors while at work in the field and whipped "so cruelly that the shirt upon his back, though made of the most substantial material, was literally cut to pieces." His employer, who was a Presbyterian clergyman, took the matter in hand and had them brought to justice, and they were severely punished by the court. This put an end, he says, to persecution on that circuit.

Gatch was too much devoted to the work of preaching the gospel to be turned aside by persecution. "He has been heard to say, judging, probably, from the rage and cruelty of the mob, into whose hands he had fallen the day before, and from the severe manner in which they had whipped the young man in the field, that, had he fallen into their hands when lying in wait for him, his life would probably have been taken; 'for,' said he, 'I should never have made the promise that they intended to extort from me.'" Sometimes, he says, he felt great timidity at the prospect of danger, but, when the hour of peril came, his fears vanished. This he considered a clear fulfillment of the promise, "Lo, I am with you always."

We will take our leave of this Methodist pioneer and hero with the following tribute by his son:* "When he went to Virginia,† persecution did not rage to the same

* Rev. George Gatch, in Christian Advocate and Journal, 1835, p. 136.

† He was appointed to Hanover, Virginia, at the Conference in 1776.

6

extent, but his health soon failed from excessive labor, and exposure to the open air in field preaching; so that at the Conference, in 1778, he received no appointment; and January 14, 1778, he was married to Elizabeth Smith, of Powhattan county, daughter of Thomas Smith. Though he received no regular appointment after this time, he had the superintendence of some of the circuits in the vicinity of his residence, and spent a considerable time in traveling and preaching at large; until the stability of the work, and the cares of his family reconciled his mind to a more circumscribed sphere.

"He was received into full connection at the Conference in 1774, and acted as an assistant; and when the preachers from England were under the necessity of returning, he was one of five who were chosen to superintend the work. When the controversy* arose, which led to the present organization of the Church, he was one of three who superintended the southern part of the work, and to whom the present state of things, in part, is to be attributed. He was the mover and vindicator of the rule for trying members by a committee, and from his labors in the business department and in the pulpit, it may be said, he bore the burden and heat of the day.

* This controversy was concerning the administration of the ordinances, a summary account of which will doubtless be given in the History of American Methodism.

" He resided in Powhattan county sixteen years and then removed to Buckingham county. He was led, after a residence of five years in Buckingham county, to hazard a removal to the Northwestern territory. This was in the fall of 1798; and in the succeeding winter he settled his family on the Little Miami, nine miles from the mouth—the place of his residence till his death. He began immediately to hunt up the lost sheep in the wilderness, and was among the first to establish Methodism north of the Ohio. He was chosen, in 1802, from Clermont county to assist in the formation of a constitution for a state government; and was chairman of the committee to whom were referred the propositions of Congress for becoming a state. After the organization of the state he served twenty years as associate judge. As one of the pioneers, he was useful in the settlement of the country, and was looked to for advice on all common matters, by the many who soon began to settle in his neighborhood; while his house was a refuge for the weary wanderer. In his political and civil relations he maintained the dignity of the gospel, and carried religious influences, thereby, into many minds, which, probably, otherwise would not have been brought under its control.

" He was all the time industrious, as a local preacher, and continued his religious services after he had declined all civil and domestic labors and responsibilities.   I believe he preached his last sermon on the second of January 1834, on which he was eighty-four years old.

"He was taken on the 25th of December quite ill with the prevailing epidemic.   He appeared sensible of his situation, and said but little.   He remarked, a few hours before his dissolution, four of his children standing by his bed, that on the morning before he was taken he had an unusual flow of Divine feelings, such as he had rarely experienced; but that, during his affliction, his pain had been so great that he could hardly compose his mind while he could send a wish to the throne of grace; but that we must all pray for him, as he had often prayed for us.   When asked, however, he expressed an unshaken confidence in God.   He fell asleep in the arms of Jesus, without a struggle or a groan, or the least apparent agitation; while his spirit silently forsook the long abode in which it had experienced so many vicissitudes, and found a safe retreat in the bosom of its God."

CHAPTER V.

DARK DAYS IN THE HISTORY OF NEW JERSEY METHODISM.

AT the Conference of 1775 there still remained two circuits in New Jersey, and three preachers were appointed to labor in the State. John King and Daniel Ruff were sent to Trenton circuit and William Duke to Greenwich. They were to change in one quarter. It would appear that, led by so brave and earnest a champion of the cause as King, they labored zealously to carry the work forward; yet there appears at the close of the year a very remarkable and painful decrease of members—a decrease of one hundred and fifty, one half from the number reported the previous year.

It is not probable that this mournful declension was the result of ordinary backslidings; but the excitement of war, and the arousement of a martial spirit, which was beginning to be felt over the whole country, called the minds of the people away from religious contemplations and caused them to neglect the ordinances of the gospel. While their minds and hearts were absorbed by thoughts and schemes of carnal warfare it is not strange that many ceased to fight the good fight of faith. It is a sad duty to record too, that the preachers on the Trenton circuit, were not as attentive to the work as its exigencies required, else, it may be, there had not been so serious a declension in the membership. On the 16th of April 1776, Asbury, in his Journal says, "I received a letter from friend E. at Trenton, complaining that the societies in that circuit had been neglected by the preachers." There may have been reasons which rendered this neglect, in some degree, justifiable, or possibly, unavoidable.

During those early and troublous times it was a common thing for preachers to locate. Accordingly the three who traveled in New Jersey this year soon retired into the local ranks. King, as we have seen, located at the end of the year, but afterward returned to the work, Ruff located in 1781 and Duke in 1779.

Enough has already been said of King to give the reader a tolerably just idea of his character as a minister. We will however give an additional incident which shows how powerful was the influence which he exercised. A German, named Henry Rowman, was induced one day to attend a Methodist meeting. It was in the year 1768. He went under the influence of strong prejudice ; and, after reaching the place, determined to go away without hearing the preaching ; but, on seeing a group of decent, well dressed persons approach the place, he supposed it could be no disgrace to him to be found in their company, so he returned and seated himself. John King was the preacher. He took his position and stood a few minutes with his hand before his face, engaged in devotion. Bowman was forcibly struck with the conviction that he was a messenger from God, and that he himself was a sinner. Distress seized his mind, and he turned his attention to the subject of his personal salvation and anxiously sought pardon until he obtained it. He united with the Methodists, and after maintaining his profession fifty-nine years he finished his course with joy.

DANIEL RUFF entered the ministry at a very early period in the history of the cause. He was received on trial at the Conference of 1774, the second held in America, but he was very usefully engaged in the work previously to that time. Nearly three months before that Conference was held, Bishop Asbury, being in the region of Baltimore, speaks of preaching at the "upper ferry," and says : "Honest, simple Daniel Ruff, has been made a great blessing to these people. Such is the wisdom and power of God, that he hath wrought marvelously by this plain man, that no flesh may glory in his

289374

presence." More than two months afterward he writes; "Rode to Susquehannah and many of the leading men were present, with a large congregation. Simple D. R. [doubtless meaning Daniel Ruff,] has been an instrument of real and great good to the people in these parts."

When Mr. Ruff traveled Trenton circuit Benjamin Abbott's house was one of his preaching places. The latter was much engaged for the blessing of sanctification. Ruff went to his house and preached, and in the morning, in family prayer, he prayed that God would sanctify them soul and body. "I repeated," says Abbott, "these words after him, ' Come, Lord, and sanctify me, soul and body !' That moment the Spirit of God came upon me in such a manner that I fell flat to the floor, and lay as one strangling in blood, while my wife and children stood weeping over me. But I had not power to lift hand or foot, nor yet to speak one word ; I believe I lay half an hour, and felt the power of God running through every part of my soul and body, like fire consuming the inward corruptions of fallen, depraved nature. When I arose and walked out of the door, and stood pondering these things in my heart, it appeared to me that the whole creation was praising God; it also appeared as if I had got new eyes, for everything appeared new, and I felt a love for all the creatures that God had made, and an uninterrupted peace filled my breast. In three days God gave me a full assurance that he had sanctified me, soul and body. 'If a man love me he will keep my words; and my Father will love him and we will come unto him, and make our abode with him,' (John xiv. 23,) which I found day by day manifested to my soul by the witness of his Spirit."

Ruff did not long remain in New Jersey, as in June of this year we find him in Maryland, preaching in the neighborhood of Freeborn Garrettson's residence. Rev. J. B. Wakeley quotes the following from the Life of Garrettson: " On the Tuesday following, in the afternoon, I went to hear Mr. Daniel Ruff preach, and was so oppressed that I was scarcely able to support my burden. After preaching I called in with D. R. at Mrs. G's. and stayed till about nine o'clock." " On his way home on horseback that night," continues Mr. Wakeley,* "after a most desperate struggle with the enemy, Mr. Garrettson was accepted in the Beloved. He says, 'I knew the very instant when I submitted to the Lord and was willing that Christ should reign over me. I likewise knew the two sins which I parted with last, pride and un belief.' "

* Lost Chapters Recovered from the Early History of American Methodism.

After enduring severe mental conflicts in regard to his duty to preach the gospel, and having reached a satisfactory conclusion about the matter, "I received," says Mr. Garrettson, "a letter from brother D. R. desiring me to come and take the circuit a few weeks while he went to Philadelphia. I had no doubt but the Lord directed him to write thus."* He complied with the request. When Mr Ruff returned he resumed his labors on the circuit and Garrettson went to form a new one. Mr. Ruff solicited Garrettson to attend the Conference of 1776 at Baltimore, which he did, and was received on trial and appointed to a circuit.†

In 1776, Mr. Ruff was appointed to New York. He was the first American preacher that was stationed at Wesley Chapel, the first Church built in that city. Several reasons conspired to render this a difficult appointment. The preacher stationed there the previous year had left the Methodists and the society had become greatly diminished, as they were left destitute of the advantages of pastoral attention and oversight: and "the revolutionary troubles were increasing. New York was beginning to be the theatre where awful tragedies were performed. The curtain was raised and the actors were performing their parts, at which humanity

* The experience and travels of Mr. Freeborn Garrettson, etc. ; Philadelphia, 1791. † *Ibid.*

shudders. We cannot wonder that Mr. Ruff considered it unsafe to remain in New York and therefore abandoned a scene of so much confusion and suffering."*

Mr. Ruff labored in New Jersey at four different times. During one of the periods of his ministry there an incident occurred, which may, perhaps, be regarded as illustrative of the command which Jesus once gave to a certain man to not tarry to bury even the dead of his household, but to go and preach the Kingdom of God. A man by the name of Robert Turner, went from New Jersey into the peninsula and was useful there in preaching. Lewis Alfrey, who had been an extravagant sinner, was convinced through his labors, and afterward became a useful preacher. Turner returned to his family for the purpose of settling his affairs, intending to give himself wholly to the ministry after a few weeks. Ruff pressed him to go into the circuit before the time he intended, saying, "Suppose you had but a fortnight to live would you not go?" He replied he would. By the time Ruff came round again, about a fortnight, Turner died of the small-pox.† In 1780 Mr. Ruff was stationed in Baltimore in connection with Freeborn Garrettson and Joshua Dudley. At the ensuing Conference he located. He probably labored more in New Jersey than any other preacher of his time.

* Wakeley's Lost Chapters. † Asbury's Journal.

WILLIAM DUKE joined the Conference in 1774, and was appointed to Frederick circuit with Philip Gatch. He was then quite a youth. This year, 1775, he is sent to New Jersey, and in 1776 to Brunswick; in 1777 he was stationed in Philadelphia, and in 1778 he was sent to Carolina. He joined the Protestant Episcopal Church and resided in Elkton, Maryland, where he died in 1840. Mr. Duke was intimately acquainted with Captain Webb, and often heard him preach. He greatly admired him, though he thought him a little visionary. He was accustomed to relate many interesting anecdotes concerning him. Captain Webb entertained a high regard for Mr. Duke and presented him with his Greek Testament, which he kept for many years, and then gave it to Rev. J. B. Hagany, and he presented it to Bishop Scott, who preserves it as a memento "of the old soldier, who fought so nobly the battles of the cross."

Before the close of this Conference year, Asbury again appears in New Jersey, rallying the feeble and broken detachments of the cause to more earnest battle. On Tuesday, the 22nd of April, 1776, he rode to Burlington from Philadelphia, and on the way he says, "My soul was filled with holy peace, and employed in heavenly contemplations; but found to my grief that many had so imbibed a martial spirit that they had lost the spirit of pure and undefiled religion. I preached from Rom. xiii.

2, but found it a dry and barren time. And some who once ran well now walk disorderly. On Wednesday I rode to Trenton, and found very little there but spiritual deadness. Had very little liberty in preaching among them; thus has the Lord humbled me amongst my people. But I hope through grace to save myself, and at least some that hear me."

The next day he rode about eleven miles, and preached to a people who manifested very little feeling under the word; "but at I. B's. the next day there was more sensibility amongst the congregation; and, though very unwell, I found my heart warm and expanded in preaching to them. It is my present determination to be more faithful in speaking to all that fall in my way, about spiritual and eternal matters. The people were very tender at friend F's. on Saturday. And on the Lord's day I spoke feelingly and pointedly to about three hundred souls at the meeting house. Afterward I returned, through the rain, to Trenton, and was well rewarded in my own soul, while preaching to the congregation at night. I felt every word, which seemed to cut like a two edged sword, and put me in mind of some of my former visits. May the Lord revive his work amongst them again, and make the time to come better than the former time!"

While Asbury was abundant in labors for the cause of

God and Methodism, in New Jersey and elsewhere, he was the subject of mighty assaults from the adversary. During his present tour in New Jersey, he writes, "Satan beset me with powerful suggestions, striving to persuade me that I should never conquer all my spiritual enemies, but be overcome at last. However, the Lord was near, and filled my soul with peace. Blessed Lord, be ever near me, and suffer me not to yield to the tempter; no, not for a moment!"

On the 30th of April he attended a Quarterly-meeting at Hopewell. The love-feast was an interesting and powerful season. Many related their Christian experience. He lectured in the evening at I. B's. though very weary, "but my heart," he says, "is with God, and I know we cannot tire or wear out in a better cause." The following day he rode back to Trenton, where he preached to about a hundred souls, and then traveled about thirty miles to another stopping place.

On the second of May he preached at Mount Holly. "Some melted under the word, though, at first, they seemed inattentive and careless." He says, "The grace of God kept my spirit this day in sweet seriousness without any mixture of sourness." The next day but one he was at New Mills. A Chapel was already erected there, and he preached in it with fervor but not with freedom from Matt. vii. 7; it was, probably,

1876

in process of being completed, as he says, "I found brother W. very busy about his Chapel, which is thirty-six feet by twenty-eight, with a gallery ten feet deep." He spent the Sabbath at New Mills, and preached, and it was a heart-affecting season. He then returned to Philadelphia, but went, he says, under a heavy gloom of mind, and found his spirit "much shut up."

During this year, Abbott, with apostolic zeal, marvelous faith, and overwhelming eloquence, was storming the citadel of the enemy in West Jersey. It was at about this period that he bore the banner of Methodism into the town of Salem. A gentleman there invited him to preach at his house, and on the next Sabbath after he received the invitation he proclaimed the truth there with characteristic energy and power to a large congregation. Some cried out under the sermon; many were in tears. He made another appointment in two weeks from that day at eleven o'clock. An elder in the Presbyterian Church, who was present, asked him if he would preach at his house. He told him he would that day two weeks, at three o'clock. At the time appointed he was at his post and preached at both places to many people. At the first, he enjoyed much freedom in speaking, and after the sermon, found that both the man and his wife, in whose house the service was held, were awakened. At the next, great power attended the word, several cried

aloud and one fell to the floor.   After meeting he asked
the man of the house if he knew what he had done?
"What have I done?" he replied.   Said Abbott, "You
have opened your door to the Methodists, and if a work
of religion break out, your people will turn you out of
their synagogue."   He replied he would die for the truth.
He repeated the appointment at both places.   On his
way home he met with one of Whitefield's converts, who
had known the Lord forty years.   He was, says Abbott,
an Israelite indeed.   They enjoyed great comfort in conversing on the things of God.   He afterward died at
Abbott's house, "happy in God."

The following Sabbath he preached at Hell Neck, a
place which received its name on account of the wickedness of the people.   One said he had heard Abbott
swear, and had seen him fight, and now he would go and
hear him preach.   He was awakened under the word,
and soon after was converted.   Abbott received several
invitations to preach through the neighborhood, and a
revival of religion followed.   Among those who were the
subjects of the work was a lad of fifteen.   His father
was a great enemy of religion, and determined to prevent his being a Methodist, and even whipped him for
praying.   This resulted in leading him to the borders of
despair, and he was tempted to think he had sinned
against the Holy Ghost.   Abbott heard of it and went

to see him. He told him his temptations, and cried out, " There, I have now done it!" and clapped his hands on his mouth. Abbott told him he had not done it, and would not do it for the world. His father soon came in, and he warned him against such conduct towards his son, but he replied that it was all delusion. "Who told you so?" said Abbott. "D. P., " said he, "and he is a Presbyterian and a good man." "Tell D. P. that he is a deceived man," said Abbott, "for that is the true work of God upon your son." The son then cried out, " The Lord is here! The Lord is here!" The father, addressing Abbott, said, "Benjamin, are you not a Free Mason?" He replied no; that he knew nothing of Free Masonry, but he knew this was the operation of the Spirit of God. The father then wept. Abbott prayed, and the family were all in tears. After this the son went on joyfully.

Abbott then went to another of the neighbors, and talked and prayed with them. The man kneeled, but the woman continued knitting during the prayer. When he arose he took her by the hand and said, " Do you pray?" then, looking steadfastly at her, added, "God pity you." This pierced her heart, so that she had no rest until she obtained mercy of the Lord.

The excitement reached such a height that the whole neighborhood seemed in a state of alarm. A Quaker

went to hear him, and asked him to his house. He
went, and when he entered he said, "God has brought
salvation to this house." While at prayer in the evening, a daughter of his host was convicted, and soon after,
the Quaker, his wife, three sons, and two daughters experienced religion, and as the fruit of the revival they
had a considerable society in the place.

He extended his labors also into Mannington, where
great congregations assembled to hear him preach. At
one place where he preached, the minister of the parish attended. "I felt, at first," he says, "a great cross to preach
before him, he being a learned man, and I supposed had
come to hear me with an evil design, as appeared afterward to be the case. However, I prayed to the Lord
not to let me be confounded. After I began, my cross
was but light, and the minister, who sat before me, was
no more than another sinner. The power of God rested
upon us, and several cried out aloud, and two fell to the
floor, agonizing for salvation. I tarried all night, and
the minister and five or six of the heads of the Presbyterian meeting, spent the evening with me, in order to
dispute, and pick me to pieces if possible. The minister
asked me if I was a Wesleyan: I answered, Yes. 'Then,'
said he, 'you deny the perseverance of the saints.' God
forbid, said I, for none can be saved unless they perse-
vere to the end. 'Then,' said he, 'you believe the pos-

sibility of falling from grace.' I answered, Yes. He
then, in a very abrupt manner, gave me the lie; but,
when I told him that I could prove the doctrine by the
word of God, he very passionately gave me the lie again.
I quoted sundry scriptures, particularly that of David's
fall, and turned to Ezek. chapter iii., verses 20 and 21,
and wished him to read and explain the passage; but he
would not touch the Bible. His elder said it read as I
said, and he ought to explain it. He, in a passion, said
he was brought up at a college, and certainly knew; but
I was a fool, and he could cut such a fellow's throat;
then turned to his elder and said, 'If there was a dog's
head on your shoulders, I would cut it off. Do not you
know the articles of your own Church? I will teach
you better.' I told him the curse of God was upon all
such watchmen as he was, who did not warn the people
against sin; that if they lived and died in sin, they could
not be saved, and by his doctrine souls might fall away
and perish, but their blood would be found in his skirts.
He replied, 'I could cut such a fellow's throat; it makes
my blood boil to hear the perseverance of the saints denied.' I then handed him the Bible, and desired him to
clear it up. 'But,' said he, 'you are a fool, you know
nothing at all. I was brought up at college, and I will
have you before your betters.' He got so angry that he
could say but little more. I told him that if we were

ambassadors for Christ, we ought to go on hand and heart to attack the devil in all his strong holds. And then asked the man of the house if I should preach there again; but the answer was, No. So this place was shut against me through the influence of the minister. But, glory to God, there were doors opened in Mannington, so that I was at no loss for places to preach at."

One of his old companions invited him to preach in his house at Woodstown; he accepted the invitation and preached there to a crowded house. While he was speaking, a mob of soldiers came with their guns, and bayonets fixed, and one rushed in, while the rest surrounded the door; the people fled every way, and the soldier presented his bayonet to Abbott as though he would pierce him through; it passed twice close by his ear. "If ever I preached the terrors of the law," he says, "I did it while he was threatening me in this manner, for I felt no fear of death, and soon found he could not withstand the force of truth; he gave way and retreated to the door. They endeavored to send him back again, but in vain, for he refused to return. However, I went on, and finished my discourse, and then asked the man of the house if I should preach there again. He said No, for they will pull down my house. But Dr. Harris told me I might preach in his house. In two weeks I attended at the Doctor's, and found about one hundred men under arms. When I began to preach, they grounded their arms, and heard me in a quiet, orderly manner."

In 1776 the Conference was held in Baltimore. It commenced on the twenty-first of May. Asbury was prevented from attending this Conference, much to his regret, on account of bodily indisposition. Watters, who was present, describes it as a good and refreshing season. "We were of one heart and mind," he says, "and took sweet counsel together, not how we should get riches or honors, or anything that this poor world could afford us; but, how we should make the surest work for heaven and eternal happiness, and be the instruments of saving others. We had a powerful time in our love-feast, a little before we parted, while we sat at our Divine Master's feet, and gladly heard each other tell what the Lord had done for us in the different places in which we had been laboring."

Owing, doubtless, to the declension of the cause in New Jersey, the work there was again thrown into one circuit, which Robert Lindsay and John Cooper were appointed to travel. The causes of the last year's decrease still existed, so that no marked progress was made. Still, the cause did not retrograde, but there was an increase of ten members during the year. Lindsay, the preacher in charge, was an Irishman by birth. He went to Europe during the Revolutionary war, and in

1778 his name disappears from the minutes, but Lee says he traveled and preached until 1788.

One of the heroes of his day was JOHN COOPER, a modest, unpretentious man, of good abilities, and of a self sacrificing spirit. The early Methodists were remarkable for their habits of devotion; illustrating in a good degree the apostle's injunction, to "pray without ceasing." When Cooper obtained religion and united with the Methodists, he became a man of prayer. His father, finding him at one time engaged in this exercise in an apartment of his dwelling, and being enraged at this exhibition of his religion and Methodism, threw a shovel of burning embers upon him. Not content with this he afterward expelled him from his house. Persecution, however, could not destroy his attachment to the cause of his Saviour, nor turn him away from the path of duty.

He entered the itinerancy when it promised its votaries nothing but extensive travels among strangers, frequent removals, hard labor, poor fare, and the contempt of the ungodly world. But with a resolute faith he threw himself into the ranks, and heroically fought at the various posts assigned him, until he fell with a wreath of glory upon his brow, a victor on the field. During fifteen years of the most trying period in the history of the cause, he went to and fro, traveling circuits which, in extent, were greater than some whole Conference territories at present are, the area of his labors reaching from New Jersey to Virginia.

He suffered from poverty, being often in want, as the labors of a Methodist preacher, in those days, were not productive of pecuniary gain, as they have never been, nor in many instances did those hard-working itinerants always then enjoy the commonest comforts of life. But with all his afflictions (for he was a man of affliction) and his privations he murmured not, nor would he even make his wants known until they were observed by his friends, and relief afforded him. He was admitted on trial at the Conference of 1775, having been recommended by Philip Gatch, with whom he was appointed to labor on Kent circuit, in Maryland. He closed his sufferings and toils in 1788 or 1789. He was a man of grave and fixed countenance, and his public exercises were solemn. He was quiet, inoffensive, and blameless, and subject to dejection. His end was peace.

This year the tempest of war swept terrifically over New Jersey, and such was the alarm and suffering among the people that it seemed, to human eyes, absolutely out of the question for religion, and especially Methodism, to prosper. Indeed, could it have maintained its position only, it would have been a great success. Though the decrease the last year was great, yet, as we have seen, there was a little gain realized this year. This was a triumph. The preachers were generally considered unfriendly to the American cause, on account of the imprudent conduct of the English preachers, who were compelled to leave the country; and the word Methodist, to the popular ear, was the synonym of tory. That this was unjust, of course the world now knows; for Methodism has always been as loyal to the cause of human liberty as any other Christian sect. But as is often the case, the improper conduct of a few subjected the rest to unmerited reproach and suffering.

As Washington retreated into Pennsylvania, nearly the whole of New Jersey was abandoned to the British troops, who chose their winter quarters where they pleased. The sufferings of Jerseymen were consequently terrible. Women and children fled, in winter, not knowing whither they went, while many a brave hearted man abandoned his well furnished house and farm to destruction rather than remain and trust himself to the mercy of the invading foe. This portentous year closed, however, victoriously on the side of America. The Rev. Thomas Ware, who was a Revolutionary soldier, says; "Washington, by two masterly strokes of generalship, first on the Hessians at Trenton, and secondly on the rear of the British army at Princeton, where another part of the army was compelled to lay down their arms, completely turned the tables on our enemies, and closed the campaign of 1776 with shouting on the American side.

"Many have heard the fame of these great transactions, and some I have heard talk of them as if Washington thereby barely wiped off the reproach of his late retreat: but had they lived in that portentous day, and felt the throb I felt, and millions more, they would tell a different tale. Each stroke was death. The first was death to British pride; for, by it all the fame of their mighty deeds that had gone out over the floods was blasted, and by the second all their sanguine hopes of conquest were at an end. The first stroke swept our whole western hemisphere; the proud forgiver of our sins fled from those they came to pardon; and the second compelled the mighty subduers of our continent to retreat, and shut themselves up in New Brunswick."*

Before this distressing period Methodism had been introduced into East Jersey, but such was now the state of things, no Methodist preacher could travel there. It was a long time before they could resume their labors in that part of the state; and consequently they turned their attention to West Jersey, which was open to reli-

* Rev. Thomas Ware's article entitled "The Introduction of Methodism in the Lower part of West Jersey," Christian Advocate and Journal, 1831, p. 118.

gious culture, and which has yielded more abundant fruit to Methodism than the eastern portion of the state.

The Conference of 1777 was held at Deer Creek, Harford county, Md. The minutes say it was held in the "preaching house," but Mr. Watters says it was in his eldest brother's house. There were now twenty-seven traveling preachers in the connection, twenty of whom were present at this Conference. It was a gracious and memorable occasion. Asbury preached on the charge which our Lord gave to his apostles, which was peculiarly appropriate to their circumstances, "Behold, I send you forth as sheep in the midst of wolves : be ye therefore wise as serpents, and harmless as doves."

Both the "public and private business was conducted with great harmony, peace, and love." As there appeared to be no prospect of a speedy termination of the contests between this country and Great Britain, several of the English preachers thought they would return home, if the way opened in the course of the year, and to provide against such an event a committee, consisting of five of the American preachers, viz. : Watters, Gatch, Dromgoold, Ruff, and Glendining, was appointed to act in the place of the general assistant, in case he should leave before the next Conference. It was also submitted whether, as few ministers were left in many of the parishes to administer the Sacraments, the preachers should not administer them themselves, and thus avoid being dependent upon other denominations for them; for while the greater part received them from the Episcopal. Church, some received them from the Presbyterians.* "In fact," says Watters, "we considered ourselves, at this time, as belonging to the Church of England, it being before our separation and our becoming a regularly formed Church." After much conversation upon the subject, it was finally agreed unanimously to lay the question over until the next Conference. The Conference ended with a watch-night and love-feast. Asbury says it was "a great time—a season of uncommon affection." "I never saw," says Watters, "so affecting a scene, at the parting of the preachers, before. Our hearts were knit together, as the hearts of David and Jonathan, and we were obliged to use great violence to our feelings in tearing ourselves asunder. This was the last time I ever saw my very worthy friends and fathers, Rankin and Shadford."

At this Conference Henry Kennedy and Thomas M'Clure were appointed to New Jersey, which still remained one circuit. Kennedy's name appears on the minutes, for the first time, this year, and after being appointed to Caroline the following year, he must have desisted from traveling, as his name disappears from the

* Life of Watters.

minutes; but in Asbury's Journal of April 14, 1780, it is written, "Thomas M'Clure is confined sick in Phila-delphia, Henry Kennedy and William Adams* are dead; so the Lord cuts off the watchmen of Israel. But sure I am that it is better to die early than to live, though late, to dishonor God." M'Clure was admitted on trial at the Conference of 1776, and appointed to Fairfax, the next year he was sent to New Jersey and the year following to Baltimore. In 1779 he was appointed to Kent cir-cuit. In 1780 his name does not appear in the minutes. In 1781 he was appointed to Somerset, and in 1782 his name is again absent from the minutes. Asbury speaks of him in a way which indicates that he sustained a very respectable position in our early ministry.

At the end of this year the members in the whole con-nection are reported in the aggregate, so that we cannot determine what was the number in New Jersey. The entire number of members, however, reported at the Conference of 1778, was six thousand and ninety-five, being an increase, in five years, for the whole Church, of five thousand nine hundred and thirty-five, an average of one thousand one hundred and eighty-seven a year. There were also twenty-nine traveling preachers in the con-nection, being an increase of nineteen in the same period.

At the Conference of 1777, it was asked in Confer-ence, "As the present distress is such, are the preachers

* Adams was brother-in-law to Watters.

resolved to take no step to detach themselves from the work of God for the ensuing year?" To which it was answered, "We purpose, by the grace of God, not to take any step that may separate us from the brethren, or from the blessed work in which we are engaged." None of the English preachers appear to have remained in the country longer than 1778, except Asbury.

In 1778 the storm of the revolution raged so high that Asbury and Shadford agreed to make it a matter of prayer and fasting whether they should remain in this country or return to England. The latter concluded that it was his duty to leave the country, but Asbury believed that the intimations of the Divine will to him were that he should remain; accordingly he replied to Shadford, "If you are called to go, I am called to stay; so we must part." "From that moment," says Rev. E. Cooper, "he made America his home. He resolved to abide among us, and at the risk of all, even of life itself, to continue to labor and to suffer with and for his American brethren.

"Oppositions, reproaches, and persecutions rushed in against them, from every quarter in various forms, like a tempest and a flood. During the whole period of conflict and danger his manner of life was irreproachable. His prudence and caution, as a man and a citizen; his pious and correct deportment, as a Christian and a minister, were such as to put at defiance the suspicious mind and the tongue of persecuting slander. They were never able to substantiate any allegation, or the appearance of a charge against him that was incompatible with the character of a citizen, a Christian, or a faithful minister of the gospel. He never meddled with politics. But in those days of suspicion and alarm, to get a preacher or a society persecuted they only had to excite suspicion, sound the alarm, and cry out, 'Enemies to the country,' or, 'tories.' The Methodists, at one period, were generally called tories by those who either knew not the people, or the meaning of the word."

After giving some account of the persecutions inflicted upon the preachers in Maryland, the venerable Cooper says, "During those perilous times where was our Asbury? How was he employed? and what was the manner of his life? After having traveled and preached at large, with all the zeal, fidelity, and caution, which prudence and wisdom, situated and circumstanced as he was, could dictate; he being greatly embarrassed and perplexed, and, withal much suspected as an Englishman, had, at length, to retire, in a great measure, for a season, until the indignation was overpast. The spirit of the times, the passions and the prejudices of the people, and the jealousies and suspicions subsisting against him as an Englishman, and as a principal Methodist preacher, were such that he could not, with safety, continue to travel openly and at large. In the year 1778, when the storm was at its highest, and persecution raged furiously, he, being in serious danger, prudently and advisedly confined himself, for personal safety, chiefly to the little state of Delaware, where the laws were rather more favorable, and the rulers and influential men were somewhat more friendly. For a time he had, even there, to keep himself much retired. He found an asylum as his castle of safety, in the house, and with the hospitable family of his firm friend, Thomas White, Esq., one of the judges of the Court in Kent county, Delaware. He was a pious man, and his wife one of the holiest of women; they were great friends to the cause of religion, and to the preachers generally. From this place of retreat and protection, as in a castle of repose and safety, he could correspond with his suffering brethren who were scattered abroad in different parts. He could also occasionally travel about, visiting the societies, and, sometimes, preaching to the people. He was accessible to all the preachers and his friends who came to see him, so that by means of correspondence and of visits, they could communicate with each other for mutual counsel, comfort, and encouragement."*

In his journal Asbury makes the following statement:

* Cooper on Asbury.

"From March 10, 1778, on conscientious principles, I was a non-juror and could not preach in the state of Maryland; and therefore withdrew to the Delaware state, where the clergy were not required to take the state oath; though, with a clear conscience, I could have taken the oath of the Delaware state, had it been required; and would have done it, had I not been prevented by a tender fear of hurting the scrupulous consciences of others. Saint Paul saith, 'When ye sin so against the brethren and wound their weak conscience, ye sin against Christ.' 1 Cor. viii. 12."

The following passage from his journal of Sept. 15, 1778, will indicate somewhat the nature of his feelings while confined in Delaware. "This was a day of peculiar temptations. My trials were such as I do not remember to have experienced before; and, for some time, it seemed as if I scarcely knew whether to fight or fly. My usefulness appeared to be cut off; I saw myself pent up in a corner; my body, in a manner, worn out; my English brethren gone, so that I had no one to consult; and every surrounding object and circumstance wore a gloomy aspect. Lord, must I thus pine away, and quench the light of Israel? No! though he slay me yet will I trust in him." His necessary seclusion was not spent in idleness. "On the contrary," he says, "except about two months of retirement from the direst necessity, it was the most active, the most useful, and the most afflictive part of my life."

The Conference of 1778 was held at Leesburg, Va., on the 19th of May. Asbury was not present, and for prudential reasons, doubtless, his name does not appear on the minutes for that year. The fact of his being an Englishman "was enough with some," says Watters, " why he should be suspected as unfriendly to our cause and country, though I will venture to say that his greatest enemy could allege nothing else against him, nor even that with propriety." Daniel Ruff was the only traveling preacher appointed to labor in New Jersey, but Abbott was still laboring most energetically as a local preacher, and did more work probably, than is now performed by any regular Methodist clergyman in the state. His labors were productive of large and glorious results. It was probably not far from this year, and perhaps during it, that he attended a quarterly meeting at Morris River. It was a powerful season. "The slain," he says, " lay all through the house, and round it, and in the woods, crying to God for mercy; and others praising God for the deliverance of their souls. At this time there came up the river a look-out boat; the crew landed and came to the meeting; one of them stood by a woman that lay on the ground crying to God for mercy, and said to her, 'Why do you not cry louder?'

8

She immediately began to pray for him, and the power of the Lord struck him to the ground, and he lay and cried for mercy louder than the woman. This meeting continued from eleven o'clock till night."

At another appointment he attended, so great was the display of divine power among the people that many fell to the floor. Sinners sprang to the doors and windows and fell over one another in getting out; five jumped out at a window, and the cries of the slain were very great. One woman went close by Abbott and cried, "You are a devil!" A young man cried out, "Command the peace!" but a magistrate who was present, answered, "It is the power of God." Another, with tears in his eyes, entreated the people to hold their peace; to which an old woman replied, "They cannot hold their peace, unless you cut their tongues." "Glory to God!" says Abbott, "this day will never be forgotten either in time or eternity. I was as happy as I could contain." He preached at a Mr. Smith's on Tuckahoe river and one fell to the floor. He then asked the people what they thought of such manifestations, and whether they did not think they were of the devil. "If it is of the devil," he said, "when she comes to she will curse and swear, but if it is of God, she will praise him." The people looked on in amazement while she lay struggling on the floor. At length she came to, praising the

Lord with a loud voice, and declaring that God had sanctified her soul. Abbott then met the society and impressed sanctification upon them. A woman who had been fifteen years a professor of justification fell to the floor, and after some time arose and declared that the Lord had sanctified her soul. Abbott exhorted those around her to claim the promise, and while she was yet speaking six or seven were prostrated upon the floor.

He threw open the doors and windows and called the wicked to come and witness for themselves the displays of divine power, telling them that if they would not believe when such manifestations were given, they would not believe if God Almighty were to speak to them, as he did to Moses, in a flame of fire. Before the meeting closed, six or seven professed to obtain sanctification.

The next morning he went to another place "and preached with great liberty." The meeting commenced at eleven o'clock and lasted until midnight. Before it was over seven professed to find peace, and joined the society. "Here I was as happy in my own soul," he says, "as I could wish either to live or die." On the day following, "I preached," he says, "at brother Hew's to a precious, loving people; and as soon as I had kneeled down, before I had uttered one sentence, they all cried out, Amen. After preaching, in class, I endeavored to teach them the meaning and nature of the term Amen." At one of his appointments, before preaching, he retired in secret. So mighty was the Divine influence that rested upon him, he lost the use of his physical powers, and "cried out" in such a manner that the people who had not seen the like before were alarmed. After recovering a little, he went and preached to them, and had a "precious time."

Do any say, Abbott was a fanatic? We reply, Was Tennent then a fanatic? Was not he, the Presbyterian pastor of Freehold, the subject of exercises not dissimilar to those which Abbott experienced? Before service one Sabbath morning, Tennent went into a grove near his Church, to commune with God, and so singularly and powerfully was he wrought upon, that, finding he did not come to address the waiting congregation, his elders sought him out and conveyed him to his pulpit, where he preached under the influence of this powerful baptism with the Holy Ghost sent down from heaven. Who ever dreamed of charging Tennent with fanaticism because he thus sank under the power of God? And why should Abbott, because to him was given so great an unction from the Holy One, be stigmatized with this charge? A man possessed of an extraordinary faith and a bui. 'ng zeal which prompts him to abound in sacrifices and labors for God and humanity, especially if he be a Methodist, is exceedingly liable to the charge of fanaticism.

But it is not new. Many centuries ago was it said by a fit representative of a class who are swift to pass their judgment upon God's heroes, "Paul, thou art beside thyself, much learning doth make thee mad."

In 1779 there were two Conferences, one for the Northern and one for the Southern section of the work. The Northern Conference was held at the house of Thomas White, Esq., in Kent county, Delaware. All the preachers on the northern stations were present and united. "We had," says Asbury, "much prayer, love, and harmony; and we all agreed to walk by the same rule and to mind the same thing." At this Conference New Jersey was united with Philadelphia, and three preachers were appointed to the laborious field. They were Philip Cox, Joshua Dudley, and Daniel Ruff.

Freeborn Garrettson visited New Jersey this year, where he labored a short time with considerable success. He says, "I bless and praise my dear Lord for the prosperous journey he gave me through the Jerseys; several were awakened, and some brought to know Jesus. One day, after preaching, an old man came to me and said all in tears, ' This day I am an hundred and one years old, and this is my spiritual birth-day.' The dear man's soul was so exceedingly happy, that he appeared to be ready to take his flight to heaven.

"I preached at a new place, where the congregation

consisted mostly of young people, from, ' The Son of man is come to seek and to save that which was lost.' Luke xix. 10. We had a wonderful display of the power of the Lord. After I had finished, the young people hung around each other, crying for mercy; and I believe many will praise the Lord eternally for that day."

Asbury records in his journal this year a remarkable account of the case of ACHSAH BORDEN, who appeared to be possessed of a dumb spirit. "From her childhood," he says, "she was attentive to reading her Bible, and ofttimes had serious thoughts of eternity; one day, reading and meditating, an uncommon light and comfort flowed into her heart. Her soul cried out, ' Sweet Jesus !' and was convinced Christ was her Saviour; her friends observing for a season that she was very serious feared a melancholy; which to prevent, they gathered their friends and neighbors, with music and dancing, thinking to arouse her (as they said) from her stupidity, or charm off her religious frenzy. Through various temptations she was prevailed upon to go into company, of course, into sin. She lost her comfort, and afterward fell into deep distress. She had heard of the Methodists, and was anxious to go to them that they might pray for her. Those with whom she was, paid no regard to her importunity, but locked her up in a room, and ordered all the knives to be taken away. She knew their meaning, but says she was under no temptation to destroy or lay violent hands upon herself. Soon after this her speech failed her, so that she only spoke half sentences, and would be stopped by inability; but by grasping anything hard in her hand, she could speak with difficulty and deliberation; but soon lost this power, and a dumb spirit took perfect possession of her; she said then it was impressed on her mind, 'The effectual and fervent prayer of a righteous man availeth much.' She heard the Methodists were a people that prayed much, and still retained her desire to go amongst them, and by signs made it known to her friends. And after about one year's silence, her mother was prevailed upon to go with her to New Mills, New Jersey, (about thirteen miles distant,) where there was a society and meeting-house; they knew no Methodists, nor could get any one to tell them where to find any, notwithstanding they were now in the midst of them. Satan hindered; inquiry was made among the B——ts, who knew the Methodists, of whom we might have expected better things. They returned home, and after another year's waiting in silence, by signs her mother was persuaded to come to New Mills again; they fell in with the B——ts again, but turning from them, with much difficulty, and some hours' wandering, they found one to direct them. They went where a number were met for prayer; the brethren saw into her case, believing it was a dumb spirit, and that God would cast him out.   Prayer was made part of three days; the third day at evening she cried for mercy, soon spoke and praised God from a sense of comforting, pardoning love.   During the two years of her silence, she would not work at all, nor do the smallest thing."

Garrettson, in his journal, gives an account of this case, though he does not give her name; but there can be no doubt of its being the same person, notwithstanding there is a slight difference in some points between the two statements; yet substantially they agree.   Mr. Garrettson says she was a young woman, brought up a Quaker, and that Mr. Ruff, one of the preachers, was present when she presented herself to the society.   He says, "Sometime after, I came into this neighborhood and sent word to her mother I would preach such a day at her house.   When the day arrived I took the young woman home, accompanied by many friends, and we were received like angels; some thought the Methodists could work miracles.   Many of the friends and neighbors came, and could not but observe how angelic this young woman appeared to be; who was now able to speak and work as well as usual.   I bless the Lord who gave me great freedom in preaching on this remarkable occasion. The people seemed to believe every word which was delivered, and a precious, sweet season it was.   The old lady was ready to take us in her arms, being so happy, and so well satisfied with respect to her daughter."

At the end of this year there were one hundred and forty members in New Jersey, which was a decrease in the two years last past of twenty. Yet from the slight information we obtain concerning its progress, we infer that the cause assumed a more encouraging and favorable appearance during the year. On the 7th of October, Bishop Asbury, in his journal, says, "I received a letter from brother Ruff; he says the work deepens in the Jerseys." Again on the 24th of April, 1780, he says, "Received three epistles from the Jerseys, soliciting three or four preachers, with good tidings of the work of God reviving in those parts. The petitioners I shall hear with respect."

Those few words tell of prosperity, and they are about all we are able to learn in regard to the general condition of the work this year, with the exception of what is indicated by the report of members given at the Conference. It is evident that though there was strong opposition against them, and their discouragements were great, the zeal of these earnest Christian ministers and Methodist heroes did not flag, but in the face of obstacles sufficient to cause the stoutest heart to shrink, unless it were nerved by an apostle's faith, they bravely prosecuted their labors, praying for and expecting success.

PHILIP COX was a native of Froome, Somersetshire, England. He must have been converted about the year 1774, as Philip Gatch speaks of preaching at a certain place when he traveled Kent circuit, that year, and says, "At this place Philip Cox, who afterward became a useful preacher, was caught in the gospel net." He must have entered the itinerant connection in the year 1778, as at the Conference of 1779 he was among the number that were continued on trial. In 1780 he was sent to Fairfax, Va., and in 1781 to Little York. His subsequent appointments, so far as known, were as follows:—In 1782 and 1783 Frederic and Annamessex Md.; 1784, Long Island; 1785, Northampton, Md.; 1786–7–8, Brunswick, Sussex, and Mecklenberg, in Va.

On this last circuit he had for his colleague the Rev. Wm. M'Kendree, who was in his first year in the ministry. In 1789 he received the appointment of Book Steward and was reappointed to the office in 1790. We are not able to ascertain his appointments for the last three years of his life. While Mr. Cox traveled as book steward, Enoch George, who subsequently became bishop, commenced traveling with him. Cox treated his young companion with paternal kindness, for which the latter cherished, it is said, a sense of lifelong obligation.

Shortly after he commenced preaching, while traveling with Mr. Cox, they met Bishop Asbury. Cox said to the bishop, "I have brought you a boy, and if you have anything for him to do you may set him to work." Asbury looked at him for some time, and at length called him to him, and laying his head upon his knee, and stroking his face with his hand, said, "Why he is a beardless boy and can do nothing." George then thought his traveling was at an end, but the next day the bishop accepted his services and appointed him to a circuit.*

Mr. Cox was a man of very small stature. At one time he felt badly and concluded to retire from the field. But on being weighed he found his weight amounted to an hundred pounds. He then remarked, "It shall never be said I quit traveling while I weigh an hundred weight."†

He was eminently successful as a minister of Jesus Christ. When he traveled Sussex circuit in Virginia, in 1787, the people were converted in multitudes. Having hurt a limb he had resolved to take a day's rest, but being sent for to attend the funeral of a little child, he went and spoke to a congregation of a hundred persons from the words, "Except ye be converted and become as little children, ye cannot enter into the kingdom of heaven." Although he was compelled to preach sitting

* Heroes of Methodism. † Lee's Hist. of Methodists.

upon a table, and fifty of his auditors were old professors, thirty of the other fifty professed to find peace before the close of the meeting. The next day he sat in a chair on a table in the woods and preached, when "above sixty souls were set at liberty." At another time, at a Quarterly meeting held in Sussex circuit, he says; "Before the preachers got there the work broke out, so that when we came to the chapel, above sixty were down on the floor, groaning in loud cries to God for mercy. Brother O'Kelly tried to preach, but could not be heard for the cries of the distressed. It is thought our audience consisted of no less than five thousand the first day, and the second day of twice that number. We preached to them in the open air, and in the Chapel, and in the barn by brother Jones' house, at the same time. Such a sight my eyes never saw before, and never read of, either in Mr. Wesley's Journals, or any other writings, concerning the Lord's pouring out the Spirit, except the account in Scripture of the day of Pentecost. Never, I believe, was the like seen since the apostolic age: hundreds were at once down on the ground in bitter cries to God for mercy. Here were many of the first quality in the country wallowing in the dust with their silks and broadcloths, powdered heads, rings, and ruffles, and some of them so convulsed that they could neither speak nor stir; many stood by, persecuting, till the power of the

Lord laid hold of them, and then they fell themselves, and cried as loud as those they had just before persecuted. We are not able to give a just account how many were converted, and as we had rather be under than over the just number, we believe that near two hundred whites and more than half as many blacks professed to find Him of whom Moses and the prophets did write."

It was believed that nearly two hundred whites and more than half as many blacks professed to receive forgiveness of sins at this meeting.* In his Journal, January 8th, 1788, Bishop Asbury says, "Brother Cox thinks that not less than fourteen hundred, white and black, have been converted in Sussex circuit the past year." Rev. Philip Bruce, in a letter published in the Arminian Magazine (American), dated nearly three months later, says: "Brother Cox informs me, that between twelve and fifteen hundred whites have been converted in his circuit, besides a great number of blacks."

The last services of Mr. Cox were great, it is said, in circulating books of religious instruction.

The methodist preachers of that day were not content merely to preach the truth, but encouraged the people to read religious books, regarding the latter as a most important auxiliary to the former. Instead of being opposed to the spread of knowledge among the people, the

* Arminian Magazine, vol. ii. pp. 92–3.

preachers of the Methodist Episcopal Church have done more, probably, than any other single body of men, to promote the cause of literature and learning, by their example and their direct personal labors. By placing good books in the hands of the people, they were instrumental in settling and fortifying the faith of those who were converted by their preaching, and of saving many more, perhaps, who would not have been reached by their public ministry.

Mr. Cox was delirious in his last illness, but on Sunday, a week preceding his death, he said, "that it was such a day of peace and comfort to his soul as he had seldom seen." He died in peace on the Sunday following, the 8th of September, 1793. He was a man of great spirit, quick apprehension, and sound judgment.

He who was instrumental in turning so "many to righteousness" must have a brilliant coronet of stars in the day of the Lord Jesus.

JOSHUA DUDLEY must have traveled in 1778, as at the Conference of 1779, at which he was appointed to the Philadelphia and New Jersey circuit, he was continued on trial, though his name does not previously appear in the minutes. In 1780 he was sent to Baltimore; in 1781 to Amelia; in 1782 to West Jersey; in 1783 his name is not in the minutes. At this period, the question, "Who have located this year?" was not asked in the minutes, and consequently when preachers, on account of ill health or for any other reason, desisted from traveling, there is no mention made of the fact.

Mr. Dudley could not have remained very long upon the circuit this year, as in September he was employed in Delaware. On the ninth of that month, Asbury writes, "I was unwell and was relieved by Joshua Dudley who took the circuit." Nine days afterward he writes, "Brother Dudley being detained by his father being sick, brother Cooper is come in his place."

He received still another appointment before the close of the Conference year, as on the fourth of March 1780, Asbury records in his Journal that he had appointed Joshua Dudley for Dorset. He evidently occupied an honorable position as a preacher, but our information concerning him is excedingly meagre. When he traveled in New Jersey, Benjamin Abbott heard him preach, and he has left the very brief tribute to his effectiveness as a preacher, which is as follows: "The next appoint-was made at J. D's., for brother Dudley; he came and preached with power."*

Thus have we passed the first decade in the history of New Jersey Methodism. We have witnessed its rise, its reverses, and at the same time some of its noblest tri-

* Life of Abbott. p. 81.

umphs in rescuing souls from the dark depths of guilt, who otherwise, perhaps, would never have been reached by redemptive agencies. With this decade passed its severest and darkest days, and though the progress of the movement appears inconsiderable, yet during this time the foundations were slowly but securely laid on which has since been reared that beautiful and majestic temple which is now the spiritual refuge of forty thousand souls.

The sufferings and labors of the preachers during this decade were great. They literally had no certain dwelling place but went to and fro, everywhere encountering hardship and obloquy, in order that they might save redeemed but perishing men. The societies were few, and feeble both in numbers and means, and were nearly all without churches. This last fact alone was a formidable obstacle to the advancement of the cause. One of the arguments employed by the opponents of the movement was that as the Methodists were without houses of worship and were not able to build, they would soon dwindle away, and by this means much of the fruit of Methodist toil and sacrifice was appropriated by other sects. Still, many in the face of poverty and reproach adhered to the Church which had travailed in birth for them. One whose devotion was unswerving, in reply to the prediction that the Methodists would soon become extinct, said,

"Well, if they do come to nothing, as long as I live there will be *one* left." Both the preachers and people were looked upon as fanatics, as deceivers of the people, and tories; yet in the midst of all God was with them, and through him they originated influences which are still potent with Omnipotent energy, and which will continue to bless and elevate humanity until the final victories of the militant Church shall be celebrated in the endless hallelujahs of the heavens.

9

CHAPTER VI.

METHODISM IN NEW MILLS.

IN the year 1826, the name of this village was changed from that of New Mills to Pemberton, but as during the period embraced in this volume it was New Mills, we shall use that name only.

There has long been a tradition that the first Methodist society in New Jersey was formed in that village, but fidelity to the facts of history requires us to say that this tradition is without foundation. It is justly claimed by the tradition that the society was formed there in the year 1772, Methodism having been introduced during that year by Mr. Asbury. His first recorded visit there was in the early part of that year. In his Journal he says it was on the thirtieth and thirty-first days of February, overlooking the fact, doubtless, that February has never thirty days. This of course was merely a slip of the pen.

We have already shown that both the Burlington and

Trenton societies were formed previously to the year 1772, the former having been formed on the 14th of December, 1770, and the latter in 1771. New Mills must therefore rank, at most, as the third society in point of time in New Jersey.

Ex-Gov. Fort of New Jersey, in a private note says, "The tradition was that the M. E. Church there was the first in the State and the third in the United States, in point of time. John Street, N. Y., being first; a Church in Maryland (Strawbridge's), second; and New Mills, third." This agrees with an article published by Gov. Fort in the Christian Advocate and Journal of February 14, 1834, in which he claims that the Church at New Mills was "the first Methodist meeting-house erected in the State." I am exceedingly sorry to dispel this pleasing illusion, which has been fondly cherished in many a devout heart, and transmitted from parent to child for perhaps three-fourths of a century, and I would not do it, did not candor require that I should present the facts of history as they are.

Asbury speaks of seeing the foundation of a Church laid in New Jersey in April, 1773. This could not have been the Church at New Mills, because its dimensions were not the same as those of the New Mills Church, and it is not claimed that that Church was built before the year 1774. Asbury gives explicitly the dimensions of both these Churches. The former was 35 by 30 feet, and the latter (New Mills) was 36 by 28 feet. On Saturday and Sunday the fourth and fifth of May, 1776, Asbury was at New Mills, and says he "found brother W. very busy about his Chapel." The Church was then built, as he preached in it at that time, but from this remark it would appear that it was not yet finished. The deed of purchase, says Gov. Fort, is dated the 31st of December, 1774, the very last day of that year. The evidence arising from a comparison of these dates, and the dimensions of the Churches, appears conclusive in favor of the priority of the former. Evidence adduced in a foot note on page 53 appears to fix the location of that Church at Trenton.

There is considerable ground for the opinion that there was a Church built in New Jersey at a period still earlier than this. Methodism was introduced at an early period into the township of Greenwich, Gloucester county, and on the 14th of May, 1772, Asbury, being in that locality, says, "Went to the new Church. Surely the power of God is amongst this people. After preaching with great assistance I lodged at Isaac Jenkins's, and in the morning he conducted me to Gloucester; and thence we went by water to Philadelphia."*

* See Asbury's Journal, vol. i. p. 30.

That this was a Methodist Church is probable from the fact that he speaks of it in connection with the power of God being amongst the people, and with preaching there with great assistance. None will question, I suppose, that the people who were thus distinguished for their spirituality were Methodists, and if not, I know not how it can be questioned that this "new Church" was built by that people. Had it been any other than a Methodist Church it does not seem probable that Asbury would have mentioned it in the connection he does in his Journal, or if he did, it would seem probable that he would have said something to indicate that it was not a Methodist Church. The evidence thus presented supports, we think, the following positions, viz:

1. That the first Methodist meeting-house, or Church, in New Jersey was built in the township of Greenwich, Gloucester county.

2. That the second Church in the state was built in Trenton in the year 1773.

3. That the third Methodist Church in New Jersey was built in New Mills in 1775. Gov. Fort says it was built in 1774, but as he also says the deed of purchase bears date of Dec. 31, 1774, and as Asbury speaks of finding it in an unfinished condition in 1776, we are inclined to the opinion that 1775 was most probably the year in which it was built. Still, allowing it to have

been built in 1774, it must yet rank as the third Church erected by Methodists in the province.

Although New Mills cannot claim the priority which tradition has assigned it, it can claim the more important and enviable honor of having been for years a strong-hold of Methodism in New Jersey. Some of the mightiest battles which distinguished the early history of American Methodism were fought there, and some of its sublimest victories were won. Most of the preachers of note, during the first years of its history, preached in this Church; among whom were Asbury, Captain Webb Thomas Rankin, Strawbridge, Gill, Garrettson, Abbott and others.

The original trustees of the Church were John Budd, Eli Budd, Andrew Heisler, Samuel Budd, Peter Shiras, Jonathan Budd, Daniel Heisler, Joseph Toy, and Lambert Willmore. "They were only to permit the Rev. John Wesley, or the ministers delegated by him, to preach in it. After his death the like privilege was extended to the Rev. Charles Wesley, and after the death of the latter, to the 'yearly Conference of London and North America.'"*

When Asbury preached his first sermon there, one of the above mentioned trustees heard it, and "remarked that he was a great preacher, but was afraid he might

* Ex Gov. Fort's article in Ch. Advocate and Jn'l., Feb. 14, 1834.

be one of the false prophets. Such was the prejudice against Methodism at that time. Nevertheless numbers flocked to hear him; some from curiosity, some with evil, others with good intent, and many, through his instrumentality and of those who followed him, became subjects of converting grace; among the rest, the trustee and his associates."*

Daniel Heisler, one of the first trustees, came from Holland and settled on a farm near New Mills. He was the great grandfather of Hon. George F. Fort, and of Rev. J. P. Fort of the Newark, and of Revs. John Fort and John S. Heisler of the New Jersey Conference. The first represented Methodism for three years in the Executive chair of the State, while the last named are worthy and useful ministers in the Church.

Captain Webb was so imprudent when in this country in speaking against the opposition of the colonies to Great Britain, that he was compelled, it is said, to conceal himself for some months in the premises of a reputed tory near New Mills, before he could make his escape to England.†

The fame of Abbott reached New Mills at an early period in his ministry, and they sent for him to visit them. He accordingly went, though he was but a local

* Ex Gov. Fort's article in Ch. Advocate and Jn'l., Feb. 14, 1834.

† Raybold's Reminiscences of Methodism in West Jersey. p. 197.

preacher, laboring without pecuniary reward, and the distance from his home in Salem county was about sixty miles. The first time he preached there, "God worked powerfully," he says. There was considerable weeping and one fell to the floor. This alarmed the people, as they had never seen such demonstrations before. "Next day," he says, "I preached, and the Lord poured out his spirit among us, so that there was weeping in abundance, and one fell to the floor: many prayers being made for him, he found peace before he arose. He is a living witness to this day. [Probably a number of years afterward.] I saw him not long since, and we had a precious time together."

He attended at another time a Quarterly meeting in New Mills. He says: "After our meeting had been opened and several exhortations given, brother C. Cotts went to prayer, and several fell to the floor, and many were affected, and we had a powerful time. After meeting, brother J. S. and several others went with me to I. B.'s, where we tarried all night. Here we found a woman in distress of soul; after prayer, we retired to bed. In the morning brother S. went to prayer, and after him, myself. The distressed woman lay as in the agonies of death near one hour; when she arose, she went into her room to prayer, and soon after returned and professed faith in Christ. She and her husband went with us to brother H.'s, where about forty persons had assembled to wait for us in order to have prayer before we parted. As soon as I entered the house, a woman entreated me to pray for her, and added, 'I am going to hell, I have no God.' I exhorted her and all present, setting before them the curses of God's law against sin; and likewise I applied the promises of the gospel to the penitent; then a young woman came to me and said, 'Father Abbott, pray to God to give me a clean heart.' I replied, 'God shall give you one this moment.' How I came to use the word *shall*, I know not, but she dropped at that instant into my arms as one dead. I then claimed the promises and cried to God, exhorting them all to look to God for clean hearts, and he would do great things for them, at which about twenty more fell to the floor. When the young woman came to, she declared that God had sanctified her soul. I saw her many years after, and her life and conversation adorned the Gospel. Prayer was kept up without intermission for the space of three hours; eight souls professed sanctification, and three Indian women justification in Christ Jesus."

The Church at New Mills, during the first years of its existence enjoyed remarkable prosperity. William Watters returned to New Jersey in the spring of 1782 to visit his friends there, and he says:

"At the New Mills, I thought it very extraordinary; seven years before I left a large society, and now found all alive, and but one of them had in that time left the society, while they had become double or treble the number!" * This testimony speaks much for the stability and devotion of its early members.

JACOB HEISLER was one of the first members of the Church in New Mills. When he united with the society there were but four in class beside himself. He was but sixteen years of age when he experienced religion. He assisted in building the first Church in New Mills, and lived to see it decay, and another larger and better occupying its place, and its membership greatly increased. Having fought the good fight for sixty years, he made a glorious and happy exit to heaven on the 17th of August, 1834, in the 76th year of his age.

"He was a sample of primitive Methodism," says Gov. Fort in an obituary sketch, "in the discharge of his duties, and in his conduct as a Christian and a man. He was alike punctual in attendance on public worship, family prayer, and reading God's holy word. He discharged with fidelity and success the active duties of a trustee, class leader, and exhorter for a number of years. Amid all his difficulties, trials, and severe afflictions, which to use his own language, 'equaled if not exceeded

* Life of Watters.

those of Job,' he never lost his confidence in God, nor did religion cease to be his 'chief concern.' He passed through them all with almost unexampled patience and resignation. As the period of dissolution approached, his piety shone brighter, his love grew warmer, his zeal increased, and his whole soul seemed more impressed with the image of the living God. About a week before his death, he told me that his bodily afflictions were so great he could not realize that fullness of joy and spiritual comfort which he earnestly desired; but still all was calm and peace within."

In a private letter Gov. Fort remarks concerning him as follows:—"Jacob Heisler was a man of remarkable piety. I have often heard him, when quite a child, speak in class and love-feast. He obeyed the apostolic injunction, to 'pray without ceasing,' nearer than any man I ever knew. He prayed seven times a day habitually in family and private, had strong emotions, and enjoyed the blessing of perfect love. He was always ready for death, walked with God as Enoch, and often made me think he would, like Enoch, not taste death."

CHAPTER VII.

JAMES STERLING.

FOREMOST among the most honored and distinguished laymen of his time was James Sterling, a man who was identified with New Jersey Methodism for nearly half a century.

He was born in Ireland in the year 1742, but came to this country when very young. His mother was a member of the Presbyterian Church, and her godly example and admonitions produced religious impressions on his mind at an early age. As he grew up, however, he fell into gay and trifling company, and imbibed the spirit and adopted the practices of the vain world, thus illustrating the Scripture declaration that "evil communications corrupt good manners."

He was trained to the business of a merchant by his uncle, James Hunter of Philadelphia, to whom he was much indebted for his success in life. Having reached the age in which it seemed expedient that he should enter business for himself, he removed to Burlington, New Jersey, and established himself as a merchant under the counsel and patronage of his uncle, depending, however, upon his own energy and industry for success. He withdrew from such society as was of questionable character, and formed such acquaintances as were likely to be of service to him.

He married a Miss Shaw who was an Episcopalian, himself being a member of the Presbyterian church, but agreeing to avoid all contention about differences of opinion in religion, they established the worship of God in their family, and maintained the form of godliness though for some time they remained without its power.

About the year 1771 he heard Mr. Asbury preach, and was brought under deep conviction of sin. He now became a constant hearer of the Methodist preachers, and soon joined the society, and for a considerable time he was connected with both the Methodist and the Presbyterian Churches. When the Revolutionary struggle commenced, he held the office of justice of the peace under the royal authority, "but when the government of England declared that the Colonies were no longer under his Majesty's protection, he very justly concluded that where there was no protection there could be no obligations to allegiance. He then took a decided and active part in the American cause as a firm and zealous whig. He was the Captain of a company, and went with his company to Staten Island and other places in the public service.   He embarked his reputation, his fortune, and his all in the support of the Independence of the United States."*

During the war his religious fervor abated, and his connection with the Methodist society ceased.   But, notwithstanding he made no profession of vital religion, he preserved his attachment to the cause and followers of Christ.

Having enjoyed prosperity in his business, he abandoned "mercantile pursuits and bought a valuable farm in Salem county, and furnished it with stock and everything necessary to become a complete and great farmer. He moved on his farm with flattering anticipations," but not being contented in his new sphere of life he did not continue very long in it; but "about the close of the war he returned to Burlington and again went into the mercantile business where he continued to reside till the close of his valuable life."

During his residence in Salem county he renewed his attention to spiritual concerns and was made the partaker of a "peace that passeth all understanding."

* "Obituary Notice of James Sterling, Esq., of Burlington, New Jersey, which was published in the American Daily Advertiser, (Philadelphia,) January 19, 1818."

Benjamin Abbott, in his Life, p. 45, says, "On a Saturday night I dreamed that a man came to meeting, and stayed in class, and spoke as I never had heard any one before. Next day James Sterling came to meeting, stayed in class, and spoke much as I had seen in my dream. After meeting I said to my wife, that was the very man I had seen in my dream, and the Lord would add him to his Church. Soon after he was thoroughly awakened and converted to God." Years after this event Mr. Abbott, speaking of Mr. Sterling, says, "He yet stands fast among us a useful and distinguished member, known by many of our preachers and members." Having obtained the knowledge of salvation by the remission of sins he had to endure a severe conflict, in order to subdue his pride of spirit. He was a man of position and of fortune; but the Methodist society there at that time was composed chiefly of persons in the humble walks of life, and was generally regarded with disrespect by the polite and refined world. "However, he humbled himself, or rather, was humbled by grace, and became and continued to be a member of the persecuted and reproached society, and the Lord blessed his soul very remarkably, and in such a gracious manner as he had never before experienced, with pardon, and peace, and joy in the Holy Spirit. He professed and no doubt possessed justifying grace by faith in his Lord and

Saviour, the Spirit of grace bearing witness with his spirit, that he was born of God. He became very bold, zealous, and active in the cause of religion ; and he frequently spoke in public by way of exhortation, warning his fellow creatures to flee by repentance from the wrath to come, and to fly by faith to the Lord Jesus Christ for salvation.

He yet continued to be a member for some time both of the Presbyterian and the Methodist connections. But about that time some objections were raised by a part of the Presbyterian Church Session to his continuing to be a member of both communities ; that if he continued in the Methodist society, and to speak in public, by virtue of authority or permission from the Methodists, they objected to his communing with them ; and also they objected to some tenets which he held in opinion with the Methodists as true and Scriptural, which some of the Session considered as contrary to their Confession of Faith. The Session, however, was divided on these questions. Some were for his continuing among them as he had done ; others were for his not communing with them unless he left the Methodists. He had been recommended to them in terms of high approbation in his certificate from a sister Church, and they had no charge of immorality against him, and were probably unwilling to part with him. Yet the foundation was laid in that dispute for him to leave the one or the other society for the sake of peace; he therefore voluntarily made his election, or choice, to withdraw from the Presbyterians, as he had resolved to continue among the Methodists. Henceforward to the day of his death he was closely and firmly united with the Methodist Episcopal Church, in fellowship and communion."*

Probably no layman in the State ever did more to advance the cause of religion and Methodism than Mr. Sterling. Not content with laboring for the cause in the community where he lived, he was accustomed to go abroad to aid in the work of God. He was a "true yoke fellow" of Abbott, and more than once they together shook the gates of hell. One day Abbott had an appointment at the house of a Baptist. When he arrived the man of the house declined permitting him to preach on account of the offence which had been given him by a piece on baptism which one of the Methodist preachers had published. "I remained perfectly composed and easy," says Abbott, "whether I preached or not. Brother Sterling, who had met me here, reasoned the case with him until he gave his consent." Abbott then preached and "the people wept all through the house and the man of the house trembled like Belshazzar."

* Obituary Notice of James Sterling, Esq, of Burlington, N. J.

10

Abbott made a preaching tour in Pennsylvania, and his ministry produced its accustomed effect. At one of his appointments, "I met," he says, "with my worthy friend and brother in Christ, James Sterling, of New Jersey, whom I was glad to see, having written to him some days before and informed him how God was carrying on his work. In two days after he had received the account he met me here. We had a crowded house and the Lord laid to his helping hand; divers fell to the floor and some cried aloud for mercy." After the people began to recover from the physical suppression produced upon them, doubtless, by intense religious emotions, Abbott appointed a prayer-meeting at the house of a friend in the neighborhood. He says, "I gave out a hymn and brother S. [Sterling] went to prayer, and after him myself. I had spoken but a few words before brother S. fell to the floor." All in the house were prostrated shortly except Abbott and three other men. One of these was a Presbyterian, who opposed the work, attributing these marvelous phenomena to Satanic agency. Abbott arose and began to exhort, "and the two men," he says, "fell, one as if he had been shot, and then there was every soul down in the house except myself and my old opponent. He began immediately to dispute the point, telling me it was all delusion, and the work of Satan. I told him to stand still and see the salvation of the Lord. As they came to they all praised God, and not one soul but what professed either to have received justification or sanctification, eight of whom professed the latter." It thus appears that Mr. Sterling either enjoyed the blessing of sanctification previously to this time or he received it on this occasion. Our authorities do not determine which was the case.

At one time he was subjected to the operations of the Spirit to such a degree that his physical powers entirely gave way, and the friends being alarmed called a physician who treated him for a physical disorder, applying blisters, &c. When he recovered sufficiently he made known to them the cause of his being thus affected, assuring them that it was the result of a powerful Divine influence and not an " infirmity of the flesh."

He once went to Pott's Furnace where Abbott had an appointment and met him there. The place was remarkable for its wickedness, being in this respect, as Abbott affirmed, "next door to hell." The furnace men and colliers swore they would shoot Abbott, but undaunted by their threats he " went into the house and preached with great liberty." Some of the colliers were so deeply affected under the word that their blackened faces were streaked with the tears which streamed from their eyes. Mr. Sterling exhorted, and was very happy in declaring the truth. After meeting they went to a

Mrs. Grace's at the forge. "The old lady took me by the hand," says Abbott, "and said, 'I never was so glad to see a man in the world, for I was afraid that some of the furnace men had killed you, for they swore bitterly that they would shoot you.'" At another time Mr. Sterling went into Maryland where Abbott was making one of his tours. They met at a Quarterly meeting which was held in a barn. Abbott preached on Sabbath morning and many cried aloud under the word and some fell to the floor. After the service he went to the house of a friend taking Mr. Sterling with him. On their arrival they were congratulated by the gentleman in a complimentary style, to which Mr. Sterling replied " as became the Christian and gentleman." At family worship the kitchen door was opened so that the colored people, who assembled there in numbers, might participate in the devotions without entering the parlor. Abbott announced a hymn and Mr. Sterling led them in prayer. When he ceased Abbott prayed. The power of the Lord was displayed in a wonderful manner among the colored people; "some," says Abbott, "cried aloud, and others fell to the floor, some praising God and some crying for mercy; after we had concluded, brother S. went among them, where he continued upward of one hour, exhorting them to fly to Jesus, the ark of safety."

Mr. Sterling was, as the above acts show, an earnest

and indefatigable Christian laborer. He felt a deep interest for the religious welfare of all classes, and though a man of wealth and position, he did not think it below his dignity to labor in a kitchen with the enslaved children of Ham, and point them to Him who is no respecter of persons, but who accepts all of every nation that fear Him and work righteousness.

He was particularly devoted to the spiritual interests of his own household. He kept a watchful eye over those in his employ as well as over those to whom he sustained a more intimate and endearing relation. A rule of his house was that all who were able should attend Church on the Sabbath. When the hour of service arrived he was not only there himself, but it was his custom to rise and look over the congregation to see if all the members of his family, which included his clerks and servants as well as his own children, were present; and if not, when he returned home the absent ones were called to an account, and if they could render a satisfactory excuse it was well, but if not they received from their parent or employer, as the case might be, such a reproof and exhortation as they were not likely soon to forget.

Mr. Sterling was a man of large benevolence, making his money as well as his time and energies subservient to the cause of religion. He contributed much during his life towards building Methodist houses of worship, and his Christian hospitality was unbounded. Twenty-four Methodist preachers, who were on their way to General Conference, stopped at a hotel in Burlington to spend the night. He heard of them being there, and immediately he proceeded to the place, introduced himself and told them he desired them to repair to his house and spend the night. They inquired if it would be convenient for him to entertain so many at once. He replied, Perfectly, and as many more if it were necessary. Of course the clerical company exchanged their quarters at the hotel for the more genial accommodations of his attractive Methodist home. On Quarterly meeting occasions it was no uncommon thing for a hundred persons to dine at his house, and he frequently lodged as many as half that number at those times.

In the obituary sketch of him, which is attributed to Rev. Ezekiel Cooper, it is said, "It is supposed and believed that he has entertained in his house and contributed towards the support of more preachers of the gospel than any other man in the State, if not in the United States; and that he has done as much, if not more, in temporal supplies towards the support of religion, than any other man in the circle of our knowledge. In this work of benevolence he had been zealously, diligently, and regularly employed for about half a century. His heart, his purse, and his house were open to entertain, not only his acquaintances, but to show hospitality to strangers; especially to those who came in the name of the Lord; and particularly to the ministers of Jesus Christ, of any denomination, who were always made welcome under his roof, where, with his family, they found a hospitable home and a comfortable resting place. The writer speaks in part from his own observation and knowledge, for more than thirty years.

"As a merchant and a man of business he was equaled by few. He conducted his affairs upon a large and extensive scale with great diligence, perseverance, punctuality, and integrity for more than fifty years. Probably no other man in the State, and but few in the United States, ever transacted so much business in the mercantile line as he did; nor with more honor and honesty, and general satisfaction to those with whom he had dealings. He was particularly distinguished as an extraordinary and supereminent man of business for more than half a century.

"To take him all and in all perhaps his like we shall seldom see again. Not that we presume to intimate that he had no faults, or was without the infirmities of human nature which are the common lot of man; but he was unquestionably an extraordinary man, in the several circles of his long, active, useful, and devoted life."

He died firm in the faith of Christ, and in hope of a blissful and glorious immortality, on Tuesday, the sixth of January, 1818, in the 76th year of his age, after a long and painful illness "which he bore with great patience and Christian resignation." In his will he requested that on his grave stone should be inscribed the following lines :—

> " Christ is to me as life on earth,
> And death to me is gain,
> Because I trust through him alone
> Salvation to obtain."

Mr. Sterling was the father of Mrs. Porter, the estimable wife of Rev. John S. Porter, D.D. ; and the excellent Robert B. Yard of the Newark Conference is his great-grandson, and the only one of his descendants whose life has been devoted to the ministry of the Church of which he was so long an ornament.

HE RESTS FROM HIS LABORS AND HIS WORKS DO FOLLOW HIM.

CHAPTER VIII.

DAWNING OF BRIGHTER DAYS.

THE Conference of 1780 met in Baltimore the 24th of April. It was a most important and trying session. The Virginia preachers seemed determined to administer the ordinances themselves to their people, arguing that those who were instrumental in converting men by their ministry had a right to give them the Sacraments, notwithstanding they were without Episcopal Ordination. They had even gone so far as to appoint a Committee, who first ordained themselves and then proceeded to ordain their brethren. The Northern preachers could not approve of this extraordinary measure, and at this Conference it was feared that the controversy would result in a division of the Church. Before the close of the session, however, the Conference appointed a Committee consisting of Asbury, Watters, and Garrettson, to attend the Conference of the Southern preachers in Virginia, with a view to effect, if possible, a reconciliation. "But as nothing less than their suspending the administering the ordinances," says Watters, "could be the terms of our treaty with them, I awfully feared our visit would be of little consequence; yet I willingly went down in the name of God, hoping against hope."

"We found," continues Watters, "our brethren as loving and as full of zeal as ever, and as fully determined on persevering in their newly adopted mode; for to all their former arguments, they now added (what with many was infinitely stronger than all the arguments in the world), that the Lord approbated, and greatly blessed his own ordinances, by them administered the past year. We had a great deal of loving conversation with many tears; but I saw no bitterness, no shyness, no judging each other. We wept, and prayed, and sobbed, but neither would agree to the other's terms. In the mean time I was requested to preach at twelve o'clock. As I had many preachers and professors to hear me, I spoke from the words of Moses to his father-in-law, 'We are journeying unto the place of which the Lord said, I will give it you; come thou with us and we will do thee good: for the Lord hath spoken good concerning Israel.'

"After waiting two days, and all hopes failing of any accommodation taking place, we had fixed on starting back early in the morning; but late in the evening it was proposed by one of their own party in Conference, (none of the others being present,) that there should be a suspension of the ordinances for the present year, and that our circumstances should be laid before Mr. Wesley, and his advice solicited in the business; also that Mr. Asbury should be requested to ride through the different circuits and superintend the work at large. The proposal in a few minutes took with all but a few. In the morning, instead of coming off in despair of any remedy, we were invited to take our seats again in conference, where with great rejoicings and praises to God, we on both sides heartily agreed to the above accommodation. I could not but say, It is of the Lord's doing and it is marvelous in our eyes. I knew of nothing upon earth that could have given me more real consolation, and could not but be heartily thankful for the stand I had taken, and the part I had acted during the whole contest. I had by several leading characters, on both sides, been suspected of leaning to the opposite; could all have agreed to the administering the ordinances, I should have had no objections; but until that was the case, I could not view ourselves ripe for so great a change. In a letter received from Mr. ——, in the course of the year, he observed, amongst other things, nothing shakes Bro. —— like your letters. You will, I hope, continue to write and spare not. We now had every reason to believe that everything would end well, that the evils which had actually attended our partial division, would make us more cautious how we should entertain one thought of taking any step that should have the least tendency to so great an evil.   It is an observation that I have seen in some of Mr. Wesley's works, None can so effectually hurt the Methodists as the Methodists. The more I know of Methodism, the more I am confirmed in the correctness of the observation.   The Lord make and keep us of one mind and heart."

Let it not be said that this brief account of the settlement of this dispute, given by one of the chief actors in the scene, is irrelevant to our work.   This was a matter in which every section of the Church was interested. The prospect of a division was like a cloud of densest gloom, which spread itself over the whole horizon of the Church, and this amicable adjustment of the difficulty was as if the cloud gathered up its black folds and calmly rolled itself away without discharging against the palaces of Zion the terrible artillery which it concealed in its bosom.   The Church in New Jersey could not but blend its exultant notes with the thanksgivings of American Methodism at large, for so happy a deliverance from the direful catastrophe which threatened it.

At this Conference the connection of New Jersey with Philadelphia ceased, and William Gill, John James, and Richard Garrettson were appointed to the State.   None of the preachers however were appointed for a longer time than six months, as at the end of that period all were directed to change their field of labor. Who supplied the work the latter half of the year we are not able to tell, but according to Rev. Thomas Ware, George Mair volunteered this year to labor as a missionary in the eastern part of the State, in which for some time the Methodist preachers had not been permitted to travel. This was probably in the latter part of the year, as he was appointed by the Conference this year to Philadelphia. His labors were productive of much good, and at the ensuing Conference two preachers were appointed to East Jersey.

The condition of the country was not such this year as to render the prospects of religion much more favorable than they had been during the war; the American army of the North being quartered at Morristown in deep privation and distress, and the spirit of war being rife throughout the province. The winter was terribly severe, so that "the earth was frozen so deeply that in many places the ground opened in vast chasms, of several yards in length and a foot wide, and three and four feet deep." It was also difficult to obtain provisions; "the rivers, creeks, and other water ways were frozen almost to their bottom, so that oxen, and sleds loaded, passed over the water as on solid ground. The birds and the wild animals of the West Jersey forests died in vast numbers." Notwithstanding the unpropitiousness of the circumstances, the work advanced gloriously this year, and a brighter day than it had ever known dawned upon the infant Methodism of the province. At the close of the year five hundred and twelve members were reported, which was an increase of three hundred and sixteen, and almost treble the number reported the previous year.

The tidings of the revival reached Asbury, who, in his Journal, says, "I rejoice to hear that the work of God is deepening and widening in the Jerseys." Shortly after he was in the province, where he was told "there is daily a great turning to God in new places, and that the work of sanctification goes on in our old societies."

While in New Jersey he met with an old German woman with whose simplicity he was much pleased. She said she had "lived in blindness fifty years, and was at length brought to God by the means of Methodism." She was rejoicing, he says, in the perfect love of God; her children were turning to the Lord, while she preached, in her way, to all she met.

While in New Jersey this time he heard Benjamin Abbott. He says, "His words came with power, the people fall to the ground under him, and sink into a passive state, helpless, stiff, motionless. He is a man of uncommon zeal, and (although his language has somewhat of incorrectness) of good utterance." Such is the opinion the sagacious and thoughtful Asbury has recorded concerning this "wonder of his generation," the most remarkable man, probably, in faith, zeal, and success, that American Methodism has ever produced.

WILLIAM GILL stands first among the preachers appointed to New Jersey this year. He was one of the greatest men of the Church in his day, and would have been great at any period in the cause. Lee mentions him in a very laudatory style as a man, a Christian, and a minister. Dr. Rush of Philadelphia warmly admired him, and is said to have remarked that William Gill was the greatest divine he had ever heard. He was a native of Delaware, and was admitted on trial by the Conference in 1777, and was appointed to Baltimore; in 1778 he was sent to Pittsylvania, in Virginia; in 1779, Fairfax; 1781, Kent, Delaware; 1782, Sussex, Virginia; 1783, Little York; 1784, Baltimore; 1785–6, Presiding Elder in Maryland; 1787, he and John Hagerty were "Elders" over a district which included only two "appointments"—Philadelphia and Little York. In 1788 he was appointed to Kent circuit as preacher in charge, and before the next Conference he finished his labors and went to his reward. He was somewhat deficient in physical strength, but he possessed a keen, strong, and subtle intellect, a clear judgment, "and by those whose powers of vision were strong like his," says Mr. Ware, "he was deemed one of a thousand. But by the less penetrating his talents could not be appreciated, as he often soared above them. * * In conversation, which afforded an opportunity for asking questions and receiving explanations on deep and interesting subjects, I have seldom known his equal." He was a man of blameless deportment, possessed a meek spirit, and was "resigned and solemnly happy in his death." One of his cotemporaries, who knew him personally, says, "His death was truly that of a righteous man. After witnessing a good confession, leaning upon the bosom of his God, he closed his own eyes, and sweetly fell asleep. This was characteristic of the man." Though a man of eminent abilities, it appears from a passing remark by Asbury, that in common with most Methodist preachers of his time, he was subjected to the stern discipline of poverty. Asbury says, "I feel for those who have had to groan out a wretched life, dependent on others—as Pedicord, Gill, Tunnell,* and others whose names I do not now recollect; but their names are written in the book of life, and their souls are in the glory of God."

Even a grave stone with an inscription sufficient to

* These were all eminent ministers, and they each labored in New Jersey.

designate his resting place was denied him. A person who visited his grave writes in the Christian Advocate: " He died in Chestertown, Kent Co., Md.; and when a few more of the older men of this generation pass away the probability is no one will know the place of his sepulchre, as I was unsuccessful in endeavoring to persuade the Methodists there to erect at his grave only a plain head and foot stone; but his record is on high."

JOHN JAMES entered the Conference this year on trial, and the following year he was appointed to Amelia, in Virginia. In 1782 the question is asked in the minutes, " Who desist from traveling this year?" and the answer is, " John James." Mr. Ware, in his Life, gives an account of a preacher visiting Cumberland and Cape May during the time that East Jersey was inaccessible to Methodist laborers, and the editor of the book says he learned from Mr. Ware that the name of the preacher was James. As no other preacher of that name was appointed at this period to New Jersey, nor indeed was in the traveling connection, the inference is that it was the colleague of Gill and Garrettson. Mr. Ware's account of his proceedings there is as follows: " His manner was to let his horse take his own course, and on coming to a house, to inform the family that he had come to warn them and the people of their neighborhood to prepare to meet their God; and also to direct them to notify their

11

neighbors that on such a day one would, by Divine permission, be there to deliver a message from God to them, noting his appointment in a book kept for that purpose; and then, if he found they were not offended, to sing and pray with them and depart. Some families were much affected, and seemed to hold themselves bound to do as he directed. Others told him he need give himself no further trouble, for they would neither invite their neighbors, nor open their doors to receive him if he came.

"This course soon occasioned an excitement and alarm through many parts. Some seemed to think him a messenger from the invisible world. Others said, 'He is mad.' Many, however, gave out the appointments as directed; and when the time came he would be sure to be there. By these means the minds of the people were stirred up, and many were awakened. While thus laboring to sow the seed of the gospel, he came one evening to the house of Captain Sears, and having a desire to put up for the night, made application to the captain accordingly. Captain S. was then in the yard, surrounded by a number of barking dogs, which kept up such a noise that he could not at first hear what the preacher said. At this the captain became very angry, and stormed boisterously at them, calling them many hard names for which the preacher reproved him. When they became silent so that he could be distinctly heard, he renewed his request to stay over night.   The captain paused a long time, looking steadily at him and then said, 'I hate to let you stay the worst of any man I ever saw ; but as I never refused a stranger a night's lodging in all my life, you may alight.'

" Soon after entering the house, he requested a private room where he might retire.   The family were curious to know for what purpose he retired, and contrived to ascertain, when it was found that he was on his knees.   After continuing a long time in secret devotion, he came into the parlor and found supper prepared. Captain Sears seated himself at table, and invited his guest to come and partake with him.   He came to the table, and said, ' With your permission, captain, I will ask the blessing of God upon our food before we partake,' to which the captain assented.

" During the evening the preacher had occasion to reprove his host several times.   In a few days the captain attended a military parade ; and his men, having heard that the man who had made so much noise in the country had spent a night with him, inquired of him what he thought of this singular person.   ' Do you ask what I think of the stranger ?' said he, ' I know he is a man of God.'   ' Pray how do you know that, captain ?' inquired some.   ' How do I know it ?' he replied, ' I will tell

you honestly—the devil trembled in me at his reproof.'
And so it was.   The evil spirit found no place to remain
in his heart.   I have spent many a comfortable night
under the hospitable roof of Captain Sears.   He lived
long an example of piety—the stranger's host and comforter, and especially the preacher's friend.   By such
means the work was commenced in this region, and
spread among the people."

RICHARD GARRETTSON probably entered the ministry
in 1778, as in the minutes of 1779, in which his name
first appears, he stands continued on trial.   His travels
in the work were quite extensive until 1783, when his
name disappears from the minutes.   He was a brother of
Freeborn Garrettson, and is represented as having been
a good and zealous man and a useful minister.   In 1781
he was sent to labor in Virginia, and towards the close of
that Conference year Mr. Garrettson says, "I attended
my brother Richard Garrettson's Quarterly meeting ; and
we both had great freedom to preach the word, and a
precious, powerful time.   My brother traveled several
days with me, and we had sweet times together."   Afterward he remarks, "I perceived that the Lord had
blessed my brother Richard's labors in this place."

GEORGE MAIR was admitted on trial by the Conference this year, and was appointed to Philadelphia, but,
as we have seen, voluntecred as a missionary to East

Jersey. He was "grave, undaunted," and "invincible to everything but truth." Mr. Ware describes a love-feast held by Mr. Mair, which affords a good illustration of his labors and success in that unpromising portion of the province which he had the bravery and zeal to enter. The account, without which our work would be incomplete, is as follows :—

"In the year of our Lord 1780, when we were contending for independence, not with Great Britain alone, but with her Indian and Hessian mercenaries, and what was worse, with many of our fellow citizens who despised independence, or, in despair of obtaining it, had joined the enemy; when our country was laid waste by fire and sword, and many hundreds who had embarked in the cause of freedom were perishing in captivity, with hunger and cold; when many bosoms were agitated with the thoughts of revenge on our cruel and unnatural enemies, and resolved with independence to live or die—it was at such a time as this, when little was known, or thought, or said about the way to heaven, a missionary of the Methodist order volunteered for East Jersey, and was instrumental in producing a religious excitement of a very interesting character. Many who seemed to have forgotten that they were accountable creatures, and lived in enmity one with another on account of the part they had taken in the great national quarrel, were brought to follow the advice of St. Paul, 'Be ye kind one to another, tender hearted, forgiving one another, even as God for Christ's sake hath forgiven you.'

"Of this I saw a pleasing exhibition in a love-feast at a Quarterly meeting held by our missionary, Mr. George Mair, previous to his taking leave of his spiritual children in the north-west part of East Jersey. I saw there those who had cordially hated, lovingly embrace each other, and heard them praise the Lord who had made them one in Christ. The meeting was held in a barn, attended by several preachers, one of whom opened it on Saturday, and great power attended the word; many wept aloud, some for joy and some for grief; many, filled with amazement, fled, and left room for the preachers to have access to the mourners, to pray with and exhort them to believe in the Lord Jesus, which many did, and rejoiced with great joy. Such a meeting I had never seen before.

"Next morning we met early for love-feast. All that had obtained peace with God, and all who were seeking it, were invited, and the barn was nearly full. As few present had ever been in a love-feast, Mr. Mair explained to us its nature and design, namely, to take a little bread and water, not as a Sacrament, but in token of our Christian love, in imitation of a primitive usage, and then humbly and briefly to declare the great things the Lord had done for them in having had mercy on them.

"Mr. James Sterling, of Burlington, West Jersey, was the first who spoke, and the plain and simple narrative of his Christian experience was very affecting to many. After him, rose one of the new converts, a Mr. Egbert, and said, 'I was standing in my door, and saw a man at a distance, well mounted on horse-back, and as he drew near I had thoughts of hailing him to inquire the news ; but he forestalled me by turning into my yard and saying to me, " Pray, sir, can you tell me the way to heaven ?" " The way to heaven, sir ; we all *hope* to get to heaven, and there are *many ways* that men take." " Ah ! but," said the stranger, " I want to know the best way." " Alight, sir, if you please; I should like to hear you talk about the way you deem the best. When I was a boy I used to hear my mother talk about the way to heaven, and I am under an impression you must know the way." He did alight, and I was soon convinced the judgment I had formed of the stranger was true. My doors were opened, and my neighbors invited to come and see and hear a man who could and would, I verily believed, tell us the best way to heaven. And it was not long before myself, my wife, and several of my family, together with many of my neighbors, were well assured we were in the way, for we had peace with God, with one another, and did ardently long and fervently pray for the peace and salvation of all men. · Tell me, friends,' said he, 'is not this the way to heaven?

"'It is true many of us were for a time greatly alarmed and troubled. We communed together and said, It is a doubtful case if God will have mercy on us, and forgive us our sins; and if he does, it must be after we have passed through long and deep repentance. But our missionary, to whom we jointly made known our unbelieving fears, said to us, "Cheer up, my friends, ye are not far from the kingdom of God. Can any of you be a greater sinner than Saul of Tarsus? and how long did it take him to repent? Three days were all. The Philippian jailor, too, in the same hour in which he was convicted, was baptized, rejoicing in God, with all his house. Come," said he, "let us have faith in God, remembering the saying of Christ, *Ye believe in God, believe also in me.* Come, let us go down upon our knees and claim the merit of his death for the remission of sins, and he will do it—look to yourselves, each man, God is here." Instantly one who was, I thought, the greatest sinner in the house except myself, fell to the floor as one dead; and we thought he was dead; but he was not literally dead, for there he sits with as significant a smile as any one present.' Here the youth of whom he spoke uttered the word *Glory!* with a look and tone of voice that ran through the audience like an electric shock, and for a time interrupted the speaker; but he soon resumed his narrative by saying, ' The preacher bade us not be alarmed—we must all *die* to *live.* Instantly I caught him in my arms and exclaimed, The guilt I *felt* and the vengeance I *feared*, are gone, and now I know heaven is not far off; but here, and there, and wherever *Jesus* manifests himself is *heaven.*' Here his powers of speech failed, and he sat down and wept, and there was not, I think, one dry eye in the barn.

"A German spoke next, and if I could tell what he said as told by him, it would be worth a place in any man's memory. But this I cannot do. He, however, spoke to the following import:—

" ' When de preacher did come to mine house, and did say, " Peace be on this habitation; I am come, fader, to see if in dese troublesome times I can find any in your parts dat does know de way to dat country where war, sorrow, and crying is no more; and of whom could I inquire so properly as of one to whom God has given many days?" When he did say dis, I was angry, and did try to say to him, Go out of mine house; but I could not speak, but did tremble, and when mine anger was gone I did say, I does fear I does not know de way to dat goodest place, but mine wife does know; sit down and I will call her. Just den mine wife did come in, and de stranger did say, " Dis, fader, is, I presume, yourn wife, of whom you say she does know de way to a better country, de way to heaven. Dear woman, will you tell it me?" After mine wife did look at de stranger one minute, she did say, *I do know Jesus*, and is not he de way? De stranger did den fall on his knees and tank God for bringing him to mine house, where dere was one dat did know de way to heaven; he did den pray for me and mine children, dat we might be like mine wife, and all go to heaven togeder. Mine wife did den pray in Dutch, and some of mine children did fall on deir knees, and I did fall on mine, and when she did pray no more de preacher did pray again, and mine oldest daughter did cry so loud.

" ' From dat time I did seek de Lord, and did fear he would not hear me, for I had made de heart of mine wife so sorry when I did tell her she was mad. But de preacher did show me so many promises dat I did tell mine wife if she would forgive me, and fast and pray wid me all day and all night, I did hope de Lord would forgive me. Dis did please mine wife, but she did say, We must do all in de name of de Lord Jesus. About de middle of de night I did tell mine wife I should not live till morning, mine distress was too great. But she did say, Mine husband, God will not let you die; and just as the day did break mine heart did break, and tears did run so fast, and I did say, Mine wife, I does now believe mine God will bless me, and she did say, Amen, amen, come, Lord Jesus. Just den mine oldest daughter who had been praying all night, did come in and did fall on mine neck, and said, O mine fader, Jesus has blessed me. And den joy did come into mine heart, and we have gone on rejoicing in de Lord ever since. Great fear did fall on mine neighbors, and mine barn would not hold all de peoples dat does come to learn de way to heaven.' His looks, his tears, and his broken English, kept the people in tears, mingled with smiles, and even laughter, not with lightness, but joy, for they believed every word he said.

"After him, one got up and said, For months previous to the coming of Mr. Mair into their place, he was one of the most wretched of men. He had heard of the Methodists, and the wonderful works done among them, and joined in ascribing it all to the devil. At length a fear fell on him; he thought he should die and be lost. He lost all relish for food, and sleep departed from him. His friends thought him mad; but his own conclusion was, that he was a reprobate, having been brought up a Calvinist; and he was tempted to shoot himself, that he might know the worst. He at length resolved he would hear the Methodists; and when he came the barn was full; there was, however, room at the door, where he could see the preacher, and hear well.   He was soon convinced he was no reprobate, and felt a heart to beg of God to forgive him for ever harboring a thought that he, the kind Parent of all, had reprobated any of his children.   And listening, he at length understood the cause of his wretchedness; it was guilt, from which Jesus came to save us.   The people all around him being in tears, and hearing one in the barn cry, Glory to Jesus, hardly knowing what he did, he drew his hat from under his arm, and swinging it over his head, began to huzza with might and main.   The preacher saw him and knew he was not in sport, for the tears were flowing down his face, and smiling, said, 'Young man, thou art not far from the kingdom of God; but rather say, Hallelujah, the Lord God omnipotent reigneth.'   Several others spoke, and more would have spoken, had not a general cry arisen, when the doors were thrown open that all might come in and see the way that God sometimes works.''

Mr. Mair enjoyed the acquaintance and friendship of Rev. Uzal Ogden, an evangelical and zealous clergyman of the Protestant Episcopal Church, who showed much friendly regard to the Methodists at that early day, and coöperated with them in the work of disseminating truth and righteousness among the people.   He will appear more prominently in our pages hereafter. We make this allusion to him for the sake of introducing a letter addressed by him to Mr. Mair. It is dated Newtown [Newton, Sussex Co., N. J.], 10th July, 1783.

"TO MR. GEORGE MAIR, A METHODIST PREACHER."

"DEAR SIR:—Your favor of the 10th of April, I had the pleasure of receiving yesterday. The regard you express for me merits my thanks; and be assured your piety and zeal have gained you my affection. I fervently pray that you may be the peculiar object of the love of God; that yourself and family may be blessed with his spiritual and temporal favors; that you may never be 'weary in well doing;' that you may daily behold an increase of success of your 'labor of love;' and that in due season you may shine as a star of the first magnitude in the celestial regions, because you shall have been instrumental in turning many persons from the commission of vice to the practice of virtue.

"Oh! the bright, the dazzling prospects the faithful servants of God have before them, when they look beyond the things of time and sense. Let a due respect to the 'recompense of reward' of the faithful, a sense of the love of Christ towards us, and of the importance of the souls of men, cause us to be animated with new zeal to promote the interests of religion, occasion us to disregard the reproaches of the unrighteous, and with resignation and patience bear whatever cross God in his good providence may suffer to be laid upon us.

"You mention you have lately had some severe conflicts with the powers of darkness, and who is without such trials among the righteous? But, happily, you have been preserved from destruction; you have experienced the all-sufficiency of the grace of God for your comfort and safety. I praise the Lord that he hath been a 'present help to you in time of trouble.' Doubtless in future you will hereby be emboldened, whatever temptations or afflictions you may be exercised with, to 'trust in the Lord Jehovah,' as 'in him there is everlasting strength.' And for your peace and safety, in time to come, you will, I conclude, if possible, be more observant of the apostolic injunction, to 'quench not the Spirit, and to pray without ceasing.' Our security and joy depend much on our duty regarding these words of wisdom and friendship of St. Paul.

"May God, in his mercy, grant that both of us may be more circumspect in all our ways; 'redeem the time' we may yet be favored with; enjoy much of the Divine presence; glorify the Almighty on earth and be glorified by him in heaven.

"Heaven! Pleasing word! Blessed place! The habitation of the righteous. Though we meet not again here, there, even there, I trust we shall embrace each other never more to part. Delightful idea! Let it solace the soul. Let it give us that happiness we are deprived of through our separation from each other.

"I do not regret the countenance I have shown the Methodists; nor shall I cease to be friendly towards them, as I am persuaded they are instrumental in advancing the divine glory, and the salvation of mankind.

"I have not yet received the pamphlet written by Rev. Mr. Knox, though I expect to be favored with it by Mr. Roe in a few days.

"Ever shall I be happy to hear from you, and with punctuality and pleasure answer your letters. Believe me to be,

"Dear Sir,

"Your sincere friend,

"And very humble servant,

"UZAL OGDEN."

As the above letter was written in reply to one from Mr. Mair, and as it touches some points of personal experience of which he evidently had spoken in his letter, it gives us a glimpse of his interior life; slight indeed, yet interesting to such as cherish the memorials of the Methodist heroes of the olden time.

In 1784 Mr. Mair was appointed to Caroline, Md., and before the next Conference he had finished his labors and departed to his rest.   He was a man of affliction, but possessed a clear understanding and a very patient and resigned spirit.

CHAPTER IX.

THE WORK AND LABORERS IN 1781.

THE Conference of 1781 was held at Choptank, Delaware, the 16th of April, and adjourned to Baltimore the 24th of the same month.   Several preachers from Virginia and North Carolina attended, and "all but one," says Asbury, "agreed to return to the old plan, and give up the administration of the ordinances: our troubles now seem over from that quarter; and there appears to to be a considerable change in the preachers from North to South; all was conducted in peace and love."

At this Conference New Jersey was again divided into two circuits, which were called West and East Jersey. Caleb B. Pedicord and Joseph Cromwell were appointed to the former, and James O. Cromwell and Henry Metcalf to the latter.   The preachers appear to have remained on their circuits only half the year; as in November, Joseph Everett was sent by Bishop Asbury to travel in West Jersey with James O. Cromwell.   It is

12

probable that Pedicord went to the East Jersey circuit at that time, and labored there in the place of Cromwell. Everett speaks kindly of his colleague, and says that his own labors were blessed in the conversion of many souls. "In the West Jersey," he says, "I was opposed by the Baptists and beset by Lutherans. They would have put a period to my life, but my Master had more work for me to do."

Among the events of importance to the Church this year was the conversion of THOMAS WARE. He was a native Jerseyman, brought up in the Calvinistic faith, and was a revolutionary patriot. He was one of the nine thousand who were quartered at Perth Amboy in 1776.

When he heard of the brilliant victory at Trenton he felt assured that the liberties of his country were safe, but he soon felt the necessity of a higher liberty—a freedom from the bondage of sin and death. But his mind was confused by the religious opinions he had been taught in his childhood, and unable to solve satisfactorily the great questions concerning God and destiny that struggled within him, he became dejected in spirit and wandered for some time in the mazes of doubt, knowing not where he should find rest to his soul.

At length he fell into a project of going to sea. The brig was about to sail, and "impatient," he says, "for

the hour to arrive when I was to enter upon an enterprise on which I was fully bent, I wandered to a
neighboring grove, not merely to indulge in reverie, but
to think more minutely on the subject of our adventure
than I had before done.   While I was laboring to find
arguments to justify the course I was about to pursue,
a stranger passed me, though I was so merged in the
thicket that he did not see me.   As he was going by, he
began to sing the following lines :—

> ' Still out of the deepest abyss
>   Of trouble, I mournfully cry,
>   And pine to recover my peace,
>   To see my Redeemer and die.
>
> I cannot, I cannot forbear
>   These passionate longings for home.
>   Oh ! when shall my spirit be there ?
>   Oh ! when will the messenger come ?'

As he walked his horse slowly I heard every word distinctly, and was deeply touched, not only with the
melody of his voice which was among the best I ever
heard, but with the words, and especially the couplet,—

> ' I cannot, I cannot forbear
>   These passionate longings for home.'

"After he ceased I went out and followed him a great

distance, hoping he would begin again. He, however, stopped at the house of a Methodist and dismounted. I then concluded he must be a Methodist preacher, and would probably preach that evening. I felt a wish to hear; but thought I could not in consequence of a previous engagement.

"As yet I knew very little of the Methodists. My mother, who was strongly prejudiced against them, charged me to refrain from going after them; and I had heard many things said against them, especially that they were disaffected against their country. There was one Methodist in town, however, to whom I was under some obligation. This good man had noticed me; and suspecting that I was under some religious impressions, he came and told me that Mr. Pedicord, a most excellent preacher, had come into the place, and would preach that night, and he very much wished me to hear him. I told him I presumed I had seen the preacher, and mentioned the lines I had heard him sing in the road. On inquiring of him if he knew such a hymn, he replied that he did very well, and immediately commenced and sung it to the same tune; and, as he was an excellent singer, I was deeply affected, even to tears. I told him I would be glad to hear Mr. Pedicord, and probably should hear a part of the sermon, and possibly the whole, if it were not too long. I accordingly went, and was there when

the preacher commenced his service.   I thought he sung
and prayed delightfully.   His text was taken from the
24th chapter of Luke: 'Then opened he their understanding, that they might understand the Scriptures.
And he said unto them, Thus it is written, and thus it
behooved Christ to suffer, and to rise from the dead
the third day, that repentance and remission of sins
should be preached in his name among all nations,
beginning at Jerusalem.'   Soon was I convinced that
all men were redeemed and might be saved—and saved
now from the guilt, practice, and love of sin.   With this
I was greatly affected, and could hardly refrain from exclaiming aloud, 'This is the best intelligence I ever
heard.'   When the meeting closed, I hastened to my
lodgings, retired to my room, fell upon my knees before
God, and spent much of the night in penitential tears.
I did not once think of my engagement with my sea-
bound companions until the next day, when I went and
told the young man who had induced me to enlist into
the project that I had abandoned all thoughts of going
to sea.   They, however, proceeded in their perilous undertaking, were betrayed, their officers thrown into
prison, and the brig and cargo confiscated.   When I
heard of this I praised the Lord for my deliverance
from this danger and infamy, which I considered worse
than death.

"I now gave up the study of navigation, and abandoned all company but that of the pious. The New Testament I read over and over, and was charmed with the character of God our Saviour, as revealed in it; and I esteemed reproach, for his sake, more desirable than all earthly treasure."

Having experienced the blessing of pardon, Mr. Ware became at once a zealous laborer in the cause he had espoused. He traveled sixty miles to see an unconverted sister and to tell her what the Lord had done for him. In his first interview with her she became convinced of the necessity of religion, and never afterward rested until she obtained it.

Mount Holly was the place of his spiritual birth, "and on that account," he says, "it has ever been to me the most lovely spot I ever saw, not even excepting Greenwich, the place of my nativity. I was here in former years as a soldier, on my way to the army, and this was my retreat when, in a state of melancholy bordering on despair, I sought concealment. Here, now, while the joyous villagers sought me in vain on the playful green, I passed the solemn twilight in audience with my God. Here, too, I had spent the live-long day in fasting and melting thoughts on Calvary, agitated with petrifying fears and gloomy horrors; sometimes imagining sounds of ominous import, as though the mountain tops had become the rendezvous of fiends or beasts of prey. But when the disquietude of my mind was allayed by the peaceful enjoyment of the grace of life, I no longer sought concealment; and it was strange to see with what amazement many listened while I told them what the Lord had done for me. Some wept bitterly, confessed their ignorance of such a state and pronounced me happy; while others thought me *mad*, and on the Methodists, not on me, laid all the blame of what they conceived to be my derangement."

He was soon elevated to the leadership of a class and exercised his gift of exhortation. Many of his brethren entertained the opinion that he ought to preach, and expressed to him their views respecting the matter. "But I believed them not," he says. "The affectionate solicitude I felt for the salvation of sinners, which had prompted me to some bold acts that I had performed from a sense of duty, I did not construe as a call to the ministry, but as a collateral evidence of my adoption into the family of God. That a knowledge of the learned languages was essential to qualify a man to preach the gospel, as many seemed to think, I did not believe, for some of the best preachers I ever heard had it not; but they had other qualifications—a good natural understanding and discriminating powers, which fall not to the common lot of men, however pious and learned they may be. When my feelings were moved on the subject of religion and the salvation of souls, I could talk somewhat readily; and I sometimes had the eloquence of tears. My capacity and knowledge were, in my own estimation, too limited ever to think of being a preacher. I was a leader and an exhorter; and more than these I never expected to be.

"Such were my views and feelings when Bishop Asbury came to New Mills, about seven miles from Mount Holly, and sent for me to come and see him. I had not been introduced to him, nor did he previously know me. On entering his room, he fixed his discriminating eye upon me, and seemed to be examining me from head to foot as I approached him. He reached me his hand, and said, 'This, I suppose, is brother Ware, or shall I say Pedicord the younger?' I replied, 'My name is Ware, sir, and I claim some affinity to the Wesleyan family, and Mr. Pedicord as my spiritual father.' 'You then revere the father of the Methodists?' said he. 'I do,' I replied, 'greatly; the first time I heard his name mentioned, it was said of him, by way of reproach, that he had brought shame upon the Christian world by preaching up free will. Free will, said I, and what would you have him preach?—bound will? He might as well go with St. Patrick and preach to the fish, as preach to men without a will. From that time, I resolved to hear the

Methodists, against whom I had been so much prejudiced.'

" ' Sit down,' said Mr. Asbury, ' I have somewhat to
say unto thee.   Have all men since the fall been possessed of free will?'   I replied that I considered they
had, since the promise made to Adam, that the seed of
the woman should bruise the serpent's head.   ' Can man,
then, turn himself and live ?' said he.   ' So thought
Ezekiel,' I replied, ' when he said, Turn yourselves and
live,' remarking, as I understood it, that he can receive
the testimony which God has given of his Son; and
thus, through grace, receive power to become a child of
God.   ' Are all men accountable to God?' he still· further inquired.   I replied, ' The almighty Jesus says,
" Behold. I come quickly, and my reward is with me, to
give to every man according as his works shall be." '
' On what do you found the doctrine of universal ac-
countability ?' he added.   ' On the doctrine of universal
grace—" The grace of God which bringeth salvation
hath appeared unto all men," ' &c., was my reply.

" He then looked at me very sternly, and said, ' What
is this I hear of you ?   It is said you have disturbed the
peaceful inhabitants of Holly, by rudely entering into a
house where a large number of young people were assembled for innocent amusement, and when welcomed by
the company and politely invited to be seated, you re-

fused, and proceeded to address them in such a way that some became alarmed and withdrew, and the rest soon followed.' To this I answered, ' My zeal in this affair may have carried me too far. But I knew them to be generally my friends and well-wishers, and felt to do as the man out of whom Christ cast a legion of devils was directed, namely, to go and show my friends how great things God had done for me. It is true, when I entered the room, some appeared delighted to see me, and heartily welcomed me ; but those who knew me best appeared sad. And when invited to take a glass and be seated, I told them I must be excused, for I had not come to spend the evening with them, but to invite them to spend it with me. "You know me," I said, " and how delighted I have often been in your company, and with the amusements in which you have met to indulge. But I cannot now go with you. My conscience will not permit me to do so. But as none of your consciences, I am persuaded, forbid your going with me, I have come to invite you to go with me and hear the excellent Mr. Pedicord preach his farewell sermon. Pardon me, my friends, I am constrained to tell you the Lord has done great things for me through the instrumentality of this good man." The circle was not very large. Not a word of reply was made to what I said. Some were affected and soon left after I withdrew. It is true some of the citizens were offended, and said it was too much that the Methodists should give tone to the town. "Must the youth of Mount Holly," said they, "ask leave of the Methodists if they would spend an evening together in innocent amusement?" Others said, "The young man must have acted from a Divine impulse or he could not have done it, as he is naturally diffident and unassuming." But I never knew that any one of the party was offended.'

"Bishop Asbury listened to this simple explanation of the matter attentively, but without relaxing the sternness of his look, or making any reply to it. He then branched off to another subject. 'Was it not bold and adventurous,' said he, 'for so young a Methodist to fill, for a whole week, without license or consultation, the appointments of such a preacher as George Mair?' I replied that Mr. Mair was suddenly called from the circuit by sickness in his family, and I saw that he was deeply afflicted, not only on account of the distress his family were suffering, but, especially, because of the disappointments it must occasion on a part of the circuit where there was a good work going on; that some of these appointments were new, and there was no one to hold any meeting with the people whatever; that I was therefore induced, soon after he was gone, to resolve on going to some of these places and telling those who might come out the cause of the preacher's absence; and that if I was sometimes constrained to exhort these people without a formal license, it was with fear and trembling, and generally very short, unless when the tears of the people caused me to forget that I was on unauthorized ground.

"He still said nothing, either by way of reproof or commendation, more than the manner of his introducing the subjects might seem to imply. And being under an impression that his remarks were designed to mortify me for my course in the matter of the ball, and in taking the circuit in the absence of Mr. Mair, I said, 'Mr. Asbury, if the person who informed you against me had told me of my errors, I would have acknowledged them.' Here he stopped me by clasping me in his arms, and saying in an affectionate tone, 'You are altogether mistaken, my son,—it was your friend Pedicord who told me of your pious deeds, and advised that you should be sent to Dover circuit, which had but one preacher on it;' that I could tell the people if I pleased, that I did not come in the capacity of a preacher but only to assist in keeping up the appointments until another could be sent, and that he would give me a testimonial to introduce me. But if they did not cordially receive me, he said, I might return, and he would see me and compensate me for my time and expenses."

Being thus appealed to, he felt that he could not well decline entering upon the work.   He therefore promised Asbury that, if he insisted upon it, he would go to the circuit and assist in keeping up the appointments until a preacher could be sent who might perform the regular work of a minister.   Accordingly in the early part of September, 1783, he "with a very heavy heart," set his face towards the Peninsula, and, having reached his circuit, was welcomed by the people, and labored with satisfaction and success among them.   Thus was thrust into the vineyard that devoted and successful laborer, who for more than half a century ceased not to declare the whole counsel of God, and who having fought the good fight, finished his course with joy; while the benedictions of the Church, which had grown to such magnitude and strength during his period of service, attended his spirit in its triumphal passage to heaven.

CALEB B. PEDICORD was one of the serenest and most beautiful lights that has ever adorned the firmament of Methodism.   He was a man of great sweetness of spirit and of unquestioned holiness.   His devotion to the work of God was intense and absorbing, and neither the enticements nor the persecutions of the world had any power to move him from the post of duty.   There he firmly stood and bravely fought, until he victoriously laid down his armor for the crown and exaltation of a Christian conqueror. In common with the Methodist ministers of his day he was subjected to hardship and persecution. He was once beaten upon his horse, in Maryland, by a shameless persecutor, and the scars he received he carried to his grave.

One of the greatest obstacles which beset the early ministry of Methodism was the ignorance of the people respecting spiritual things. Many who had the form of godliness had no conception whatever of the deep experiences of a spiritual life. A lady in Maryland, who had been a very strict Church woman, and had observed the Sabbath and catechized her children, became convicted of sin, and so deep did her distress become that she betook herself to her bed, not knowing what was the matter. Pedicord visited her. He understood her case, and with his sweetly pathetic voice he spoke to her of the great Physician who had an infallible remedy for her anguish and sorrow. She looked to Him, believed, and her wounded spirit was made whole. That lady was the mother of the late venerated William Ryder of the Philadelphia Conference.*

To manifest strong religious emotions, or to give expression to the heart's gratitude and joy in exclamations of praise, was considered, at that time, by many, an evidence either of fanaticism or of mental aberration.

* Christian Advocate and Journal., May 12, 1837.

A lady in the eastern part of New Jersey who was awakened under the ministry of Pedicord in 1782, obtained the knowledge of salvation by the remission of sins, and so great was her joy that she shouted aloud her Saviour's praise. The people were startled. They concluded she must be insane. Her father, who had previously joined the society, was sent for, and on arriving he discovered the cause of her ecstatic expressions, which was simply the manifestation of God to her soul. Instead of participating in the alarm, or making an effort to suppress her shouting, he said he wished all present could feel as she felt. That it was not an evanescent emotion was proved by a subsequent life of devotion, extending over half a century. When she came down to the verge of Jordan, she exclaimed, "I am going home where pain and sickness never come," and passed over to the eternal shores. Thus in thousands of cases has it been demonstrated by holy and useful lives, and peaceful and victorious deaths, that the deep emotions and hearty exclamations which have been peculiarly characteristic of Methodists are not always empty cant, but are the result of " an unction from the Holy One."

That the Divine Being exercises a special providence over those that love Him is not only clearly taught in the Scriptures, but is also strikingly illustrated sometimes in the lives of his people. An escape quite as providential, apparently, as that of John Wesley from the burning rectòry, is recorded of Pedicord.   The fact is thus given by Asbury : " A remarkable instance occurred of the watchful care of God over his people. Mr. Pedicord went to bed, but could not sleep, though he tried again and again.   At last he was obliged to rise ; and going down stairs with the man of the house, he found the house on fire."   That unwelcome and singular unrest was the means, it may be, of saving his own and others' lives.

Though Mr. Pedicord was appointed to West Jersey, he seems to have labored in the interior and also in the eastern part of the State.   He must therefore have been abundant in labors as well as usefulness.   The fruit of his ministry that year was visible in New Jersey for at least half a century after he had passed to his reward, and the effects of his labors are probably felt to this day.

We have spoken of his devotion to the cause of his Master.   A passage from the Life of Abbott will show with what weight that cause pressed upon his heart.   "I removed," says Abbott, "to Lower Penn's Neck with my family, where I found a set of as hardened sinners as were out of hell.   I preached again and again, and all to no purpose.   Brother Pedicord and brother Metcalf came to my house, and I told them that I was almost discouraged. When they heard it they were so distressed that they could not eat breakfast, but retired to their room where they remained until about one or two o'clock. When they came down stairs brother P. said, ' Father Abbott, do not be discouraged; these people will yet hunger and thirst after the word of God,' and appeared cheerful. In the evening he preached to the neighbors, and next day they went on their circuits."

While Pedicord was in New Jersey, a desperado and tory of the name of Molliner, who, with his gang of confederates, had committed great ravages in their work of plunder along the Atlantic counties, was arrested and brought to justice at Burlington. His imprisonment lasted but six weeks, during which time he was tried, convicted, and sentenced to die. Though so desperate a sinner, Pedicord and his colleague visited his cell in connection with William Budd, a local preacher from New Mills, for the purpose of bearing to him salvation through the Crucified. They told him of Jesus and his cross, and of his power and willingness to save the chief of sinners. He heard their words. He looked to the Lamb of God. He flung his trembling spirit, so deeply stained with guilt, into the fountain that was opened to the house of David and to the inhabitants of Jerusalem for sin and for uncleanness. He rose, as those preachers testified, a regenerated, saved man.

13

On the day of his execution, thousands of persons, it was computed, collected from all parts of the surrounding country to witness the tragical event. The display of military, and the sounds of music that floated mournfully on the air, heightened the impressiveness and solemnity of the scene. The condemned man in company with his religious advisers, Pedicord, Cromwell, and Budd, rode in the wagon which contained his coffin, to the place of execution. "The huge procession passed out of Burlington, over Ewling's bridge, to a place called 'Gallows Hill.' The wagon halted under the fatal tree, and the soldiers were arranged around the vicinity in a square. The dense mass of spectators pressed closer and closer to the object on which all eyes were now fixed. Molliner arose and gazed upon the crowd; his countenance seemed changed; he spoke at some length, acknowledged his guilt, and begged the people to pray for him; then, closing his eyes, he sat down and appeared to be engaged in an agony of prayer.

"Rev. Mr. Pedicord, standing in the wagon beside the coffin, gave out a text, and preached a suitable sermon, which affected all hearts within hearing of his sweetly musical voice, whose melting tones seldom failed to draw tears from all eyes. The people wept and sobbed while they heard. After the sermon a prayer was offered by one of the other preachers. On standing up again,

Molliner requested them to sing, and a hymn was sung. At the close Molliner was deeply exercised, clapping his hands exultingly, and exclaiming, 'I've found Him! I've found Him! Now I am ready.' He adjusted the rope to his neck, took leave of those around, who stepped down from the wagon, and then said again, 'I am ready; drive off!' The horse started, the wagon passed from beneath his feet, he swung round a few turns, settled, struggled once for a moment, then all was still. The spirit of the daring refugee, now an humble Christian, was in the presence of God."*

Mr. Ware gives an affecting illustration of the devoutness and beauty of Pedicord's spirit, which is as follows: "Mr. Pedicord returned again to our village. I hastened to see him, and tell him all that was in my heart He shed tears over me, and prayed. I was dissolved in tears. He prayed again. My soul was filled with unutterable delight. He now rejoiced over me as a son— 'an heir of God, and joint heir with Christ.'" Ware wrote to him acknowledging him as the instrument of his salvation. "A thousand blessings on the man who brought me this intelligence. On my bended knees I owned the doctrine true, and said, It was enough—I may be happy—Heaven may be mine, since Jesus tasted death for all, and wills them to be saved! But I am

* Raybold's Methodism in West Jersey.

not myself; my hopes and fears are new. Oh! may I never lose this tenderness of heart. Yes, my friend, I am thy debtor. To me thou hast restored my Bible and my God. And shall I be ungrateful? No. I will see thee and confess the whole."

As Ware was about entering the ministry, Pedicord wrote him a kind letter. Here is an extract:

"Dear Tommy,—Brother Asbury made me glad when he informed me you had consented to come down to the Peninsula in the character of a licentiate, to spend some time on the Dover circuit, and then come to me. You have kept, in faithful memory, my earnest advice to study deeply the sacred pages, therein to learn the sum of good, Heaven kindly, though conditionally, wills to man. This you have done, and it has eventuated as I hoped; you have learned that He who claims all souls as His, and wills them to be saved, does sometimes from the common walks of life, choose men who have learned of Him to be lowly in heart, and bids them go and invite the world to the great supper. The Lord is, at this time, carrying on a great and glorious work, chiefly by young men like yourself. Oh, come and share in the happy toil, and in the great reward! Mark me, though seven winters have now passed over me, and much of the way dreary enough, yet God has been with me and kept me in the way I went, and often whispered, 'Thou art mine, and all I have is thine.' He has, moreover, given me sons and daughters, too, born not of the flesh, but of God; and who can estimate the joy I have in one destined, I hope, to fill my place in the itinerant ranks when I am gone! Who, then, will say that mine was not a happy lot? 'Tis well you have made haste; much more than I can express have I wished you in the ranks before mine eyes have closed in death and on all below.

" It is true, in becoming an itinerant you will have to sacrifice all means of acquiring property, all domestic ease and happiness, and must be content with food and raiment. Nor are the hardships and perils less appalling than those you have witnessed in our war for independence; for it is a fact known to you already, in part, that the professing world, with the clergy at their head, are in array against us. But thanks be to God! we know Him, who both died, and rose, and revived that he might be Lord both of the dead and living, and in receiving our commissions have felt a courage commensurate (may I not say?) with that with which the disciples were inspired when Jesus came and spake unto them, saying, 'All power is given unto me in heaven and in earth, go ye,' &c. &c.

" It was to the whole bench of the apostles the charge was given, so they understood it, hence they all became itinerants; why, then, is not the world evangelized? Are the clergy blameless in this matter? So thought not

Wesley, so thinks not Asbury, his coadjutor. The clergy have long since abandoned this apostolic plan; they have doubtless deemed it more than could be expected of them therein to copy the apostolic example.

"When Asbury pressed me to become an itinerant, I said, 'God had called me to preach, and wo be unto me if I preached not, but I had not conviction that he had called me to itinerate.' 'No conviction, my son,' said he to me sternly, 'that you should follow the directions of Him who commissioned you to preach? Has the charge given to the disciples, Go and evangelize the world, been revoked? Is the world evangelized?' He said no more. I looked at the world, it was not evangelized. I looked at the clergy, and thought of the rebut received from some of them who were thought the most pious, when smitten with penitential grief, and ardently desirous to know what I must do to be saved, and thought who hath said, 'The hireling careth not for the sheep, because he is a hireling.'

"The world must be evangelized; it should long since have been so, and would have been so, had all who professed to be ministers of Christ been such as were the first gospel preachers and professors; for who can contend with Him who is Lord of lords, and King of kings, when they that are with him in the character of ministers and members are called, and chosen, and faithful? Here the drama ends not, but the time we think is near, even at the door. Nothing can kill the itinerant spirit which Wesley has inspired. It has lived through the revolutionary war, and will live through all future time. Christendom will become more enlightened, will feel a divine impulse, and a way will be cast up, on which itinerants may swiftly move, and in sufficient numbers to teach all nations the commands of God."

Pedicord possessed, in an uncommon degree, the qualities of an orator. Physically, he was a noble type of manhood. His form was commanding, his countenance was indicative of intelligence and sensibility, and his voice was like the thrilling, melting murmurs of the harp. In addition to this, his spirit was pervaded by a depth of tender sympathy that flowed out in his words, and hence it is not surprising that almost immediately after he began to speak, the moistened eyes of his auditors told how resistless was his power. "He possessed," says Ware, "the rare talent to touch and move his audience at once. I have seen the tear start and the head fall before he had uttered three sentences, which were generally sententious. Nor did he raise expectations to disappoint them. If he could not bind his audience with chains, he could draw them after him with a silken cord. Never was a man more tenderly beloved in our part of the country than he; and if the decision

devolved on me I should say there was none like Pedicord. But he was my spiritual father."

In his "Heroes of Methodism," Mr. Wakeley has
given a letter, addressed by Pedicord to a young lady,
which is beautifully illustrative of the character of his
mind and heart. It shows him to have possessed a mind
clear in its perceptions, and possessed of much delicacy
and refinement, and a heart adorned with the beauty of
meekness, gentleness, and love. As it is probably, with
the exception of that already given, the only production
of his pen extant, its insertion here will not, it is hoped,
be considered contrary to the scope of the present work.
This letter, so sweet and beautiful in itself, is, in consequence of its having been written by Pedicord, invested
with an almost hallowed interest.

"VIRGINIA, *January* 12*th*, 1783.

"MISS PATTY:——Your friendly letter came safe to
hand a few days since. I have read it again and again,
and was so happy as to catch the tender spirit in which
it was written. It affords matter of real joy even to
hear from my dear friends; but to receive a letter containing an account of their spiritual welfare is cause of
more abundant consolation. You are pleased to thank
me for my former letter, and also express your approbation of the thoughts hinted in favor of early piety. I

am more than ever persuaded of the propriety of them,
though I feel myself very insufficient to give instruction
to those who are surrounded with every hopeful and encouraging circumstance.   I take knowledge from your
letter that you entertain low thoughts of yourself.   Our
souls prosper the most under the shade of the cross; and
it is well to go down the necessary steps into the valley
of humiliation.   When praying, as in the dust, our devotion is in character, but, in the mean time, let us remember, help is laid upon One that is mighty.   'Look
unto me,' is His language; He blesses the broken in
heart and comforts the contrite spirit.   He is the
strength of the weak, the overflowing fountain of all
goodness, who delights in administering suitable comfort
according to our various cases.   Let faith (which is the
eye of the soul) momently behold a reconciled God; ever
remembering that in striving to believe, and in the exercise of faith, it is obtained and increased: the secret, inward, powerful effects of living faith are almost
a mystery to those who feel them.   Salvation by faith
is what the Scripture strongly recommends.   It is true,
God is the author, Christ the object, and the heart the
subject; but, notwithstanding this, it has pleased our
great Author to bestow this precious gift in proportion
to our willingness to receive and improve it.   Love, also,
is the glorious spring of all outward and inward holi-

ness. Happy for us when we feel this holy, heavenly, active principle operating, and sweetly attracting our willing hearts into all the graces and virtues of living religion. Hope! oh, blooming hope! which constantly eyes the future promised inheritance! Oh! Patty, let these three graces be in lively exercise! Indeed, I am at a loss to describe the many blessings that flow from a conviction of our being interested in the favor of the Lord. Those comforts and graces do not naturally belong to man; it is fruit that grows not upon nature's tree. It follows that in order to abound in them, we must eye His will, who is the author and giver of them; which no doubt calls for the mighty exertions of all our ransomed powers, carefully walking in, and constantly looking through all the means of Divine institution. So shall we sail as upon broad waters, and our feet stand in a wealthy place.

"I continue a son of affliction, but still fill up my appointments. Remember me affectionately to your grandmamma, who behaved to me as a mother, sister, Christian, and friend.

"The blessed God bless you and keep you blooming for a blissful immortality. Yours, &c.,

"CALEB B. PEDICORD."

Pedicord was admitted by the Conference of 1777,

and appointed to Frederick, Md.   In 1778 his appointment is not designated in the minutes.   In 1779 he was sent to Delaware, in connection with Asbury, Garrettson, and others.   In 1780 he was again appointed to Delaware with Joseph Cromwell as preacher in charge. 1781, West Jersey; 1782, Sussex, Va.; 1783, Mecklenburg, Va.; 1784, Baltimore, as preacher in charge with Thomas S. Chew and William Gill.   Before the next Conference he ceased to labor and to live.

In describing Pedicord, a writer says, " There was one for whom Asbury looked in vain, one who had been his companion in many a long and dreary journey, one whose eloquent voice had often made the hearts of listening thousands

> ' Thrill as if an angel spoke,
> Or Ariel's finger touched the string.'

Pedicord, the gentle spirited, the generous minded, the noble souled, the silver tongued Pedicord had fallen, had fallen in his opening glory and abundant promise.   Asbury looked for him and he was not.   The grave had closed over his body, and his spirit had passed to the land where only spirits so refined, so sensitive, so ethereal as his, find congenial sympathy and rest."

His is the first obituary sketch given in the minutes. It is exceedingly brief, but very expressive.   As with a single stroke of the hand of a master artist it presents in bold relief a just outline of his beautiful character. " *Caleb B. Pedicord,—a man of sorrows; and, like his Master, acquainted with grief; but a man dead to the world, and much devoted to God.*" That is all. Is it not enough?

An original character was JOSEPH CROMWELL, but a man of zeal, and power, and distinguished success. A son of thunder, he ranged through New Jersey, Delaware, Maryland, and Virginia, summoning the people to repentance on pain of being cast into the inextinguishable flames of perdition. Multitudes heard his message and hastened their escape to Calvary, whither he unerringly directed them.

His superiority over most of his cotemporaries consisted chiefly, perhaps, in the strength of his natural endowments, his resolute and vehement earnestness, and his faithfulness in presenting the truth, urging it home upon the consciences of his hearers with a practical directness which said, " *Thou* art the man." There was, too, a kind of magic about his speech—a something that penetrated and thrilled you, while it left a deep and vivid impression of the truth. His speech and his preaching were not with enticing words of man's wisdom, but in demonstration of the Spirit and with power.

The year before he was sent to New Jersey, Asbury

says of him, " I thought it would be well for me to have a person with me always, and I think Cromwell is the man.   If I should preach a systematic, dry sermon, he would pay the sinners off."   Another of his cotemporaries, Rev. T. Ware, says he preached "with an authority few could withstand.   By his labors thousands of all classes and conditions in society" were brought to God and walked worthy of their professions.

Asbury speaks of a love-feast at which he was present in which Cromwell spoke.   He says, " His words went through me as they have every time I have heard him. He is the only man I have heard in America with whose speaking I am never tired ; I always admire his unaffected simplicity ; he is a prodigy—a man that cannot write or read well, yet, according to what I have heard, he is much like the English John Brown, or the Irish John Smith, or Beveridge's shepherd's boy ; I fear he will not stand or live long.   The power of God attends him more or less in every place.   He hardly ever opens his mouth in vain ; some are generally cut to the heart, yet he himself is in the fire of temptation daily.   Lord keep him every moment !"

But temptation, alas ! proved too powerful for him. Had the fears concerning his life, which Asbury expressed in the above emphatic tribute to his power and usefulness been early realized, his grave would have been

bedewed with the tears of thousands saved by his ministry, whose grief would not have been embittered by
the gloom which lingered over the scene of his departure.   Had he then fallen in the midst of his labors and
his triumphs, his untarnished name, crowned with imper-
ishable honors, would have gone down the generations of
Methodism among those of its noblest sons and heroes.
But he lived to furnish Methodism and the world with
another mournful example of the fact that the good and
the mighty may leap from their commanding altitude
into depths of guilt and sorrow.   And yet who can tell
but his majestic spirit which unhappily faltered in its
struggle with the flesh, may, through the abounding
grace he had so successfully proclaimed to others, have
risen from the scene of his humiliation to a throne of
celestial glory?   But of this we can only tremblingly
hope.   No visible light, alas! illumined his final hour.

After spending about sixteen years in the work, during which time he filled important appointments, including the cities of Philadelphia and Baltimore, and that
of Presiding Elder, in 1793 he located.   In a little
more than eleven years after his location, Asbury records his mournful end as follows: "After a long absence I came once more to John Jacobs'.   From him I
heard the awful account of the awful end of Joseph
Cromwell.   He had walked backward, according to his

own account; three days he lost in drunkenness; three days he lay sick in darkness—no manifestations of God to his soul; and thus he died! We can only hope that God had mercy on him. Compare this with what I have recorded of his labors and his faithfulness in another part of my Journal. Oh! my soul, be warned! Brother Jacobs preached his funeral sermon, and gave a brief sketch of his life, his fall, and his death. His text was, 'Tell it not in Gath, publish it not in the streets of Askelon;' how appropriate the choice!''

JAMES O. CROMWELL, a brother of Joseph, was admitted on trial at the Conference of 1780, and appointed to Sussex, Md. In 1781 he was sent as preacher in charge to East Jersey. In 1782 we find him on the Fluvanna circuit, Va. This was a hard field of labor— the rides were long, and a large portion of the circuit was very mountainous. The opportunities for usefulness were not flattering, yet some additions were made to the societies. Cromwell labored hard and diligently in this rugged and unpromising field, but was frequently subjected to discouragement, and even dejection. In 1783 he was sent to Pittsylvania, Va.; in 1784 to Kent, Md. At the Christmas Conference, 1784, he was ordained elder, and appointed with Freeborn Garrettson to Nova Scotia. This was a trying field, but he labored in it with zeal and success. In 1786 he and Garrettson were "elders" in Nova Scotia.   In 1787 he and two others were elders over a district that included a portion of the State of Maryland.   From 1788 to 1791, three years, he was Presiding Elder in New Jersey, his district including the entire State.   In 1792 he was appointed to Bethel circuit, N. J.   In 1793 he located.   It is said that he was a devout and laborious man, and a useful and powerful preacher.

HENRY METCALF was admitted at the Conference of 1781, and appointed to East Jersey.   In 1782 he was sent to Sussex, Va. ; in 1783 to Pasquetank, N C.   At the Conference of 1784 the question is asked for the first time, Who have died this year ?   And the answer is, William Wright and Henry Metcalf; but no notice is given of them in the minutes except the bare mention of their names.   Metcalf was considered an excellent and deeply devoted man, but he was a man of a sorrowful spirit and suffered under mental depression.   With him the habit of devotion appeared to be a ruling passion, strong in death.   When near his end, it is said, he rose from his bed, and bowed upon his knees, and while in that devout attitude his spirit ascended to God.*

* Lee's Hist. of Methodism, and Asbury's Journal.

CHAPTER X.

PROGRESS OF THE WORK IN 1782.

THE Conference met at Ellis's preaching house, Va., on the 17th of April, 1782.   Asbury says, " We amicably settled our business and closed our Conference. * * We had a love-feast—the power of God was manifested in a most extraordinary manner—preachers and people wept, believed, loved, and obeyed."   The minutes say the Conference adjourned to Baltimore the 21st of May. At this Conference East Jersey reported 282 members, and West Jersey 375.   This was a gain for the State of 145 members during the ecclesiastical year 1781.

The appointments in New Jersey this year were, East Jersey, John Tunnell, Joseph Everett.   West Jersey, Joshua Dudley, Richard Ivy.   The work continued to advance during the year, so that an increase of nearly four hundred (371) was realized in the membership.   On the 16th of September Asbury writes, " I think God will do great things in the Jerseys: the prospect is

14

pleasing East and West." He visited Burlington and
Trenton this year. The latter town he found " in a
great bustle with the Court, and the French troops."
He preached to a large and serious congregation on the
Syrophœnician woman. "Ah! poor gospel-hardened
Trenton!" he exclaims. "But a few have been converted
of late." While making his tour in the State he was
annoyed by persons who demanded his pass. In Germantown a gentleman of the committee examined his,
and those of the preachers stationed on the circuit.
"He treated us with great politeness," he says, "and
told us what the law required: brother Tunnell's pass
was pronounced valid; but mine was not, because I had
not the signature of the proper authorities in the counties through which I had traveled. I pleaded ignorance
of the necessity of this. Here appeared to be the secret—the mob had been after brother Everett with
clubs, and it was supposed, under the connivance of their
superiors; they found, however, that he was qualified
according to law: the work of God prospers, and, it is
possible, this is the real cause of offence to unfriendly
ministers." He speaks of preaching on Sabbath the
8th of September to a very gay congregation of four or
five hundred persons, and says, "The priests of all denominations, Dutch and English, appear to be much
alarmed at our success; some oppose openly, others more

secretly; the Episcopal ministers are the most quiet; and some of these are friendly."

Tunnell and Everett did not remain on the circuit only until November, when they were sent to the Philadelphia circuit.   Everett, in speaking of his appointment to East Jersey, says: "I was appointed to East Jersey with that man of God, John Tunnell, whom I loved as another self.   We labored in sweet fellowship until November; the Lord also owned his word through my weak instrumentality."*   Woolman Hickson, George Mair, and Richard Ivy appear to have labored in East Jersey the latter part of this year.

About this year a society was formed by Benjamin Abbott, in Lower Penn's Neck, in the West Jersey circuit.   The class met in an old log-house, belonging to an aged man by the name of Swanson, who was the leader.   Some of the first members were Wm. Bilderback and wife, Catharine Casper, Elizabeth Dixon, and Sarah Bright.   The manner in which Methodism was introduced there can be best given in Abbott's own language.   He says, "One day as I was preaching, I. Holladay of Lower Penn's Neck, stopped to hear, and the word reached his heart; after sermon, he asked me if I would come and preach at his house: I asked him if I should give it out for the circuit preacher; he said, Yes.   I

* Arminian Magazine, (American,) vol. ii., 1790.

did so, and after bidding the family farewell, an officer of the army being present, I took him by the hand, and said, 'God out of Christ is a consuming fire,—farewell!' and so we parted.   God pursued him from the very door, and gave him no rest; before twelve o'clock that night he was out of bed on the floor at prayer.   In about two months his soul was set at liberty, and he is a member of our Church at the present period.

" The day appointed at Mr. Holladay's, the traveling preacher came, and a great concourse attended, to whom he preached; some seemed awakened, some disputed, and some were in great consternation.   When he concluded he asked if he should give out preaching there again.   Mr. H. replied he might.   At the time appointed abundance of people attended, to whom brother Ivy preached with great power, being full of faith and the Holy Ghost.   Many of the people wept, and it was a good season.   By this time there were many doors opened.   One cried, Preach at my house; and another, Preach at my house, &c.   The next appointment was made at J. D.'s, for brother Dudley: he came and preached with power.   After meeting I told them that that day week I would declare to them, 'Even the mystery which hath been hid from ages and from generations, but now is made manifest to his saints, to whom God would make known what is the riches of the glory of this mystery, among the Gentiles; which is Christ in you the hope of glory, whom we preach, warning every man, and teaching every man in all wisdom, that we may present every man perfect in Christ Jesus,—Whereunto I also labor, striving according to His working, which worketh in me mightily.' Col. i. 26–29. The people concluded that I was going to prophesy, and would tell how the war would terminate; this brought abundance together. I preached, and God attended the word with power. I had not spoken long before a professing Quaker said it was a mystery to him; but before I concluded, himself, his wife, son, and daughter were all struck under conviction, and never rested until they all found rest to their souls, and joined the society. About six months after, the son died in a triumph of faith; the father was taken ill at the funeral, and never went out of his house again until carried to his grave. He departed this life praising God in a transport of joy. By this time there was a general alarm spread through the neighborhood. We had prayer meetings two or three times a week, and at almost every meeting some were either convinced or converted. One old woman, to whose soul the Lord had spoken peace, clapped her hands, and began to praise the creature instead of the Creator. I stepped to her and said, I have done nothing for you; if there be any good, it is the Lord that has done it, and therefore praise God. 'Oh,' said she, 'but you are a dear good creature for all!' I turned away and went among the people. At this meeting we had the shout and power of Israel's God in the camp: prayer was kept up until near midnight.

"Next morning a young man came to my house to know what he must do to be saved. I applied the promises of the gospel, and then went to prayer, and after me my wife, and then my daughter Martha; and while supplicating the throne of grace on his behalf, the Lord, in his infinite goodness, spoke peace to his soul; and we were all made partakers of the blessing. He joined the society, lived several years, and died clapping his hands, and shouting, 'Glory to God! I am going home!' That moment his hands ceased clapping, he died.

"We had now about twenty-two or three in society; but persecution soon arose, and the devil stirred up one J. N., a professor of religion among the Presbyterians, who at first appeared very friendly, and was active in bringing us into the neighborhood; but soon after, he became an instrument in the hand of the devil to oppose and lay waste the truth, and did much hurt to the cause of God, and all under the cloak of religion. He went among our young converts, and told them that God had revealed it to him that the Spirit which they professed to receive at their conversions was of the devil, and not the Spirit of Christ.   But, glory to God! it was not in the power of men or devils to extinguish the Divine flame, although they cast a cloud on many minds, and turned some out of the way.

"The height of my harvest being on our meeting day, when meeting time came I told my reapers that they must all go to meeting, and that I would pay them their wages as though they were at work.   We all went, and God wrought powerfully; several fell to the floor and two found peace; it was a great day to many.   After meeting we returned to our work again.

"I continued for about two months to preach under the trees, for the house would not contain the people. We seldom had a meeting during that period but that some were either convinced, converted, or sanctified.

"I now thought it might be expedient to make an attempt toward building a meeting-house.   A subscription was drawn for that purpose, but not being able to obtain a suitable piece of ground to build on, as those who had such refused to sell, it fell through for nearly four years, and we continued our meetings as before.

"One day while I was speaking, the power of the Lord laid hold on a Quaker woman, and as she was about to escape, she fell on her hands and knees.   Some of her friends helped her up, got her into a wagon and carried her off.   I was afterward informed that it took them two weeks to kill her convictions. The work of the Lord went on among the people, and I continued to impress the necessity of sanctification upon believers. We had, at that time, twelve children who were converted to God."

While Abbott resided in Penn's Neck, two wicked men resolved that should he attempt to preach at a certain place again they would kill him. The friends besought him not to run the hazard of doing so, but he replied, "I fear them not," and proceeded in his undertaking. "The two men came to the door of the house with heavy clubs in their hands. When Abbott saw them he called aloud on the Lord to 'strike those daring sinners.' Both became alarmed and turned and ran; one fell down; but, by the assistance of their cronies, both got away, so well frightened that they never came to kill Abbott again."*

One day Abbott went to a neighbor's (Tobias Casper's), "and told the family that all his children had embraced religion except his son Elisha; he had been praying for him, and he believed the Lord would *convert* him or *kill* him! The next day the family heard a great and strange noise, just over the Branch, which separated the two farms. Some of the family thought the British

* Methodism in West Jersey. This, and the remaining facts of this chapter are not given in Abbott's Life.

had come on shore and were about to kill the people over on that side; but Mrs. Casper went to the door, and hearing the sounds, said, 'That is the noise of shouting; it is Elisha Abbott; he is at work along the Branch.' She went over to see, and there found that the Lord had indeed converted Elisha, all alone, in the swamp or woods. Mrs. Casper found the young man leaping, shouting, and praising God. His father soon came also; and it was such a time as when the fatted calf was killed to celebrate the prodigal's return.

. "The husband of Catharine Casper, the woman named, was very much opposed to the Methodists. He hated this new sect, which was everywhere spoken against. He was violently opposed to his wife going to meetings; but she was faithful; taking up the cross daily, and never faltering in her duty. One Sabbath day, while she was gone to Methodist meeting, her husband, Tobias Casper, kindled a fire in the oven. One of his neighbors, Azariah Dixon, came to the house, and seeing the fire blazing from the great mouth of the oven, asked, in amazement, what Casper was about—what he was going to do with the oven. He replied that 'he wanted to heat it nine times hotter than it had ever been, and he intended to burn his wife in it as soon as she came from meeting.' Casper kept up the fire until his wife returned. When she saw it, and inquired what he

was going to do with the oven, he said, ' To burn you.'
' Well, if you have more power than the Master, whom
I serve, has to keep me out, I will go in it.' He, no
doubt, expected violent opposition, and the offer to go
into the fire confounded him. He looked at her a while
and then said, ' Well, you are a fool,' and walked off;
and there the affair ended.

"During the first revival in Penn's Neck under the
preaching of Benjamin Abbott, a female slave, by the
name of Phillis, was converted. She belonged to a
wealthy lady of the place, Mrs. Miles; and the lady,
displeased with her conversion, made the service of her
black slave harder than ever, ' because she had become a
Methodist.' But Phillis was faithful, and used to go to
the barn to pray. At one time her mistress took the
cowhide and went to the barn after her servant. Hearing a noise, she paused; and listening, distinctly heard
the slave praying to the Lord, and supplicating for mercy
for her hard-hearted mistress. Conviction. seized the
lady's heart; and she exclaimed, ' Can it be possible that
my slave thinks more of me and my soul's salvation
than I do myself?' She returned to the house leaving
poor Phillis at prayer ; and, retiring to her chamber, fell
upon her knees and prayed aloud for mercy. Phillis
heard the cry when she came in, and in a short time the
Lord converted the lady. The overjoyed slave ran off

to Mrs. Casper, and told her.   She came over, and found Mrs. Miles happy in God, praising him for what he had done in answer to the prayers of poor Phillis. At the death of Mrs. Miles, she left Phillis a house, and a lot of four acres of land, which, with her *freedom*, enabled her to live comfortably during her life.   She continued faithful, died happy, and is, no doubt, in the kingdom of heaven with her mistress."*

* Raybold's Methodism in West Jersey.

CHAPTER XI.

METHODISM IN SALEM.

IN giving sketches of local Churches we cannot well be confined to the chronological method, which we endeavor to preserve, as far as practicable, in our narrative. To gain a clear and just idea of the establishment of Methodism in any neighborhood or town, it is necessary to group together the events of several years, so that they may be seen in their appropriate relation to each other. On this principle we introduce our sketch of early Methodism in Salem at this period in our narrative, (1782,) which was about the time the first Methodist society was formed in that town.

As Benjamin Abbott was the most distinguished hero of Methodism in Salem county, it will not be improper here to notice some of the facts of his personal history which are not given in his Memoirs.

We have elsewhere remarked that though we had no definite proof of the fact, yet it was our opinion that he lived, at the time of his conversion, in the township of Pittsgrove, and that the class which was formed in his neighborhood, and of which he was appointed the leader, must have been the nucleus of either the Broad Neck, or Murphy's, since called Friendship, Church. We have since learned that this opinion is in accordance with the facts in the case.

"At the time of his conversion, [1772,] he lived in the township of Pittsgrove, and labored for one Benjamin Vanmeter, who employed him solely on account of his muscular strength; for otherwise he was very objectionable, being intemperate, and when so very quarrelsome. In the same neighborhood there lived one John Murphy, a member of the Presbyterian Church, a man of sterling sense and extensive reading, whose house appears to have been a home for the Methodist itinerants, and among the first preaching places in the county. After a time he became a member of the society, quite contrary to the wishes of his former friends, so much so that they cited him before the session, and wished to know why he could not be a Presbyterian. He replied, 'that he never could believe that God had ordained man to sin, and then damned him for doing what he could not help.' Being displeased at this, they commanded silence and dismissed him. At the house of John Murphy was formed the first Methodist society in this county,

and, perhaps, in all Jersey west of Pemberton. Here
for several years the circuit preachers preached, administered the ordinances, held love-feasts, &c., until the society had increased so much that they formed the purpose to build, which resulted in the erection of a log
meeting-house. On the same site there was erected,
about ten years since, a good, substantial brick building,
and is called on the Salem circuit plan, *Friendship*.
Benjamin Abbott was, no doubt, one of the first members
of this society, as John Murphy was one of his neighbors; and it was returning from a visit to J. Murphy's
that Mr. Abbott's wife was converted."

The above is the statement which Rev. Jefferson
Lewis wrote and published twenty years ago. He obtained his information, no doubt, from authentic sources,
and hence his testimony is to be believed. It agrees
precisely with the opinion given on a previous page before the writer knew that there was any such corrobora-
tive testimony in existence. Mr. Lewis, who took the
pains to investigate the subject at that time, says that
Abbott, "no doubt, was nearly the first Methodist in
Salem County."

The third society that was formed in the county,
was, it is understood, at Quinton's Bridge, about three
miles from Salem. It was formed about 1781 or 1782,
probably as early as 1781. Abbott preached there at

the house of Benjamin Weatherby, and soon formed a class, among the members of which were Henry Ffirth and John McClaskey.   The latter became a distinguished preacher, and filled several important appointments, including the cities of New York, Philadelphia, and Baltimore, and also that of Presiding Elder.   The former was a convert from Quakerism, and brother to John Ffirth, the compiler of Abbott's Memoir.   He was instrumental in the erection of the first Methodist Church edifice in the town of Salem.

Rev. John Lednum, who was stationed in Salem in the year 1826, thirty years after the occurrence, and who, therefore, had a good opportunity to learn the facts, says that Mr. Weatherby was "a zealous laborer in the cause of Methodism, and afterward fell away."   He thinks that he was the person Mr. Abbott publicly addressed at the funeral of Mrs. Paul, in Salem, a short time before his death, in which address "he called to mind the happy hours that he had spent under his roof; how much he (Mr. W.) had done for the cause of God; and how often they had rejoiced together, as fellow-laborers in Christ Jesus; and then warned him, in the most solemn manner, of his impending danger, in the love and fear of God, until tears flowed, his strength failed, and he was unable to speak any longer."   Though Mr. W. appeared angry, yet the word produced its intended effect; and, after Mr. Abbott's death, he rose in a love-feast and declared that God had healed his backslidings, and that Mr. Abbott was an instrument in the Divine hand in his restoration.*

"Whether the Penn's Neck," says Mr. Lewis, in the sketch from which we have already quoted,—"whether the Penn's Neck or Salem society has the precedence, in point of time, is difficult to determine. My own opinion, however, founded on circumstances, is, that they were formed nearly at the same time."

Methodism was introduced into Salem about the year 1774. Daniel Ruff, who was appointed that year to Chester circuit, and who, as we have before seen, exchanged for a time with William Watters, who was on the Trenton circuit, visited the town of Salem and preached in the Court-house. Thomas Ware, who was then a youth about fifteen years of age, was present and heard the sermon. He said when Mr. Ruff entered the town he walked into the porch of the tavern, which was then kept by an uncle of Mr. Ware, and with whom the latter then lived, "and sat down until the bell rang, when he repaired to the house, and opened the exercises by singing the hymn beginning,

'Fountain of life to all below,
    Let thy salvation roll.'"

* See Life of Abbott. pp. 270–71.

Sixty-five years after the occurrence of this event Mr. Ware retained a distinct recollection of these words. He also remembered having heard Abbott preach about this time. The latter, undoubtedly, preached in Salem about the same period as Ruff.

One interesting incident connected with Abbott's ministry in Salem is not given in his Life. He resided at the time, in Mannington, the township adjoining Salem, to which place he removed about two or three years after his conversion. He went into Salem with a load of wood. So far as his appearance was concerned, he presented rather a sorry figure. He wore an old tattered great-coat, girded round the waist with a rope. "Now," said the lawyers, as he advanced up the street, "here is old Abbott, let us have some fun, he'll preach for us if we will ask him." They did ask him, and he consented to preach. The room selected for the service was in the tavern opposite the Court-house, called the grand jury room. When Abbott entered the room he looked all around, and seeing but one door, he took a chair and placed himself in it in order to prevent a retreat on the part of his auditors, and announced for his text, "Ye serpents, ye generation of vipers, how shall ye escape the damnation of hell?" Mr. Ware observed that such a flood of terror "had seldom been poured from the lips of any preacher. He, however, closed in a tender, win-

15

ning manner, by directing them *how* to escape; and as
Mr. W. intimated, much to their relief.

"Mr. Abbott continued to labor as a local preacher,
in his peculiar style, throughout the county, for fifteen
years; and, although it was repulsive to many people,
and particularly so to formalists, he was greatly instrumental in the conversion, not only of the immoral,
but some who stood high, professionally, in other
religious societies, Presbyterians, Baptists, Quakers,
Churchmen, and even Roman Catholics. So great was
his fame in combating the powers of darkness, especially the sin of intemperance, that some thought the
devils existed in a kind of subjection to him. A certain
man who had been so addicted to drunkenness as to
bring on repeated attacks of *delirium tremens* imagined,
during one of these attacks, that his bed-room was full
of devils, that he saw them sticking to the tester of his
bedstead, &c.; at the same time alleging that *father*
Abbott (as saint and sinner called him) had driven them
out of Penn's Neck,* and they had come to Salem, and
nothing would answer but *father* Abbott's prayers to
drive them from his bed-room. He was accordingly sent
for."

The first meeting-house in Salem was erected in the
year 1784. Henry Ffirth superintended the enterprise.

* Abbott removed from Mannington to Penn's Neck, about 1781.

He was thought to possess some wealth at the time, but he failed shortly after, which gave occasion to the enemies of Methodism to say, "The Methodists have ruined him!" The truth was, however, he was involved beyond recovery before he became a Methodist.

When the attempt was made to build a Church in Salem, the society, which was small and scattered, found themselves too weak to accomplish the undertaking. They therefore called upon their Quaker neighbors for assistance, and they subscribed liberally. The matter was talked over at the Friends' Quarterly-meeting, and it was objected that the Methodist preachers "spoke for hire." To this it was answered, "No, it was only for a passing support." At length consent was given that *Friends* who were free to do so, might contribute towards the enterprise.*

Benjamin Abbott was baptized in this Church soon after it was finished. Although he was converted about twelve years previously, and commenced preaching shortly after, he was not baptized, in consequence of the Methodist ministry being an unordained ministry, until the Salem Church was erected.

The Rev. J. Lewis, in his sketch of Salem Methodism, published in 1839, says:—

"The planting of Methodism in Salem was accom-

* Asbury's Journal, vol. i. p. 464.

panied with many circumstances common to its introduction in other places, and some rather peculiar; one of the latter I shall mention.   The Methodists, on application to the magistrates, had obtained such effectual relief from open violence that their persecutors were obliged to have recourse to some new expedient to accomplish their purposes, without rendering themselves amenable to justice.   The method to which they resorted was this: to assemble together in a place of their own, in order to turn experimental religion into a farce.   In this burlesque on religion, the persons present acted band-meetings, class-meetings, and love-feasts to the great entertainment of the profane congregation, who, with corresponding irreverence and much apparent satisfaction, enjoyed this new species of theatrical mirth.

"It happened, one night, while they were performing a band-meeting, that a young actress stood upon one of the benches to speak her pretended experience.   At length, after having said much to command the mirth of the delighted audience, she exclaimed, with mock solemnity, at the same time beating her breast, 'Glory be to God, I have found peace, I am sanctified, and am now fit to die.'   Scarcely had the unhappy girl uttered these words before she actually dropped from the bench a lifeless corpse.

"Struck with this awful visitation the auditors were

instantly seized with inexpressible terror, and every face filled with consternation and dismay. The assembly immediately broke up; and, in consciousness of having gone beyond the bounds of common profaneness, they all silently and sneakingly retired to their respective habitations, except the mournful few left behind to take charge of the melancholy victim. From this moment all persecution was at an end in Salem, and not a tongue was afterward heard either against the gospel or any of its friends.*

"An aged member of society, who joined about ten years after this circumstance took place, informs me that the young woman did not die immediately, but was carried, after falling, first to the house of her sister, who, understanding the circumstances, refused to receive her, and, in being conveyed thence, she actually died upon the wheelbarrow with which they conveyed her. This occurrence must have taken place some time about 1792, when Benjamin Abbott and David Bartine traveled the Salem circuit, one of the seven circuits in New Jersey."

In the same territory in which there were then seven circuits, there are now two conferences, and nearly three hundred circuits and stations, and in Salem there are now two large Churches, each one supporting its own pastor. Such has been the growth of Methodism within that period.

* Dr. Coke's Journal, page 186.

CHAPTER XII.

SKETCHES OF PREACHERS.

WE meet this year for the last time in New Jersey, WILLIAM WATTERS, the first traveling preacher raised up in America, and one of the first that regularly labored in New Jersey. He returned this year simply to visit the scenes of his former toils and the friends of other days. He moved slowly, visiting several places, and proclaimed again to his delighted friends the gospel which seven years before he had preached with so much success among them. During his visit he was suffering from the ague, which rendered him, in some degree, unfit for labor; yet the demands made upon him were such that he could not well refrain from preaching, as he says, "I was obliged to preach oftener amongst my old friends than I wished, for my ague and fever attended me as constantly as the day." He speaks of the work of religion being, at this time, in a prosperous condition in the portion of the State which he visited. We cannot take our final leave of him without lingering to cast a more minute survey over the history of his useful life.

As we have already seen, he was born in 1751, (his birth occurring on the 16th day of October,) in Baltimore county, Maryland. His parents were members of the Church of England, and at the age of two years he was deprived of his father by death. The family were left in comfortable circumstances, though not rich, and at a very early age William was the subject of religious impressions, " but was naturally vain, proud, self-willed, passionate." "Cursing, swearing, lying, and such like practices," he says, "were not allowed in my mother's family; and from my infancy I always found the greatest affection for her, as one of the best of parents; and if, at any time, I was sensible that I had grieved her in any degree, I never could be at rest till I had humbled myself, and she had shown me tokens of forgiveness."

At the age of eight or nine years, he was beset with temptations to curse God, which, he says, " would often make me shudder, and with all my might, I would try to put away such troublesome thoughts out of my mind, but was not able; so that it was not uncommon for me, at such times, in the utmost distress inwardly to reply— No—no! not for the world; but would conclude that, as God knew my heart, I had actually cursed him as though I had spoken aloud, and that this was the unpar-

donable sin that our Saviour said should never be forgiven, which would greatly distress me; while I thought
myself, at such times, one of the vilest sinners on earth,
and was frequently afraid that all who saw me would
know how wicked I was.   At other times I was much
terrified with thoughts of death and the torments of
hell; though it was a very rare thing I ever heard any
one say a word on those momentous subjects.

"As I grew older, I was more and more engaged in
seeking death in the error of my ways, and by the time
I was twelve or fourteen I took great delight in dancing,
in card-playing, in attending horse-racing, and such like
pernicious practices; though often terrified with the
thoughts of eternity in the midst of them, which would
frequently so damp all my momentary joys, that I would
feel very miserable indeed.   Thus did my precious time
roll around, while I was held in the chains of my sins,
too often a willing captive of the devil; I had no one to
tell me the evil of sin, or to teach me the way of life
and salvation.   The two ministers in the two parishes,
with whom I was acquainted, were both immoral men,
and had no gifts for the ministry; if they *received* their
salary, they appeared to think but little about the souls
of the people.   The blind were evidently leading the
blind, and it was the mere mercy of God that we did not
all fall into hell together."

In the summer of 1770 the Methodists preached in the neighborhood where he was brought up, and he had frequent opportunities of hearing them. They preached the doctrine of the new birth, but he could not conceive what it meant; and for some time he gave but little thought to the truths he heard, yet he dared not despise and revile the Methodists as many then did. "By frequently being in company with several of my old acquaintances," he says, "who had embraced and professed Methodism, amongst whom was my eldest brother and his wife, (whom I thought equal to any religious people in the world), and to hear them all declare, as with one voice, that they knew nothing of heart religion, the religion of the Bible, till since they heard the Methodists preach, utterly confounded me; and I could but say with Nicodemus, 'How can these things be?' While I was marveling and wondering at these unheard-of things that those strange people were spreading wherever they came, and before I was aware, I found my heart inclined to forsake many of my vain practices, and the last place of merriment I was ever at, I remember well, I was hardly *even a looker-on.*"

The Spirit strove with him, and he soon became quite serious, read his Bible with attention, was uniform and earnest in private prayer, took pleasure in the company of the pious, and shunned the society of others. He embraced every opportunity of hearing the gospel and the last month before he was fully convinced of his real condition as a sinner, he says, he seldom, if ever, omitted bowing his "knees before the God and Father of our Lord Jesus Christ, four or five times a day." Yet all this while, he says, he was but a Pharisee, seeking to be justified by the deeds of the law, though he was sincere in all that he did.

At length, after having more than an ordinary amount of religious concern for several days, he attended a prayer meeting one Sabbath day. "While one was at prayer," he says, "I saw a man near me, who I knew to be a poor sinner, trembling, weeping, and praying, as though his all depended on the present moment; his soul and body were in an agony. Mercy—Mercy for Christ's sake! was the burden of his cry. The gracious Lord, who works by what means he pleases, blessed this circumstance greatly to my conviction; so that I felt, in a manner which I have not words fully to express, that I must be internally changed—that I must be born again, born of the Spirit, or never see the face of God in glory. Without this I was deeply sensible that all I had done, or could do, was vain and of no account, if not done as the Lord had appointed, in order to obtain this Divine change, this new nature. I went home much distressed, and fully determined, by the grace of God, to seek the salvation of my soul with my whole heart, and never rest till I knew the Lord had blotted out my sins, and shed his love abroad in my heart by the Holy Ghost. In this frame of mind, I soon got by myself, and fell upon my knees before my merciful God, who had spared me through a life of sin and ingratitude. But, oh! alas! my heart, my sinful heart felt as a rock! and, although I believed myself in the 'gall of bitterness, and in the bonds of iniquity,' and, of course, that if I died in that state, I must die eternally; yet I could not shed one tear, neither could I find words to express my wretchedness before my merciful High Priest. I could only bemoan my forlorn state, and wandered about through the afternoon in solitary places, seeking rest, but found none.

"I returned in the evening to the neighbor's, above mentioned, where we had been for public worship, and several coming in, joined in prayer, and the Lord again smote my rocky heart, and caused it to gush out with penitential sorrow for my many sins against him who so 'loved the world, that he gave his only begotten Son, that whosoever believeth in him, should not perish, but have everlasting life.' I was so melted down, and blessed with such a praying heart, that I should have been glad if they would have continued on their knees all night in prayer for me a poor helpless wretch. My concern was such, that I feared lying down or closing my eyes, lest I should wake in hell.

"The following day I was unfit for any worldly business, and spent that day mostly in private, while Christ on the cross, bleeding, and bearing the sins of the whole world in his own body, and dying to make a full atonement for the chief of sinners, that they might not die eternally, was continually before the eyes of my mind; while, in the most bitter manner, did my soul exclaim, Oh! how have I slighted the bleeding Saviour, and trampled his most precious blood under my unhallowed feet, and have done despite to the Spirit of grace! The thoughts and sight thereof, now, through Divine mercy, made my eyes to run down with tears, while my very heart was ready to burst asunder with sorrow. Thus was I bowed down and determined to wait at the foot of the cross, while I was stripped of all dependence in outward things, and was well assured that there was 'no other name under heaven given among men, whereby we must be saved.'"

He continued to seek the Lord with strong crying and tears, oppressed with the burden of his sins, and refusing "to be comforted but by the Friend of sinners." So great was his distress that for three days and nights he could scarcely eat, drink, or sleep; his flesh wasted; his strength failed, and he felt most sensibly the force of the question—"A wounded spirit who can bear?"

For a little time he feared that his state was hopeless—
that his day of grace had forever passed; but for the
most part he had a gleam of hope that at some distant
time God would be merciful to him.   At length some devout friends, who were acquainted with his state, visited
him, and after some conversation he desired them to
pray for him.   It was about the middle of the day.
The family were called in, and one gave out the hymn,

> " Give to the winds thy fears,
>   Hope and be undismayed ;" &c.

They all joined in singing, and sung with the spirit and
in faith, while with eyes flowing with tears, and his face
turned to the wall, he "felt a lively hope" that the Lord
would show him mercy.   And he was not disappointed.
"The Lord heard," he says, "and appeared spiritually
in the midst.   A divine light beamed through my inmost
soul, which, in a few minutes, encircled me around, sur-
passing the brightness of the noon-day sun.   This divine glory, with the holy glow that I felt within my soul,
I feel still as distinct an idea of, as that I ever saw the
light of the natural sun, or any impression of my mind.
*   *   *   My burden was gone—my sorrow fled—my
soul and all that was within me rejoiced in hope of the
glory of God; while I beheld such fullness and willingness in the Lord Jesus to save lost sinners, and my soul

so rested on him, that I could now, for the first time, call Jesus Christ 'Lord, by the Holy Ghost given unto me.' The hymn being concluded, we all fell upon our knees, but my prayers were all turned into praises. A supernatural power penetrated every faculty of my soul and body, and the words of the prophet were literally fulfilled in my conversion to God. 'And he shall sit as a refiner and purifier of silver; and He shall purify the sons of Levi, and purge them as gold and silver, that they may offer unto the Lord an offering in righteousness.' Such was the change, and so undeniable to all present, that they appeared greatly affected, and confident that the Lord had descended in the power of his Spirit, and wrought a glorious work in the 'presence of them all.' "

This happy change occurred in May, 1771, in the same house in which he was born. Having never known or heard of any people but the Methodists, who professed to know anything of what he now enjoyed, and as they were instrumental in leading him to the attainment of salvation, he was led to unite himself with them, "and thought it a greater blessing to be received a member amongst them than to be made a prince."

The Methodists had no regular preaching in those days, and at that time there had been only three preachers in Maryland, Strawbridge, King, and Williams, so that some times quite a long period would elapse in which they had no preaching. "But, in one sense," he says, "we were all preachers. The visible change that sinners could not but see, and many openly acknowledged, was a means of bringing them to seek the Lord. On the Lord's day we commonly divided into little bands, and went out into different neighborhoods, wherever there was a door open to receive us, two, three, or four in company, and would sing our hymns, pray, read, talk to the people, and some soon began to add a word of exhortation. We were weak, but we lived in a dark day, and the Lord greatly owned our labors; for, though we were not full of wisdom, we were blessed with a good degree of faith and power. The little flock was of one heart and mind, and the Lord spread the leaven of his grace from heart to heart, from house to house, and from one neighborhood to another; and though our gifts were small, yet was it astonishing to see how rapidly the work spread all around, bearing down the little oppositions with which it met, as chaff before the wind. Many will praise God forever for our prayer-meetings. In many neighborhoods they soon became respectable, and were considerably attended."

From the time of his conversion he felt a deep solicitude for sinners, and was drawn out in prayer for their salvation. He felt willing to make any sacrifice in order to save them, but did not think it possible that he should ever be able to labor in a public capacity for their good. Finding, however, that his humble endeavors were blessed to the conversion of souls in several different neighborhoods, and that the hearts and houses of the people were open to receive him, and at the same time feeling a conviction that it was his duty to labor for God, he sought, by fasting and prayer, for divine direction, and finally became convinced that he must go forth as a messenger of the Most High, to bear the offers of salvation, in His name, to the people.

His first regular field of labor, as an itinerant, was Norfolk, Va., where he went with Robert Williams in the autumn of 1772. They were kindly received by the friends there, but found the state of religion by no means encouraging. Hundreds of the people attended the preaching, but they were, he says, " the most hardened, wild, and ill-behaved of any people I had ever beheld in any place."

Mr. Pillmore, who was at that time in Norfolk, took a tour as far as Charleston, leaving Watters to fill his place during his absence. " As he returned through Portsmouth, two men, well dressed, at the ferry, were swearing horridly. He lifted up his hands, and with a stern voice, exclaimed aloud—' Well! if I had been brought to this place blindfolded, I should have known I was near Norfolk.'

" The Parish minister of Norfolk undertook, in a sermon, to represent us as a set of enthusiasts and deceivers. His text, for this noble purpose, was, 'Be not over righteous.' Amongst other things he told his people, (what none of them would have otherwise suspected,) that he knew from experience the evil of being over righteous. He said so much that his friends were dissatisfied. I suppose he thought that Mr. Pillmore was gone to return no more. But he found his mistake, for he returned in a few days after, and gave public notice that on such a day and hour he would preach to them from 'Be not over wicked,' the words following the parson's. On the hour appointed the town appeared in motion, and came out in crowds. After reading his text, he informed his congregation why he had given them the notice of his intending to preach from these words, and why he had made choice of them in particular. That he had been creditably informed that a certain divine of that town had given the citizens thereof a solemn caution against being over righteous. Lifting up his hands with a very significant countenance, he exclaimed, 'And in *Norfolk* he hath given this caution!' The conduct of the parson looked (as it certainly was) contemptible. Though these were severe reproofs, and from one capable of

16

forming a sound judgment, yet Norfolk continued Norfolk as long as I knew anything about it; and it was no ways strange to me that in a few years after it was consumed by fire."

Having entered the itinerant ranks, Watters continued to labor with zeal, fidelity, and success until 1783, when he located. His location was caused by his being in a feeble state of health, and not receiving that indulgence in his appointments which he thought needful under the circumstances. But he remained firm in his attachment to Methodism, and labored with as much zeal in the local sphere as he had before done in the itinerancy. As an illustration of his ministerial labors after he located, we give the following account of the first year of his location: "I attended Greenwich preaching-house, forty miles from me, every fourth Sabbath; and Leesburg, thirty miles off, every fourth Sabbath, besides the places between me and those above mentioned. And though I was much fatigued in so doing, being still in a weak state of health, yet I found the Lord's service to be perfect freedom, and feared living to no good purpose."

In 1786 he again entered upon the regular work of the ministry in Berkeley circuit; but before half a year had expired, family considerations compelled him again to retire.

As he was returning home from this circuit, he saw,

for the last time, his old friend and fellow laborer, Richard Owen (or Owings), who was dangerously ill. He says, "He was the first American Methodist preacher, though for many years he acted only as a local preacher. He was awakened under the preaching of Robert Strawbridge, à local preacher from Ireland, who, with one more, Philip Embury, were the first Methodist preachers in America. He was a man of respectable family, of good natural parts, and of a considerable utterance. Though encumbered with a family, he often left wife and children, and a comfortable living, and went into many distant parts, before we had any traveling preachers amongst us, and without fee or reward freely published that gospel to others, which he had happily found to be the power of God unto his own salvation. After we had regular circuit preachers amongst us, he, as a local preacher, was ever ready to fill up a gap; and by his continuing to go into neighborhoods where they had no preaching, he was often the means of opening the way for enlarging old, or forming new circuits in different places. Several years before his dissolution, after his children were grown up and able to attend to his family concerns, he gave himself up entirely to the work of the ministry, and finished his course in Leesburg, Fairfax circuit, in the midst of many kind friends, but some distance from his family. As his last labors were in the

circuit where I lived, I had frequent opportunity of being in his company, both in public and in private, and
had every reason to believe that he had kept himself un-
spotted from the world, and had the salvation of souls
much at heart.   I wish it was in my power to hold him
up in his real character, as an example to our present
race of local preachers.   Plain in his dress, plain in his
manners, industrious and frugal, he bore a good part of
the burthen and heat of the day in the beginning of that
work which has since so gloriously spread through this
happy continent, and was as anxious to be a general
blessing to mankind as too many now are to get riches,
and make a show in the world.   I shall need make no
apology for giving this short account of so worthy a man
to any who knew him.   I have been led to it from my
long and particular acquaintance with him, and there
not having been (I am sorry to say it) a more public account of him.   'Blessed are the dead who die in the
Lord, from henceforth; yea, saith the Spirit, that they
may rest from their labors, and their works do follow
them.' "

He returned to the regular work in 1801, in which he
continued until 1806, when he again retired from the
ranks of the itinerancy.

Watters was a man of circumspect life, and of unremitted devotion to the cause and work of God. He appeared to be but little influenced by considerations of an earthly nature, but by prayer, by fastings, by watchfulness, by labors, and by faith unfeigned, he sought the rewards of a celestial life. His memory is worthy of being cherished by the Church through all her generations; and with the lapse of ages his example will gather a brighter lustre, as it stands out serenely amidst the fading twilight of the early dawn of American Methodism, invested with a wreath which the hand of Providence wove only for him,

THE FIRST AMERICAN METHODIST ITINERANT PREACHER.

RICHARD IVY was a native of Sussex county, Virginia. He entered the itinerancy, probably, in 1777, as he stands in the minutes as continued on trial in 1778, which is the first time his name appears on the record.

He was appointed that year to Fluvanna, Va. The following year he was appointed to Brunswick, Va.; in 1780 he was sent to Pittsylvania, Va.; in 1781, to Kent, Md., with David Abbott, son of Benjamin Abbott; 1782, West Jersey; 1783, Nansemond, Va.; 1784, Camden. From 1785 to 1793 he was Presiding Elder, his districts being chiefly within the territory embraced in South Carolina and Georgia. In 1793 he was appointed

Traveling Book Steward. In 1794 he desisted from traveling to take care of his mother. In 1795 he was appointed to Norfolk and Portsmouth. He returned to his native place and was making arrangements to retire from the itinerant field, when he was taken sick, and died in the latter part of this year. "He was a man of quick and solid parts," say his brethren, in the obituary notice given of him in the minutes, and he "preached," says Lee, "with a good degree of animation." He was a devoted man, and manifested a self-sacrificing spirit. "He sought not himself any more than a Pedicord, a Gill, or a Tunnell—men well known in our connection—who never thought of growing rich by the gospel; their great concern and business was to be rich in grace and useful to souls. Thus, Ivy, a man of affliction, lingering out his latter days, spending his all with his life in the work. Exclusive of his patrimony, he was indebted at his death."*

"Soon after I joined the Methodist society," says Rev. T. Ware, "Messrs. Pedicord and Cromwell were removed from our circuit, and Dudley and Ivy appointed in their places. In one part of the circuit there were several families who had received the preachers from the beginning. Some of these were the most wealthy and

* Minutes, vol. I. p. 67.

respectable in the vicinity, only they were suspected of being unfriendly to the cause of their country. They had joined the Methodists before the war commenced ; and though they had committed no act by which they could be justly accused of opposition to the declaration of independence ; yet, as they refused to bear arms, they were considered hostile to it, and the preachers suspected of disaffection on account of continuing to preach at their houses.

"Learning that a company of soldiers, quartered near one of these appointments, had resolved to arrest the first preacher who should come there, and carry him to head quarters, I determined to accompany him, hoping, as I was acquainted with some of the officers, to convince them that he was no enemy to his country. The preacher was Richard Ivy, who was at that time quite young. The rumor of what was about to be done having gone abroad, many of the most respectable inhabitants of the neighborhood were collected at the place. Soon after the congregation were convened, a file of soldiers were marched into the yard and halted near the door ; and two officers came in, drew their swords and crossed them on the table, and seated themselves, one at each side of it, but so as to look the preacher full in the face.

" I watched his eye with great anxiety, and soon saw

that he was not influenced by fear.   His text was, '*Fear not, little flock, for it is your Father's good pleasure to give you the kingdom.*'   When he came to enforce the exhortation, 'Fear not,' he paused and said, 'Christians sometimes fear when there is no cause of fear.'   And so, he added, he presumed it was with some then present.   Those men who were engaged in the defence of their country's rights meant them no harm.   He spoke fluently and forcibly in commendation of the cause of freedom from foreign and domestic tyranny, looking, at the same time, first on the swords and then in the faces of the officers, as if he would say, This looks a little too much like domestic oppression; and, in conclusion, bowing to each of the officers and opening his bosom, said, 'Sirs, I would fain show you my heart; if it beats not high for legitimate liberty, may it forever cease to beat!'

"This he said in such a tone of voice, and with such a look as thrilled the whole audience, and gave him command of their feelings.   The countenances of the officers at first wore a contemptuous frown; then a significant smile; and then they were completely unarmed, hung down their heads, and, before the conclusion of this masterly address, shook like the leaves of an aspen. Many of the people sobbed aloud, and others cried out, Amen!   While the soldiers without (the doors and windows being open) swung their hats and shouted, Huzza for the Methodist parson! On leaving, the officers shook hands with the preacher, and wished him well; and afterward said they would share the last shilling with him.''

From the slight information we can gather respecting his pulpit abilities, we infer that they must have been of a superior order. In public exhortation he was sometimes very powerful. The man who could follow one of Abbott's successful sermons with an exhortation, and maintain the interest and feeling of the congregation must have possessed considerable power. And this Ivy did. At a Quarterly meeting in Maryland, Abbott preached on Sabbath morning with such effect that many cried aloud, and some were prostrated upon the floor, and, "after I concluded," he says, "brother Ivy gave an exhortation, and spoke very powerfully, many wept under his exhortation.''

JOHN TUNNEL was admitted on trial in 1777, and appointed to Brunswick circuit, Va., in company with William Watters and Freeborn Garrettson. These were all excellent and laborious men, yet their labors in that field were not remarkably successful. Much depends upon the circumstances under which, and the character of the people among whom, the minister labors. Sometimes there may be a large congregation to listen to the word, and yet that congregation may be mainly composed of persons who already profess to have experienced the saving power of the gospel.   In that case if a pastor builds up the flock in holiness he does a blessed work. It is not to be expected that he should have a great ingathering of souls, if but few are within the circle of his, or his Church's influence, who do not already profess religion.   Even the strongest and most effective men of our primitive ministry did not always witness, immediately, such results of their labors as they desired. This is shown by the following passage from the Life of Watters, in regard to his own and Garrettson's and Tunnell's labors in Brunswick circuit:

"In this circuit," he says, "we had many hearers, but only a few of those who were not of our society appeared to be benefited by our preaching.   There were large societies in almost every neighborhood, and generally speaking, our brethren were lively, many of them much so.   My hands were full, and my work was much greater than my strength; so that I often feared I did not pay that particular attention to every soul of my charge, that I ought.   My two brethren who labored with me were very devout and faithful men, and I was not a little comforted in the thought that they would supply my lack of service.   We endeavored to bear each other's burthens and strengthen each other's hands; and though our success was by no means equal to our wishes, yet the Lord did evidently own us in every neighborhood, both in and out of our societies. We labored to the utmost of our abilities in the good and gracious cause of our glorious Master, and daily found his service to be perfect freedom."

In 1778 Tunnell was appointed to Baltimore with Joseph Cromwell, Thomas M'Clure, and John Beck. M'Clure had previously labored in New Jersey, Cromwell and Tunnell also subsequently labored there. In 1779–80 he was appointed to Berkeley, Va., with John Haggerty; Micaijah Debruler laboring with them the second year as preacher in charge. In 1781 he was appointed to Kent, Delaware; 1782, East Jersey, as preacher in charge; 1783, Kent, Md.; 1784, Dorchester, Md.; 1785, Charleston. In 1786 he was "Elder" over a district which included East Jersey, Newark, New York, and Long Island. In 1787 he went to East Tennessee, where he labored as Elder. The circumstances under which he went to that missionary field are given by Rev. Thomas Ware, in an article published in the Christian Advocate and Journal, Feb. 28, 1834, as follows:—

"It was at a Conference in the spring of 1787 where three young men, who esteemed the reproach of Christ greater riches than all earthly treasures, volunteered to accompany the Rev. John Tunnell on a mission to East Tennessee, then called Holstein. A mission at that time to this section of country was no less perilous than one at this time is to the coast of Western Africa.

"East Tennessee, though very remote from trade, is a fine country. It is finely watered by five rivers, of which Holstein is the chief; but none of them is navigable but for small boats. The bottoms along the water courses are very rich, and here the first settlers became located, and of course the population was vastly scattered, insomuch that a parochial ministry could not be supported. And, although it had become a State, it might rather have been called a pagan, than a Christian State; for when we arrived there, there were not more than four or five sorry preaching-houses within its whole jurisdiction, two of which had been built by the Methodists.

"Here, then, was a pressing call for itinerants. And the pious father of Mr. Tunnell had written an affecting letter to his son, describing their destitution of the means of grace, and urging him to come to them, and bring with him two or three young men who counted not their lives dear, so that they might save souls, and closed with—*Let no one come who is afraid to die: their lives will often be in jeopardy from the red men of the wilder-*

ness. And the Rev. H. Willis, who had traveled one year in Holstein, said, All that good old Mr. Tunnell had said was true, and more; and in his view all that went on this mission should know all about it—should know if they traveled there, they must ford and swim the rivers at the risk of life; sleep, if they could, in the summer in blankets, and in winter in open log-cabins, with light bed-clothes, and often with two or three children in bed with you. But in particular, he should know that he was going to a frontier country, infested with savage men, cruel as the grave. Yes, continued he, the red man, seeing his possessions wasting away as the white man approaches, has become infuriated, and is resolved to sell his country at the dearest rate, and, savage-like, wreaks his vengeance indiscriminately; hence many a hapless virgin, or mother and her innocent babes, are slaughtered or led away captives; moreover, it is needful that they should know clothing is dear and money scarce."

Notwithstanding the perils that awaited them, Tunnell and his associates heroically entered that rugged field which so greatly needed their evangelical labors, and he continued there to toil until the Master said, " It is enough! Come up higher."

In 1788 he was elder over a very large district which included ten circuits and extended into North Carolina.

In 1789 he was elder in East Tennessee. This was his last appointment. He died of consumption at the Sweet Springs, in July, 1790.

Tunnell was a man of placid spirit, and "was no less tranquil in his death than in his life." He was deficient in physical strength, and his "appearance very much resembled that of a dead man," but he possessed a strong, musical voice, with which he frequently "poured forth a flood of heavenly eloquence," when he seemed like "a messenger from the invisible world." "A sailor was one day passing where Tunnell was preaching. He stopped to listen and was observed to be much affected; and, on meeting with his companions after he left, he said, 'I have been listening to a man who has been dead and in heaven; but he has returned, and is telling the people all about that world.' And he declared to them he had never been so much affected by anything he had ever seen or heard before."*

Asbury visited him during his illness, and found him very low, "but very humble and patient under his affliction." The Bishop attended his funeral, on occasion of which he recorded the following tribute in his Journal: "Brother Tunnell's corpse was brought to Dew's Chapel. I preached his funeral: my text, 'For me to live is Christ, and to die is gain.' We were much blessed and

* Life of Rev. Thomas Ware, p. 85.

the power of God was eminently present. It is about fourteen years since brother Tunnell first knew the Lord; and he has spoken about thirteen years, and traveled through eight of the thirteen states; few men, as public ministers, were better known or more beloved. He was a simple hearted, artless, child-like man; for his opportunities he was a man of good learning, had a large fund of Scripture knowledge, was a good historian, a sensible, improving preacher, a most affectionate friend, and a great saint; he had been wasting and declining in strength and health for eight years past, and for the last twelve months sinking into a consumption."

Lee, the first historian of American Methodism, pays a tribute to Tunnell's excellence and gifts as follows:— "Mr. Tunnell was elected to the office of an elder at the Christmas Conference, when we were first formed into a Church. His gifts, as a preacher, were great; and his conduct, as a pious man, was worthy of imitation. He was greatly beloved in his life, and much lamented in his death. He died about a mile to the west of the Sweet Springs. His friends took his remains over the mountain to a meeting-house about five miles east of the Sweet Springs, where they buried him."

JOSEPH EVERETT was born in Queen Ann's county, Maryland, June 17, 1732. His parents were neither rich nor poor, but were accustomed to labor, and trained their son to habits of industry. They were without religion, except the name, and called themselves of the Church of England. Until he was twenty years of age Joseph never heard a gospel sermon. The preaching he did hear had no savor of Christ and no unction of the Spirit. It consisted of such dry moral teachings as an irreligious clergyman might be expected to furnish to his hearers.

At an early age he became addicted to the vices of profanity, falsehood, &c., and continued in a course of open sinfulness until after he was married. His wife was about equally devoted to the pleasures of sin as himself, and they walked together in the downward path. He, however, had, during his career of folly, frequent unrest of soul, and was afraid of death, and sometimes felt such a sense of guilt as would cause him to resolve to reform his life, but his resolutions, he says, were but as "ropes of sand."

At length the New-lights, or Whitefieldites, entered the region where he lived, preaching the fundamental doctrines of Christianity. He went to hear them. His views of the nature of religion now underwent a change. He had thought that it consisted in breaking away from outward sin, but he now saw it was a change of the heart—the infusion of a new life into the soul. He became convinced of the necessity of the new birth, and entered upon a course of religious duties with the hope of obtaining it. He read his Bible, prayed in secret and with his family, observed the Sabbath, and attended preaching, while his mind was engrossed with the concerns of his eternity. A clearer light dawned upon his spirit, but his heart did not find rest. He felt himself to be one of the most miserable of men, and would even envy the brutes because they had no souls. Thus he continued for nearly two years, and though his outward life was greatly changed, and he entered into communion with the Church, and was regarded by many as a good Christian, yet he had not conscious peace with God. The hour of deliverance, however, came at last.

"One Sabbath day," he says, "as I was sitting in my house, none of the family being at home, meditating on the things of God, I took up the Bible, and it providentially opened at the eleventh chapter of St. Luke's Gospel; and casting my eyes on the fifth verse, read to the fourteenth. And that moment I saw there was something in religion that I was a stranger to. I laid down the Bible, and went directly up into a private chamber to seek the blessing. And everlasting praises be to Him who has said, *Seek, and ye shall find.* I was on my knees but a very few moments before he shed abroad his love in such a manner in my heart, that I knew Jesus

17

Christ was the Saviour of the world and the everlasting Son of the Father, and my Saviour; and that I had redemption in his blood, even the forgiveness of my sins. I felt these words by the power of his Spirit run through my soul, so that the tongue of a Gabriel could not have expressed what I felt; *I have loved thee with an everlasting love, therefore with loving-kindness have I drawn thee.* I felt such rapture, and saw with the eyes of my soul such beauties in the Lord Jesus Christ, as opened such a heaven of love in my breast, that I could with the poet sing the following lines:—

> ' I then rode on the sky,
>   Freely justified I,
> Nor did envy Elijah his seat ;
>   My soul mounted higher
>   In a chariot of fire,
> And the moon it was under my feet.'

So that being justified by faith, I had peace with God, through our Lord Jesus Christ. I rejoiced in hope of the glory of God."*

For some time he continued in the enjoyment of the Divine favor, but through the influence of what he afterward regarded as false teaching, respecting the deliver-

---

* An account of the most remarkable Occurrences of the Life of Joseph Everett. In a letter to Bishop Asbury. Arminian Magazine, (American) vol. II. 1790.

ance of the soul from the indwelling of sin in this life, and by neglecting the means necessary to the maintenance of a life of piety, he relapsed into formality and sin. "I went," he says, "to hear preaching, as usual, but my conscience reproached me and told me I was a hypocrite. I prayed in my family, but no life—my visits to my closet were short, and very seldom; and, withal, uncomfortable. I would talk about religion, but my heart was after my idols. In plain truth, I lived in such a manner as I thought it impossible for a Christian to live—though my principle was, there was no falling from justifying grace. And, indeed, it was impossible for me to fall, for I had shamefully fallen already."

He wandered further and further from the way of peace until he was excluded from communion with the Church, and became an open, reckless transgressor. At the commencement of the war of the revolution he became a zealous whig, and volunteered in the service of his country. Such was his courage as a soldier, that he says before he would have fled from the place of action or danger without orders, he would have fallen dead upon the spot, though his soul would have been lost for ever.

A man of so brave and resolute a spirit, if he could but be properly enlisted on the side of righteousness, and trained to use the sword of the Spirit, could not fail to make an earnest champion for the truth, nor to endure hardness as a good soldier of Jesus Christ. God had prepared the instrumentality already by means of which he was to be inducted into the arts of a spiritual warfare, and equipped for a sublimer battle than earth's heroes ever fought.

When he returned from the camp he found that a people called Methodists had entered the neighborhood, who proclaimed to the people that they all might be saved. He did not approve the doctrine and determined to oppose them, not having " the least thought that they were sent of God." When opportunity served he did not fail to manifest his decided antipathy to the new sect, but "always," he says, "behind their backs, or at a distance. As I have frequently seen since, our greatest enemies are those who will not hear us; and if at any time they do come out, they pay so little attention to what they hear, and run away with a sentence here and there, that they fill the hearts of the people with prejudice."

In this course he continued until the spring of 1778, when, after considerable hesitation, he was led to go to the house of a Mr. White, one of his neighbors, to hear a Methodist preach. Mr. Asbury was the preacher. After singing and prayer he expounded the second chapter of Judges. There was nothing in the exposition to find fault with, he says, unless he rejected it because the speaker was a Methodist. No part of the discourse produced any special effect upon his conscience, but his prejudice was shaken, and henceforth the avenues to his heart were open and he found power to pray, though for twelve or fourteen years he had not bowed his knees in secret.

He now felt the return of the Spirit to his heart, convincing him of sin, and empowering him to employ the means necessary to his salvation. He lost his attachment to the society of the wicked, and also his delight in military affairs. The Methodists noticed and encouraged him. One, particularly, who knew that he held Calvinistic opinions, used every prudent means to render his convictions effectual, and placed the writings of Wesley and Fletcher in his hands to show him the difference between the Arminian and the Calvinistic tenets. This he did with such prudence " that he entirely prevented the least prejudice, and made way for liberal principles to take place."

A single well-timed and apt remark is sometimes the means, under God, of flashing the light of volumes of truth upon the inquiring but beclouded understanding. So was it with Everett. His Methodist friend once remarked in his hearing, " that if Christ died for all the world, all the world was salvable ; and they that were lost were lost by their own fault," which, he says, gave him a better insight into the scheme of redemption than all his reading, and all the conversation, and preaching he had ever heard had afforded him.

He became more and more engaged to secure his salvation, which he "found the devil as much engaged to prevent." Often when employed in devotion it would seem as if he could hear the adversary say, "What! you are at prayers again, are you? You had better quit, for after a while you will tire and leave off as you did before." At the same time he was a by-word in the mouth of the world. But notwithstanding these "fears within, and fightings without," he went forward in the way pointed out in the Divine word until the fifth of April, 1778, when between seven and eight o'clock in the evening his soul was again set at liberty, and he rejoiced in the love of God which was shed abroad in his heart by the Holy Ghost.

He now sought to find out the truth. He read the works of Wesley and Fletcher, and attended Methodist preaching. As his peace had been restored, he wished to know how he might preserve it, and in worshiping with the Methodists he found comfort and strength. Still he did not join the society. His reason for this was, he says: "I knew that they were a despised people, and thought if I did not join them I might be more useful when it was known that I was not a member of their society. But I soon found this to be very poor logic; for the children of the devil hate the light, let it come from where it will. I read Mr. Wesley on perfection; but the mist of Calvinism was not altogether wiped from off my mind. With the Calvinists I was taught that temptations were sin. I did not attend to the law of God to find out what sin was. I could not distinguish between sin and infirmities, and hardly believe that any Antinomian can. They say all we do is sin. We are told that the sacrifices of the wicked are an abomination to the Lord. But this is no proof that the children of God commit sin. I believe with the apostle that he that is born of God sinneth not;—and he that does is of the devil. I believe that in every justified soul there is the root of every iniquity. Yet if he faithfully uses the grace and power already given to him, he thereby keeps himself from transgressing the law, which alone is sin; and therefore the evil one, the devil, touches him not. And I believe that it is the privilege of every babe in Christ to grow in grace; not only to be young men and to be strong, but to become fathers in Christ; to receive the fulness of all the rich promises of the gospel: such as the law of God on their hearts; to love the Lord with all their soul; to be dead to the world and crucified with Christ, &c., all which I believe to be the common privileges of all believers in this day; though it is to be much lamented that many live beneath them. And I praise the Lord that I am as much confirmed in the doctrine of full sanctification, as I am that a man may know that his sins are forgiven on this side the grave."

The Methodists invited him to class, but did not persuade him to join. In reading, and in conversing with them, he "began to feel," he says, "the necessity of joining the society; which I did with this view, to grow in grace myself, and to strengthen the hands of the preachers in the work of God, because I thought it to be the will of God, which ought to be our end in all we do. I saw the necessity of mortifying the corrupt cravings of the flesh, as well as using all the means of grace, in order to be perfected in love; which constitutes a Methodist."

Having united himself with the Methodists, and being well pleased with their doctrines and discipline, he was impelled by his zeal for the salvation of souls to speak to his acquaintances on the subject of religion and even to proclaim publicly the gospel of reconciliation. "Before he had been officially authorized," says Rev. Wm. Ryder, "he commenced sounding the alarm to rebellious sinners. He came truly with the thunders of the law. The Lord owned his word, and many were convinced, convicted, and happily converted to God through his labors."*

Finding that his word was rendered effectual in the accomplishment of good, he began to be deeply exercised in mind about preaching, and these impressions continually attended him. Obstacles, arising from a sense of his weakness and inability for so important a calling, rose before him, and caused him to hesitate. "Ten thousand difficulties," he says, "would shut up the way, and made it appear an impossibility, yet it constantly pursued me."

Pedicord then traveled the circuit in which he resided, of whom he says, "that man of God;" and he sent for him to meet him at an appointment in Delaware. He was well acquainted with Pedicord and complied with his request. After Pedicord preached he asked Everett to exhort, which he did, and before they parted he gave him a license to exhort.

He continued to labor earnestly and zealously for the cause, attending at the same time to his secular employment, until the latter part of the year 1780, when he entered upon his itinerant career, as the colleague of Pedicord, on Dorset circuit. Here his labors were blessed of the Lord, and he remained until February, 1781, when Pedicord received a letter from Asbury, di-

* Christian Advocate and Journal, May 12, 1837.

recting that Everett should go to Annamessex circuit. He accordingly removed to his new field of labor, where he proclaimed the truth successfully until November, when, as we have seen, he was sent by Bishop Asbury to West Jersey.   There he labored with success, having many seals to his ministry, until the Conference in May, when he was appointed to East Jersey, where he likewise labored successfully until November, when he went to Philadelphia.   He remained there, the work prospering meanwhile, until the Conference in May, 1783, when he was appointed to Baltimore.   That part of the Philadelphia circuit which profited least under their labors, he says, was the city; and for this he assigned the following reason:—" They resemble too much the Corinthians; one saying, I am of Paul, another, I am of Apollos, and another, I am of Cephas.   Where this is the case there are very few to follow Christ.   They are like weathercocks, which can never be kept at one point."

A source of severe trial to him in the beginning of his ministry was the opposition of his unconverted wife, who strongly disapproved of his traveling.   Notwithstanding, he went forward in the way of duty, praying that she might be brought to a better mind.   His prayers were now answered in her conversion.   " She saw," he says, " how she had been fighting against the Lord, in treating me wrongfully; which wounded her very sensibly; and this was sweet revenge to me. Here I saw the word of the Lord was fulfilled, to wit, 'Be not weary in well doing, for in due season ye shall reap if ye faint not.' That man should always pray and not faint. She had no more objection to my traveling."

His travels, as an itinerant preacher, extended over a very large field, embracing appointments in Virginia, Maryland, Pennsylvania, and New Jersey. He was ordained a deacon in 1786, and an elder in 1788. He filled important appointments in the connection, including that of Presiding Elder, in which office he spent a number of years of his ministerial life. In 1804 he was so worn out that he was unable to perform effective labor, and he was placed on the superannuated list, yet he continued in strictest union with his brethren of the Conference until his death.

Everett was a remarkable man. In reviewing his character and life, we have been forcibly reminded of the Apostle Paul. Some of the distinguishing traits in the character of the great apostle were strongly marked in him. He was a man of dauntless courage and heroic bravery, yet, at the same time, he possessed a meekness and tenderness of spirit becoming the lowly disciple of Jesus. He was resolute and conscientious in the performance of duty, and neither the threatenings of the wicked, nor the smiles of friends had any influence to turn him aside from the path of right. He went to Dorset circuit in 1786, where he found the work of religion declining, but the failing embers soon broke forth into a flame. This he attributed to the excluding of unworthy members and the maintaining of discipline in the Church. "I view it," he says, "as a capital fault in a Methodist preacher not to be a disciplinarian; and if ever our Church loses the life of religion, it will be for want of discipline." Utterances so weighty and truthful deserve to ring through the Church like notes from the trumpet of destiny.

"Wherever he traveled and labored," say his brethren, "he was like a flame of fire, proclaiming the thunders of Sinai against the wicked, and the terrors of the Lord against the ungodly. Few men in the ministry were ever more zealous and laborious; he was bold, undaunted, and persevering in the discharge of his various ministerial duties, and the Lord prospered his labors and gave him seals to his ministry. He was abundant in labors as long as his strength endured. He feared the face of no man, but sought the good of all."

At length, after a long life of seventy-seven years, and a ministry of nearly thirty years, remarkable for activity and success, he came down to the verge of Jordan. The Saviour, in whom he had trusted, and whose presence had cheered him amid his toils and trials, was with him to the last. The final scene was one of impressive, of sublime Christian triumph. "His last expiring breath, his last articulation with the quivering, exhausted lamp of life, were devoutly employed and closed in the solemn and pious exercise of giving honor, and praise, and glory to God; in the same important moment, his life, his breath, and his shouts were hushed in the solemn silence of death, while his enraptured spirit took its flight from the tenement of clay, or earthly tabernacle, to the habitation above, the house not made with hands, eternal in the heavens."*

On the night of his death, October 16, 1809, he awoke from a gentle slumber, and with emotions of ecstatic rapture he shouted, Glory! glory! glory! and in this holy and exultant exercise, so befitting the end of his victorious career, he continued about twenty-five minutes, when, as the sound of the last note of triumph from his lips died away in the silence of the chamber of death, his purified and heroic spirit passed through the celestial gates, to join the innumerable company of angels, and the Church of the first born in heaven.

* Minutes of Conference, vol. I. pp. 180–81.

CHAPTER XIII.

INCIDENTS AND LABORS.

THE Conference of 1783 was held at Ellis's Preaching-house, Virginia, the 6th of May. Of this Conference Asbury says, "Some young laborers were taken in to assist in spreading the gospel, which greatly prospers in the north. We all agreed in the spirit of African liberty, and strong testimonies were borne in its favor in our love-feast; our affairs were conducted in love."

The ministerial force in New Jersey was increased this year, six preachers being appointed to the State. Samuel Rowe, James Thomas, Francis Spry, and William Ringold were appointed to East Jersey, and Woolman Hickson and John Magary to West Jersey. At this Conference New Jersey reported a membership of one thousand and twenty-eight, four hundred and ninety of whom were in West Jersey, and five hundred and thirty-eight in East Jersey. The number of members in the entire connection was thirteen thousand, seven hundred and forty.

Methodism was now exerting such an influence in different parts of the State, that some of the ministers of other sects proclaimed their opposition to it. Asbury visited the southern part of West Jersey this year, and on Sunday, the 21st of September, he was at New Englandtown, a small village five miles south of Bridgeton, "but their minister," he says, "had warned the people against hearing us." He proceeded the same day to Bridgeton, and found that a Mr. Vantull had made an appointment to preach at the same hour as himself, although his appointment had been published some time previously. As he arrived there before Vantull, however, he "preached in the Court-house, and cleared out; those who remained met with hard blows." Methodism did not become established in Bridgeton until about twenty years afterward. The following evening he was at Salem, where he preached; a number of Friends being present and attending with seriousness upon the word.

The progress of the cause in West Jersey, this year, was not considerable, but it held its own, and added twenty-three to its membership.

Rev. Geo. A. Raybold gives the following concerning early Methodism in Atlantic county, in which were some of the first societies in West Jersey: "In early days, when Methodism was first introduced in the neighborhood of Hammonton, the deer were so numerous that they could often be seen from the doors of the village houses. The original proprietor of the property has often shot down with his gun the stately buck or burly bear, within a few hundred yards from the dwelling of the family. Many a thrilling narrative of hunting scenes could be recounted, if the recital would not be considered too much of an episode in the annals of Methodism. The preachers of those days sometimes went out into the deep forest to bring down the deer for the purpose of securing food for their own families. Old brother W., a Jerseyman by birth, was an expert hunter of beasts, as well as men, and this was all right. Many a rough hunter and woodsman possessed and carried with him constantly the gem of grace. Many a rough, rustic cabin of logs, contained a family devoted to God, wherein, at stated intervals, all the members gathered round the family altar, and the social fireside, where the huge pine logs, rolled into the vast, cavern-like fireplace, sent up a ruddy flame, augmented to a degree of almost fierce brilliancy, by the blaze of the pine knots, gathered for the winter fire, and used instead of candles. Perhaps the oldest grave-yard in this part of West Jersey, is that of Pleasant Mills. Ancient head-stones are standing therein, dated one hundred and fifty years since. The Church was erected on this spot by some of the very first preachers; but by which of them no record can be found. The present Church edifice superseded a log Church more than fifty years ago. The very trees, the groves, and the scenery of the river Mullica, all have an ancient appearance. To the antiquary it is quite a pleasure to gaze upon those remains of a past age. And here are found yet the children's children of some of the early Methodists. Here, some of the fathers in the ministry have held forth in by-gone days, and scores have been converted within the old walls of Pleasant Mills' Church. Not quite two miles distant is the old village of Batsto, where was an iron furnace long before the Revolution. Its large mansion-house is a good specimen of the aristocratic style of building, a hundred years ago; and it has, also, many dwellings built of huge logs, now falling into decay, which were put up long ago, for the accommodation of the workmen of the furnace. Cannons were cast here for the army of Washington, and a military corps was formed by the workmen of the village. Here, also, the venerable Asbury, in passing over all parts of the vineyard of the Lord, proclaimed the glorious doctrines of the gospel, and in the hospitable mansion of Mr. R. found a most cordial welcome. This family, even to the present third generation, are possessors of the immense estate originally pos-

18

sessed by their ancestor, and to this day they are hearty supporters of Methodism. Amidst this village congregation, rich and poor, educated and illiterate, all meet as upon one common platform : the wealthy owners, and their poorest workmen, unite sincerely in the worship of the great God."

A society must have been formed at New Germantown, Hunterdon county, in 1783 or some time previously. A Quarterly meeting was held there about this year which was productive of good. Mr. Mair, probably, introduced Methodism there. The love-feast, which Mr. Ware has described, was probably held in that neighborhood, or not very far distant. A daughter of Nicholas Egbert, who told his experience in that love-feast, professed religion about that time, and after walking more than fifty years in the way of life, peacefully finished her pilgrimage in the month of May, 1837.

In East Jersey, while most of the ministers of other denominations opposed Methodism, some of the Episcopal ministers were friendly. One, especially, to whom allusion has already been made, the REV. UZAL OGDEN of the Protestant Episcopal Church, showed himself to be the friend of the weak and struggling cause. He resided at this time at Newton, Sussex county, and cultivated a very extensive field, embracing about forty appointments in the counties of Sussex, Morris, Essex, and Hunterdon, in New Jersey, and Northampton, in Pennsylvania. He was a successful minister of the gospel, and an assistant and counselor of the Methodist preachers. He sympathized with the doctrines of Methodism, as they agreed substantially with the creed which he deduced from the Scriptures. " When I began to preach the gospel," he says, "I endeavored to obtain a just idea of it, without regard to any man's notions concerning it ; and, though I do not mean to mention here all the conceptions I have of the doctrines of Christ, I shall observe, that I think it is incumbent on me, as a teacher of religion, among other things :

" 1. To declare to men their fall from a state of innocence ; and that in themselves they have no ability to regain that moral excellence which they lost, nor to obtain the Divine favor and affection.

" 2. That Christ hath not only made an atonement for our sins, but also merited for us eternal life.

" 3. That through the aids of the Divine Spirit alone, and the means of grace, we are enabled to accept of salvation as offered in the gospel; and obtain newness of heart, or a qualification for celestial enjoyments.

" 4. That every person to whom the gospel shall be preached, who shall die impenitent, will be most justly condemned; he giving the preference to death when life was offered to him."*

His first acquaintance with the Methodists, and the feelings with which he regarded them, are stated by himself, as follows, in a letter to Bishop Asbury: "A few months past, some of the preachers, styled Methodists, were recommended to me by the Rev. Mr. Magaw,† of Philadelphia. Believing, in this day of irreligion, their wish to advance the interests of virtue, I have given them such countenance and advice as I deemed expedient, and I humbly hope and fervently pray, that they and their successors in this country may be instrumental in 'turning many souls from darkness to light, and from the power of Satan unto God.'

"Oh! when shall prosperity attend the kingdom of the Prince of Peace? When shall vice, religious prejudice, bigotry, and enmity be banished from the earth? When shall we be Christians indeed, possess the same amiable and divine temper which was in Christ Jesus our Lord? Father of mercies, compassionate a guilty world, and make bare among us the arm of thy salvation! Pluck, oh! pluck sinners, through the means of grace, as

---

* Methodist Magazine, vol. v., p. 384.

† Dr. M'Gaw was a friend to the Methodists, and rendered them ministerial assistance. He was on very friendly terms with Asbury. At one time he was Rector of St. Paul's Church, Philadelphia.

brands from the burning, and deliver them from the wrath to come!

"I am happy to add that your preachers here do honor to the cause they profess to serve; and by one of them, my good friend Mr. Hickson, I send you a sermon just published, on Regeneration, which I beg your acceptance of."

This letter, bearing date of April 11th, 1783, reveals the fact that Mr. Hickson labored in East Jersey in the ecclesiastical year, 1782. Mr. Ogden's letters are our authority for the assertion, elsewhere made, that Hickson, Ivy, and Mair, were the preachers that supplied the work in East Jersey, after Tunnell and Everett left for the Philadelphia circuit, in November of that year. In his Journal of June 2, 1783, Asbury acknowledges the receipt of this letter, and the sermon as follows:—"I had the pleasure of receiving a letter (with a sermon) from Mr. Ogden, a man of piety, who, I trust, will be of great service to the Methodist societies, and the cause of God in general." Before he received this letter, however, he wrote to Mr. Ogden, to which the latter replied by the following epistle, dated Newtown, 10th July, 1783.

"DEAR AND WORTHY SIR:—Last evening I was favored with your letter of the 28th of May.

"I am obliged to you for the expression of friendship contained in your epistle, and am happy that my conduct to your people hath received your approbation. My deportment towards them proceeded, I humbly hope, from the love of God, which, for near thirty years, I trust, though I am not quite forty years old, hath been diffused into my heart.

"Some ill-natured things have been said of me on account of the favor I have shown to Methodists; but I can truly say that it is a very trivial circumstance, in my estimation, thus to endure the judgment of men.

"I do not mean, in any instance, to omit an opportunity of advancing the Divine glory and the salvation of mankind, whatever may be the consequence of such conduct with regard to myself; and I do not repent that I have shown friendship to your people, but rejoice in it, as I cannot but be of opinion that the countenance I have given them hath, in some measure, advanced the interests of the kingdom of the Prince of Peace. And I am happy to mention that the clergy of our Church, in this state, are disposed to be friendly to the Methodists; and, with cheerfulness, if called on, will administer to them the Divine ordinances.

"I cannot but applaud the unremitted diligence of yourself and those preachers of your community, who, without any worldly expectations, 'go about doing good;' regardless of danger, toil, and the reproaches of men.

"But well you may thus act, when you consider what Christ hath done for you. How ought we, indeed, to rejoice, that the merciful Saviour deigns to employ us in his service, and that we have an opportunity to evince, in some sort, our gratitude to *him* who, in goodness ineffable, 'hath loved us, and washed us' from the pollution of iniquity, 'in the fountain of his own blood, and made us kings and priests unto God his Father, forever and ever!'

"Let us, my dear sir, more and more, if possible, contemplate the stupendous love of God towards us, and our own demerits! Let us consider what it hath cost to redeem souls, and that, in a short period, we must 'render an account to God of our stewardship!' And, impressed with these ideas, let us *endeavor* to be more faithful in the discharge of the duties of our 'high and holy calling.'

"May we add zeal to zeal, diligence to diligence, in the performance of the offices of our vocation; and when our 'labors of love' shall cease, may we hear from the lips of our Divine Master the happy plaudit, 'Well done,' &c.

"I need not say it would afford me great pleasure to enjoy your conversation. It will not, however, be in my power to meet you at the Rariton. I expect to be in Newark, which is ten miles from New York, the 25th and 28th of August next; perhaps at Newark I may there be favored with your company."

Mr. Ogden lived to a good old age, and finally left the Protestant Episcopal Church, and joined the Presbyterians. The Methodist preachers found a retreat in his dwelling, and enjoyed with him the delights of Christian and ministerial fellowship. He corresponded with several of them, and his letters uniformly breathe the spirit of true Christian catholicity, and religious and ministerial devotion. He was the author of several publications, among which was a treatise on Revealed Religion, designed to be an antidote to the infidel writings of Paine. Of this work Asbury says; "The Rev. Mr. Ogden was kind enough to present me with his first volume, On Revealed Religion: it contains a soft, yet general answer to the deistical, atheistical oracle of the day, Thomas Paine; it is a most excellent compilation, taken from a great number of ancient and modern writers on the side of truth; and will be new to common readers. So far as I have read, I can recommend it to those who wish for full information on the subject." Mr. Ogden was, it is said, a sound preacher, and rather eloquent in his palmy days. He was also successful in accomplishing the true end of the ministry, that of saving souls.

We shall hereafter witness further illustrations of his fraternal sympathy with Methodism.

The work appears to have not advanced in East Jersey, this year, as there was a decrease in that circuit of eighty-eight in the membership.

CHAPTER XIV.

METHODISM IN FLANDERS.

FLANDERS, a small village, beautifully situated in a lovely valley in Morris county, surrounded by majestic hills, and a grand and varied natural scenery, is one of the very oldest fortresses of Methodism in the eastern part of the State. It was about the year 1783 that the Methodist itinerants began to sound the trump of the gospel there, which soon echoed among all the surrounding hills, and over all the adjacent mountain summits.

The first Methodist that is known to have dwelt there was a lady. Her name was MARY BELL. She was born in the city of New York, October 25, 1753, and was awakened under the ministry of Joseph Pillmoor, sought and obtained pardoning and renewing grace, and united with the Methodist society.

In the commencement of the war of the Revolution she suffered many hardships, and was finally pillaged of her property by the soldiers, and to secure the safety of her person, she was obliged to flee from the city, when she sought a refuge amid the tranquil, yet inspiring scenes of the quiet valley of Flanders. Here she remained between thirty and forty years, when she removed to Easton, Pennsylvania, where, on the 19th of August, 1836, she finished her pilgrimage and ascended to her rest.

Mrs. Bell was a Christian of high spiritual attainments, and was active and zealous in her Master's service. Her religious example was a living, practical illustration of the excellence and power of Christian faith. Though her religious life was commenced in New York, and was consummated in her exaltation to glory, in Pennsylvania, yet to New Jersey was much of the hallowed savor of that life given, and how much it contributed to the success of Methodism in the eastern section of our State is reserved for the disclosures of eternity.

One of the most important characters in the early Methodism of Flanders was DAVID MOORE, the leader of its first class. He was born at Morristown, N. J., November 25, 1749. At an early age he was bereaved of his father, but being placed in a pious family, he was early taught the fear of the Lord. When about nineteen years of age he experienced religion and joined the Presbyterian Church. He lived in the fellowship of this Church, an acceptable member, about fifteen years. He resided in Flanders when the Methodist preachers first visited the place. He opened his doors for preaching, and they continued to preach there once in two weeks for several years. A society was formed, with which he united, and was appointed the leader. He fulfilled the responsible duties of this office about sixteen years.

During his leadership the first meeting-house in Flanders was erected, and the society increased, so that it numbered thirty members. It is not known with certainty in what year the meeting-house was built, but it was some years before the close of the last century, and was certainly not later than 1793,* and, possibly, as early as 1785. It was, in all probability, the first Church erected in East Jersey. "For many years it remained in an unfinished condition, without walls or doors, the floor itself being but partially laid, yet it was occupied as a place of worship every two weeks. It was finally completed under the administration of Rev. Elijah Woolsey, who is said to have been a very popular minister."† So strict was Mr. Moore in attending Divine worship that for seven years together he was not known to ne-

* See Christian Adv. and Jour., 1828, p. 108.

† Reminiscences of Methodism in Flanders, prepared for the writer by REV. EDWARD W. ADAMS.

glect being at this house of prayer, though it was a distance of six miles from his residence.

In the year 1800, he removed with his family to Cayuga county, New York. He there united with the Church, and was soon appointed a Steward, in which office he served the Church more than twenty years, when the infirmities of age compelled him to resign his charge.

He worthily represented the religion he professed. "Frequently, when it was mentioned in love-feasts, 'Let him first speak who feels most in debt to grace,' whom should we see but father Moore, with streaming eyes and a heart big with gratitude to God, saying that he thought himself the man; that he had found the Lord in his youth, who had supported him through middle age, and was still precious to him in the decline of life? It is worthy of remark, that a little more than a year before his death, he was frequently heard to say he had for many years been privileged with meeting with his brethren in class, but he was rationally taught that he could not long continue here; that his prayer to God was that he might live to see one more reformation, and so true is that text, 'The desire of the righteous shall be granted him,' that in the last year of his life he saw a glorious work of God in his vicinity, and more than

thirty souls professed to be brought from the kingdom
of darkness to that of God's dear Son; and, although
in the seventy-eighth year of his age, he not only saw,
but was engaged in it, for scarcely a meeting was held
in the society but father Moore made one of the number,
praying and laboring for God and souls.   With an un-
deviating constancy and uniformity of life, he persisted,
in spite of age and infirmity, to shine with unabating
lustre, until his sun set in death.   The Sabbath before
his death, in love-feast, he rose and said, that for more
than fifty-eight years the Lord had been with him.   On
Thursday morning following, about one o'clock, he was
violently attacked with excruciating pains, which greatly
alarmed his family.   A physician was immediately called,
but to no effect.   He must take his departure.   And
was he ready?   Hear his own words: 'I thought I
should not live till morning, and oh, how should I feel
if I had no hope?   Bless the Lord!'   Soon after his
speech began to fail.   He said, 'I have nothing here,'
and continued to repeat it several times, when one present asked him if he would wish to say,

> 'I've nothing here deserves my joys,
> There's nothing like my God,'

to which he assented.   On Saturday evening, Dec. 15th,

1827, about half past eight o'clock, he ceased to live as an inhabitant of earth."*

The reader will be interested in the following reminiscences of early Methodism in Flanders, from the pen of Rev. E. W. Adams:

"In those days to kneel during prayer, and stand during the singing were sufficiently contrary to general usage to bring down upon those guilty of such supposed irregularities, severe persecution from the opponents of Methodism.

"Miss Baxter, afterwards the wife of Judge Monroe, and mother-in-law to Rev. M. Force, was one of the earliest, and most devoted members of our Church in this vicinity. Subsequently to her marriage she was much opposed by her husband on account of her Methodistic principles. This was carried to such an extent that for peace sake she agreed to unite with the Presbyterian Church. But she found, after all, that to change her Church relation was not an easy matter. She had no rest day or night. In the mean time the pastor, the Rev. Mr. Fordham, being notified of her intention, called to see her. She frankly told him 'that, after all, she did not know what to do, she could not believe *their doctrines.*' He replied, 'If you cannot conscientiously subscribe to them, I do not wish you to do so.' Still,

* Obituary notice in Christian Adv. and Jour., March 7, 1828.

by her husband and others, she was urged to relinquish
Methodism.   About this time she was taken seriously
ill.   It was supposed she must die.   But one day, as
her husband came to her bedside, addressing him, she
said, 'Monroe, I am impressed with the thought, that if
you will cheerfully allow me to continue a Methodist,
the Lord will restore me to health.   I believe he will do
it.'   Recognizing the probable cause of her sickness, he
answered, 'Woman, I have nothing more to say.   Do as
you please.'   In a few hours her fever abated, she was
restored to health, and lived and died a worthy member
of the Church of her choice.

    "There was no place in the neighborhood where a
Methodist preacher could find entertainment; consequently they had to ride a distance of seven miles after
preaching, in order to find a stopping place.   At this
period the Rev. Mr. Bostwick* was one of the circuit
preachers.   While holding meeting on one occasion, his
horse being hitched a short distance from the Church,
and near the residence of Mr. Monroe, the latter concluded that he would take pity on the horse and give him
something to eat, not intending, however, to invite the
preacher.   He put the animal in the stable and fed him,

---

    * Mr. Bostwick travelled Flanders circuit in 1794.   It is probable,
therefore, that the fact mentioned by Mr. Adams occurred in that
year.

sending word to the minister where he might find his horse. Upon further meditation, he concluded that for *once* he would ask the preacher himself to come and take something to eat; which invitation was gladly accepted. When the other preacher* came round, Mr. M. thought he would not show partiality, so he invited him in like manner. But the early Methodist itinerants understood human nature, and knew how to improve a providential opening. Accordingly, when Mr. Bostwick came round again, he at once came to Mr. Monroe's, who subsequently became a valuable member of the M. E. Church, and for fifty years furnished a comfortable home for Methodist traveling preachers.

"At this same time there was living in the place a man of considerable means, who was a member of the Methodist Church, but refused to take in the preachers, fearing it would be too heavy a burden. Some time after this he sold out, and moved to Sussex, and there purchased considerable property. But it seemed as though the hand of God was upon him. His family was much afflicted, and finally he disposed of his possessions there at a sacrifice, came back to Flanders, paid an advanced price for his former property, and ultimately died in limited circumstances.

* According to the minutes, Samuel Coate was the colleague of Mr. Bostwick.

19

"Col. —— was a man of note, and of large means in this neighborhood.   Hearing that Mr. Monroe had invited the Methodist preachers to his house, he came to advise him on the subject.   Among other things, he said, 'If you tolerate these Methodist preachers on your premises, they will ride you to death.'   This man ran through all his property, and died in abject poverty. On the other hand, Judge Monroe declared that from the time he took in the Methodist preachers, God seemed to prosper him in every respect.   After a long life of liberality and usefulness, he died in affluent circumstances, and even now his name is as 'ointment poured forth.'"

The old Church in Flanders, in which so many of the early Methodists of East Jersey worshiped, and so many of the early heroes of Methodism proclaimed the gospel, and which was honored as the spiritual birth-place of many now in glory, stood until 1857, when, through the skilful management and indefatigable efforts of the Rev. J. B. Heward and Rev. M. Force it was substituted by a new and beautiful house of worship, with a spire and bell, which is an ornament to the village, and a credit to Flanders Methodists.

CHAPTER XV.

SKETCHES OF PREACHERS.

THE name of SAMUEL ROWE is first on the list of those who were appointed to labor in East Jersey in the year 1783. He was admitted on trial at the Conference of 1779, and appointed to Amelia, Virginia. His appointment in 1780 is not designated in the minutes, but on the 12th of November of that year, Asbury writes: "I am kept in peace of soul; expecting my ministering brethren, that we may consult about the work of God. Samuel Roe is going to Sussex—one that has happily escaped the separating spirit and party in Virginia, and the snares laid for his feet." In 1781 he was sent to Pennsylvania; 1782, Dorchester, Md.; 1783, East Jersey; 1784, West Jersey. In 1785 he located.

Speaking of the location of ministers, the Rev. Thomas Ware says, " The first on this list, after the organization of the Church in 1784 was Samuel Row.*

---

* The orthography of the name is not uniform. In the minutes it is spelled *Rowe;* by Asbury, *Roe;* and by Ware, Lee, and Bangs, *Row.*

He had traveled five years. Three desisted from traveling in 1785; but Row was the most conspicuous of the number. He was, while with us, a man of amiable and dignified manners, both as a Christian and a minister. He had the most tenacious and retentive memory of any man I ever knew; and the use he made of this noble faculty evinced that the bent of his youthful mind had been toward piety. He thought, as he used sometimes to say, if the Bible were lost, he could replace by his memory the four Evangelists, the Acts of the Apostles, the Epistle to the Romans, and the greater part of the Epistle to the Hebrews. He was a great admirer of Young's Night Thoughts, and never did I hear any person repeat them with such effect. He was much admired by many as a preacher; but some believed he dealt too much in flowers and in other men's thoughts."

JAMES THOMAS stands in the minutes as continued on trial, in 1783, and was appointed to East Jersey; his appointment for 1784 is not ascertained; in 1785 he was appointed to Philadelphia, which was his last appointment. Before the next Conference he had finished his course. He was an amiable and sprightly young man, and esteemed as a good preacher. The obituary notice of him in the minutes is as follows: "James Thomas,—a pious young man, of good gifts, useful and acceptable, blameless in his life, and much resigned in his death."

FRANCIS SPRY was received on trial at the Conference of 1783, and appointed to East Jersey; his appointments for 1784—5—6 are not given in the minutes; in 1787 he was appointed to Caroline, Md.; in 1788 he was appointed to Baltimore with Ezekiel Cooper. During this Conference year he finished his labors. It is said of him, in the obituary notice of him in the minutes, that he was "skillful and lively in his preaching, sound in judgment, holy in his life, placid in his mind; of unshaken confidence and patience in his death."

The name of WILLIAM RINGOLD appears on the minutes of 1783 for the first time. In 1784 he was appointed to Somerset, Md.; in 1785, to Frederick, Md.; in 1786 he located. We regret that we have no further knowledge concerning him.

WOOLMAN HICKSON was received on trial at the Conference of 1782 and appointed to Somerset, Md., but was afterward changed, there is reason to believe, to East Jersey; in 1783 he was appointed to West Jersey; in 1784, to Orange, Virginia; in 1785, Georgetown; in 1786, Baltimore. On the 24th of December of this year he was ordained elder by Bishop Asbury. His appointment for 1787 is not given in the minutes, but we learn from Rev. J. B. Wakeley's "Lost Chapters" that he labored in the city of New York that year.   Mr. Wakeley says that Baltimore was the last station to which he was regularly appointed, and in consequence of failing health he was left without an appointment in 1787, but one of the preachers appointed to New York failing to fill his appointment, Mr. Hickson labored there in his place.

While in New Jersey, Mr. Hickson enjoyed the acquaintance and friendship of the Rev. Uzal Ogden, and corresponded with him.   He appears to have stood high in Mr. Ogden's confidence and regards.   In a letter bearing date of 25th April, 1783, addressed to Mr. Hickson, Mr. Ogden says: " Your kind letter I have received by Mr. Mair, and it is with pleasure I now devote a moment in this way, to converse with you.

"Believe me, Mr. Hickson, I have a most affectionate regard for you.   Your many good and engaging qualities attach you to me very sensibly; and, 'though absent in body, I shall often be present with you in spirit;' and, I hope, not unmindful of you in my addresses to our heavenly Father.   And, O! Sir, let me be so happy as to be favored and that continually, with an interest in your petitions at the throne of Divine grace!

"I cannot but admire your zeal in forsaking all earthly considerations, all worldly connections and prospects, for Jesus! and that too in the flower of youth!

The sacrifice, on your part, is great; but remember the oblation of our blessed Saviour was infinitely superior to this. And as he hath 'bought us with a price,'—a price above all earthly computation, let us consider that we are, indeed, his in every respect, and rejoice to render him his own. And is it not an honor, an unspeakable favor, that he will graciously compensate our imperfect services with a reward that is ineffable, divine, eternal? Though conscious, 'when we have done all which is in our power to do for God, we are but unprofitable servants,' yet are we permitted to have 'respect to the recompense of reward.' Let this support us under every pressure of affliction; knowing that tribulation, also, will 'work for us a far more exceeding and eternal weight of glory!' Let the thoughts of a celestial crown animate us, likewise, to act with redoubled vigor in the service of our Divine Master. And, oh! let us consider that his eye is ever upon us, and that he will demand—with severity demand—an improvement of each talent committed to our care. Let us be mindful of the day wherein we must 'render an account of our stewardship;' consider the happiness of the plaudit, 'Well done, thou good and faithful servant; enter thou into the joy of thy Lord!' And contemplate the unhappiness of the sentence, 'O! thou wicked and slothful servant,' &c.

* * * * * *

"But let me reply to some particulars in your letter. I rejoice in the prosperity of religion at the southward; and to be informed that my sermon at Black river against bigotry hath been useful.

"I suppose some, perhaps many, unfriendly things are spoken of me on account of the countenance I show your people; but I can truly say, 'it is a small matter with me, to be thus judged of man's judgment.' I trust, in this instance, I have a conscience void of offence towards God, and all rational, pious men.

"I have formed some religious societies, and believe they will be singularly useful, and prosper in the Lord; they are, however, evil spoken of by some, by reason it is by them conceived they are *Methodistical.* How dreadful to the ears of some persons, is the word *Methodist.*"

This epistle shows that the Methodists had to contend against much opposition in laboring for the salvation of the people in New Jersey.

We will give one other letter addressed by Mr. Ogden to Mr. Hickson, which is of historical importance in our work. It bears date of September 4th, 1783, and also the following inscription:

"TO MR. WOOLMAN HICKSON, A METHODIST PREACHER, NOW IN THE COUNTY OF CAPE MAY, IN JERSEY."

"DEAR AND WORTHY SIR:—Your kind letter of the 21st of June last, I had the pleasure of receiving a few days ago. I was happy to be informed that Mr. Hickson, who is still high in my esteem, was in the enjoyment of health, and that his friends and relatives were also well. May every blessing attend him and them, in such manner as shall seem meet to Divine wisdom.

"I cannot say I have had *great* trials, in the manner you *fear*, since I was at the Quarterly meeting at Germantown; but am happy to mention that I hear this meeting hath been *blest* to many persons; and I rejoice to be told that your Annual Conference was so agreeable.

"With us, religion, in several places, flourishes. At Mr. Howell's, a few months past, I admitted about fifty persons to the Lord's table on one day, who before had not approached this blessed ordinance. May numbers daily, in every place, be added to the Church of Christ.

"I am happy you have found some of our clergy to the southward, who are disposed to countenance your preachers in their attempts to reclaim sinners from the error of their ways. And why should not the ministers of the gospel of every denomination, rejoice to have it in their power to *do good;* to demolish the empire of sin and Satan, and to give prosperity to the kingdom of the Prince of Peace? I do not, in any sort, repent of the favor I have shown the Methodists; but regard it as a happiness, that through them, I have had it in my power to aid the cause of religion.

"You inform me that many of the people of Maryland request I would visit them; that you think my labors among them would be blest; and that they would make most ample provision for my support, if I could settle with them. As to my moving from Sussex, money would not induce me to do this. I am here, I think, very useful; and as long as I can obtain a maintenance for my family, among these indigent, but affectionate people, it will not, I conceive, be my duty to leave them: and, as to my visiting the peninsula, this would be very agreeable to me, but I do not think it will be in my power to effect it, especially this fall, as my labors here daily increase; and as my appointments to preach the gospel, in various parts of this State, now extend to about two months to come. However, if possible, I shall endeavor to comply with this request next spring; and as Mr. Roe gives us some hopes that you will soon ride in this circuit, we shall then confer on the subject.

"I applaud the continuance of your zeal to promote the interests of Christianity, and ardently pray that you may ever enjoy the Divine presence and protection.

"Believe me to be,

"Dear and worthy sir,

"Your sincere friend

"And very humble servant,

"UZAL OGDEN."

Mr. Hickson, it is said, introduced Methodism into the city of Brooklyn, L. I. "Captain Webb had preached there many years before, but he formed no class. Mr. Hickson's first sermon in Brooklyn was delivered in the open air, from a table, in what is called Sands street, directly in front of where the Methodist Episcopal Church now stands. At the close of his sermon Mr. Hickson said that if any person present would open his house for preaching, he would visit them again. A gentleman, by the name of Peter Cannon, accepted the offer, and promised to prepare a place for the reception of the congregation. This place was no other than a cooper's shop. In a short time Mr. Hickson formed a class of several members. This was the first class formed in Brooklyn."*

Mr. Hickson was ardently devoted to the cause and

* Wakeley's "Lost Chapters."

work of God.   Though sinking under the wasting power of consumption, he contemplated going to Nova Scotia to labor for the salvation of souls, and Bishop Asbury found it necessary to prevent him.   He possessed fine capabilities for usefulness, but he soon finished his work and gained his reward.   "His last labors," says Lee,* "were mostly in the country, a small distance from New York, and on the east side of the North river.   He then returned to the city of New York, and died; and was buried in the city."   The society there provided him a nurse in his last sickness, and gave, also, to defray the expense of his funeral.   Poverty, exposure, and hard toil were the portion of the Methodist itinerant in those days.   Hickson gained not earthly treasures in his laborious life as a minister, but his crown is as bright and his rest is as sweet in heaven as if he had died possessed of wealth.   The brief memorial of him in the minutes is as follows :—

"Woolman Hickson :—of promising genius, and considerable preaching abilities; upright in life, but soon snatched away from the work by a consumption, and in the midst of his usefulness :—seven years in the work."

He is thus described by Rev. Thomas Ware :—

"Woolman Hickson, distinguished by his thirst for knowledge, both human and divine, traveled our circuit

* History of the Methodists.

soon after I became a Methodist; and from his excellent example I profited much. Few men among us ever observed with greater exactness 'the rules of a preacher,' especially these:—'Be diligent. Never be unemployed. Never be triflingly employed. Be serious. Let your motto be, Holiness unto the Lord. Avoid all lightness, jesting, and foolish talking.' Having a strong and discriminating mind, by his diligence and application according to these rules, he could not but make proficiency both in gifts and grace. But his physical powers were feeble; and nothing but a miracle, with the exertion he made, could save him from an early grave. Accordingly the term of his labors was short. But to such a man as Hickson it must be 'gain' to 'die.' "

The name of JOHN MAGARY first appears in the minutes in 1782, and his appointment that year was to Somerset, Md.; in 1783 he was appointed to West Jersey; 1784 to Frederick, Md. His name now disappeared from the minutes. He was an Englishman and returned to Europe.

In September, 1784, Mr. Wesley says, "I had a long conversation with John Magary, one of our American preachers. He gave a pleasing account of the work of God there continually increasing, and vehemently importuned me to pay one more visit to America before I die." In 1787 Dr. Coke informed Mr. Garrettson, in a letter, that he had been sent by Mr. Wesley to New Foundland; but in 1788 Mr. Wesley mentions a Mr. Magary as principal of the Kingswood school, which may have been the same person.

CHAPTER XVI.

THE ECCLESIASTICAL YEAR 1784–5.

THE Conference was held this year at Ellis's Preaching-house, in Virginia, on the 30th and 31st days of April, and adjourned to Baltimore the latter part of May. "It was," says Lee, "considered as but one Conference, although they met first in Virginia and then adjourned to Baltimore, where the business was finished." The "business was conducted with uncommon love and unity," says Asbury of the Conference in Virginia. East Jersey reported 450 members, and West Jersey 513. The appointments for New Jersey were as follows: East Jersey, Samuel Dudley, William Phoebus. West Jersey, Samuel Rowe, William Partridge, John Fidler. Trenton, John Haggerty, Matthew Greentree.

Asbury traversed the greater portion of the State this year, looking after the interests of the work. He preached at Burlington and Trenton, and also visited Newton, Sussex county, and preached in the Court-house. He was kindly entertained by Mr. Ogden. While in this region he preached at a place called New Market Plains, to about a hundred people, and spoke freely in vindication of Methodism. He regarded this as a singular circumstance, as he did not know till afterward that there were those present who did not attend at other times. He proceeded to New York by way of Newark, and afterward went to West Jersey, visiting and preaching at several places, including Penny Hill, New Mills, and Haddonfield. At this last place he "found a dearth. A poor sot came in and muttered awhile; after meeting he acknowledged he was a sinner, and seemed sorry for his conduct, drunk as he was."

About the year 1625, the time of the great persecution of the Puritans, a number of persons fled from England to seek a refuge and a home in the new world. The way in which they effected their escape was by raising a leaky vessel which was sunk in a dock, stopping the leak, fitting her out indifferently, and setting sail in the night. Directing their course toward the western continent, they found themselves the following morning but a short distance from the land. Their enemies were unable to discover them, however, in consequence of a thick fog which had risen between them and the shore, and which remained until they had sailed beyond the reach of their vision. They were favored with a safe voyage until they reached their desired haven which seems to have been New York bay.   "The ship grounded on the shoals of Amboy."   After discharging her noble cargo, without any loss of life she sunk at once into the deep.   It is said they purchased lands from the Indians, the title for which was afterward ratified by Great Britain.   It is believed that Elizabethtown, N. J., stands upon ground included in this purchase.

Methodism was introduced into Elizabethtown during the present ecclesiastical year.   The Rev. Uzal Ogden was at that time pastor of the Episcopal Church there. When the Methodist preachers visited the town he gave them a kind reception, and "gladly united with them in preaching a crucified and risen Saviour to perishing sinners.   A gracious work of God directly ensued."

One of the laborers in this new movement was ELIAS CRANE, a descendant of Stephen Crane, one of the company above mentioned, who fled from persecution in England, and landed in New Jersey.   Elias was awakened under the ministry of Mr. Ogden, sought and obtained religion, and united with Mr. Ogden's Church. This was a short time previously to the introduction of Methodism there.   Now that the Methodist preachers proclaimed a present and impartial salvation to the people of Elizabeth, he "went out into the streets and lanes of the city, to hunt up the poor, the maimed, the halt,
20

and blind, and invited them to the gospel feast; and thus in early life contracted that useful habit of laboring with mourners in Zion, in which pious and highly honorable work he was pre-eminently useful." In 1788 he married Elizabeth, daughter of Dr. Elihu Lassell of Elizabeth. In 1791 he removed to Uniontown, Pa., and with his companion united with the Church in that place. He was soon after appointed Class-leader, and promoted to the office of local preacher in which sphere of labor he was remarkably zealous and useful. Asbury, Coke, and Whatcoat, shared the kind hospitalities of his home. In 1813 he removed to Leesburg, where he opened his doors for itinerant preaching, and through his efforts, in connection with those of others, a society of about a hundred members was raised up, and a commodious house of worship erected. He died June 4th, 1830.

John Haggerty was the first preacher, so far as we are informed, that bore the ensign of Methodism into Elizabeth. He was sent by Bishop Asbury to form the Newark circuit, and early in the year 1785 he visited Elizabeth. He was directed to the house of Thomas Morrell's father, where he was kindly entertained, and proclaimed his message. Thomas Morrell, who was then thirty-eight years of age, was present and heard the sermon. It was from the text, " God so loved the world," &c. He was awakened under the sermon, and after a few months was converted. The foundation of Methodism in Elizabeth was laid at that time, and it continues still to prosper there, notwithstanding its formidable obstacles.

Mr. Haggerty was the first Methodist preacher Mr. Morrell ever heard. At his earnest solicitation, about three months after his conversion, the latter abandoned a lucrative business, "and commenced preaching in different places, his appointments being made by Mr. Haggerty, as he passed round the circuit." One of his first efforts as a preacher was made "at the house of his uncle, at Chatham, Morris county, New Jersey. Having been an officer in the army of the Revolution, and for several years subsequently a merchant in Elizabeth, he was widely known, and a very large assembly convened to hear the 'major' preach, especially as he had joined the sect everywhere spoken against. This, I think, was his third or fourth effort, and was, by himself, deemed an *utter failure*. He then concluded that he was not called of God to preach, and would not make the attempt again. Early the ensuing morning, while at breakfast at his uncle's, there was a knock at the door. A lady entered desiring to see the preacher of the previous evening. In a few moments another came, and then an old man upon the same errand, all of whom had been awakened under the sermon deemed by him a failure.   They had come to learn the way of salvation more perfectly.   The doctrine to them was new, having been brought up under Calvinistic influences.   He, of course, recalled his purpose to preach no more, and was encouraged to go forward.

"About this time such was the excitement all through that part of the State, occasioned by Methodist preaching, that some of the ministers of the Presbyterian Church became alarmed.   One of them, a young man, advising with an elder brother in the ministry, asked the question, 'What shall be done to counteract the influence they are exerting?'   'Why,' said the elder brother, 'we must out preach and out pray them.'   'That,' replied the young preacher, 'is impossible, for there is Mr. Haggerty, he can split a hair.' "*

Chatham is about the oldest society in Morris county except Flanders, but whether there were any Methodists there at the time Mr. Morrell preached the sermon above mentioned we are unable to say.   But very soon afterward there was a society of Methodists there, and some time previous to 1790, probably about 1786 or 1787 they moved toward building a Chapel.   But their number being small and their means limited, they were led to accept a proposal made by some persons not members of the society, but who appeared friendly, which

* Letter of Rev. F. A. Morrell to the writer.

was that they would assist them in building the Chapel, providing it should be free to all denominations. To this the Methodists consented, and one person gave timber, another boards, &c., and the house was accordingly erected. The Methodists held their public services in it for a considerable time, but in the course of years the free enterprise resulted in dissatisfaction and bickering, and at length the house was pulled down. In 1832 the present Methodist Church in Chatham was erected. Mr. Brainerd Dickinson was, we are informed, the leader of the first class, and the chief man in the society for a number of years. He was a Revolutionary soldier, and was engaged in the battle of Monmouth. He died about 1819. From this Church the venerable Manning Force, of the Newark Conference, went forth to the itinerancy, and Mr. Isaac Searles, father-in-law of Rev. Dr. Whedon, was for years, during the first part of the present century, an important and useful man in the society. He died in December, 1856, in the city of Washington, aged about 80 years. The venerable Matthias Swaim, father of Rev. John S. Swaim, now about ninety years of age, has been a member there since 1803. He is still one of the chief pillars of the Church. He became a resident of Chatham in 1791, and to him we are indebted for most of the above facts.

An event of great importance to Methodism in

America occurred this year.   It was the organization of
the Methodist Episcopal Church as a distinct and independent ecclesiastical body.

"In 1782, by virtue of the Preliminary Articles of
peace, hostilities ceased between the United States and
Great Britain—and in 1783 the Definitive Treaty of
Peace was signed, ratified, and carried into full effect.
The Independence of the United States being acknowledged by Great Britain, and our civil and religious rites,
liberties, and privileges, being established and secured,
and peace being restored again to the land; the state of
things was amazingly changed.

"In 1784, Mr. Wesley, who had been applied to for
advice and counsel, considered the situation of the Methodist societies in the United States; and on mature deliberation, advised and recommended his American brethren, who were totally disentangled, both from the British civil government, and from the English Church hier-
archy, that it was best for them 'to stand fast in that
liberty, wherewith God had so strangely made them
free.'   And he and us being at full liberty, in this matter, to follow the Scriptures, and the usages of the
primitive Church; he being clear in his own mind, took
a step, which he had long weighed in his thoughts; and,
not only advised and recommended his American brethren, but took a decided part in aiding them, to become a

distinct and independent Church. Accordingly he set apart, and appointed THOMAS COKE, Doctor of Civil law, late of Jesus College, Oxford, who was a regular Presbyter of the English Church, and vested him with full Episcopal authority, to come over to America on this business; and Richard Whatcoat and Thomas Vasey, presbyters, to come with him; and to confer ordinations, and to assist the Methodist societies in becoming, and organizing themselves an independent Church. At the same time he recommended the Episcopal form and mode of Church government; and that Dr. Thomas Coke, and Mr. Francis Asbury, be received and acknowledged, as joint superintendents or bishops. The same year, Mr. Wesley executed the famous deed of settlement, or declaration, of one hundred preachers, of whom Dr. Coke was one, and first on the list after the two Wesleys, as members of the British Conference in regular succession, to be known in law, and to hold the Chapels, preaching-houses, and other property in behalf of the connection in Europe. Next to his brother Charles, no man stood higher in the esteem and confidence of Mr. Wesley than Dr. Coke; and in America, no man stood so high with him as Mr. Asbury.

"September 18th, 1784, Coke, Whatcoat, and Vasey sailed from Bristol for America, and landed in New York the 3d of November following. Dr. Coke and

Whatcoat, leaving Vasey behind, hastened on to the south with all expedition. On the 14th of the same month they met Mr. Asbury, and about fifteen of the American preachers, at a Quarterly meeting, held in Barrett's Chapel, Kent county, State of Delaware.

"It was at that meeting, at Barrett's Chapel, that by mutual consent and agreement of the preachers there, that the General Conference, was called to meet in Baltimore, on the Christmas following, to take into consideration the proposals and advice of Mr. Wesley. Intelligence was sent off to every part of the connection. Brother Garrettson was appointed to go through Maryland, into Virginia, and to give the information to the south and west, and to call the preachers together.

"The Conference met the 27th of December, 1784, and continued their deliberation and sitting until some time in January, 1785. It was unanimously agreed, that circumstances made it expedient for the Methodist societies in America to become a separate body from the Church of England; of which, until then, they had been considered as members. They also resolved to take the title, and to be known in future by the name of THE METHODIST EPISCOPAL CHURCH. They made the Episcopal office elective; and the bishops or superintendents, to be amenable for their conduct to the body of preachers or to the General Conference. Mr. Asbury, though appointed by Mr. Wesley, would not be ordained unless he was chosen by a vote, or the voice of the Conference.   He was unanimously elected, and Dr. Coke was also unanimously received jointly with him, to be the superintendents, or bishops, of the Methodist Episcopal Church.   From that time the Methodist societies in the United States became an independent Church, under the Episcopal mode and form of government.   Designing, professing, and resolving 'to follow the Scriptures, and the primitive Church, according to the advice and counsel of Mr. Wesley, and in perfect unison with the views, the opinions, and wishes of Mr. Asbury.   This step met with general approbation, both among the preachers and the members.   Perhaps we shall seldom find such unanimity of sentiment, in a whole community, upon any question of such magnitude, proposed to be adopted by them."*

The Rev. Thomas Ware was present at this memorable conference, and he speaks of it in the following language :

" Nearly fifty years have now elapsed since the Christmas Conference, and I have a thousand times looked back to the memorable era with pleasurable emotions. I have often said it was the most solemn convocation I ever saw.   I might have said, for many reasons, it was sublime.   During the whole time of our being together

* Rev. Ezekiel Cooper's work on Asbury, pp. 102–3–4–8–9.

in the transaction of business of the utmost magnitude, there was not, I verily believe, on the Conference floor or in private, an unkind word spoken, or an unbrotherly emotion felt.   Christian love predominated ; and, under its influence, we 'kindly thought and sweetly spoke the same.'

" The annual meetings of the preachers, sent, as they hold themselves to be, to declare in the name of the almighty Jesus terms of peace between the offended Majesty of heaven and guilty man, were to them occurrences of interesting import.   The privilege of seeing each other, after laboring and suffering reproach in distant portions of the Lord's vineyard, and of hearing the glad tidings which they expected to hear on such occasions, of what God was doing through their instrumentality, encouraged their hearts every step they took in their long and wearisome journeys, and served as a cordial to their spirits.   But never before had they met on so important and solemn an occasion as this.   Fifteen years had passed away since Boardman and Pillmoor arrived in America, in the character of itinerants, under the direction of Mr. Wesley.   This was the fifteenth Conference.   During all that time, those of us who would dedicate our infant offspring to the Lord by baptism, or, would ourselves receive the holy sacrament, must go for these sacred rites to such as knew us not, and were entirely mistaken respecting our character. The charge preferred against us was not hypocrisy, but enthusiasm. Our opposers did not blame us for not living up to our profession outwardly, but for professing too much—more than is the privilege of man in this life, in speaking with Christian confidence of the knowledge of a present salvation by the forgiveness of sins, and the witness of the Spirit. There were, indeed, a few who harmonized with us in sentiment and in feeling. But, in the general estimation, we were the veriest enthusiasts the world ever saw.

" Humiliating indeed was our condition. Not a man in holy orders among us; and against us formidable combinations were formed, not so much at first among the laity as among the clergy. But being denounced from the pulpit as illiterate, unsound in our principles, and enthusiastic in our spirit and practice—in a word, every way incompetent, and only to be despised—the multitude, men and women, were emboldened to attack us ; and it was often matter of diversion to witness how much they appeared to feel their own superiority.

" All these things, however, we could have borne without concern, as the work of God was prospering, and the societies increasing more rapidly than any other denomination in the country ; but the want of orders had a tendency to paralyze our efforts. Many, very many, who had been brought to the knowledge of God through our instrumentality, were kept from uniting with us because we could not administer to them all the ordinances.

"At the Christmas Conference we met to congratulate each other, and to praise the Lord that he had disposed the mind of our excellent Wesley to renounce the fable of uninterrupted succession, and prepare the way for furnishing us with the long desired privileges we were thenceforward expecting to enjoy. The announcement of the plan devised by him for our organization as a Church, filled us with solemn delight. It answered to what we did suppose, during our labors and privations, we had reason to expect our God would do for us; for in the integrity of our hearts we verily believed his design in raising up the preachers called Methodists in this country was to reform the continent and spread scriptural holiness through these lands; and we accordingly looked to be endued, in due time, with all the panoply of God. We, therefore, received and followed the advice of Mr. Wesley, as stated in our form of Discipline.

"After Mr. Wesley's letter, declaring his appointment of Dr. Coke and Mr. Asbury joint superintendents over the Methodists in America, had been read, analyzed, and cordially approved by the Conference, the question arose, 'What name or title shall we take?' I thought to myself, I shall be satisfied that we be denominated, The Methodist Church, and so whispered to a brother sitting near me. But one proposed, I think it was John Dickens, that we should adopt the title of METHODIST EPISCOPAL CHURCH. Mr. Dickens was, in the estimation of his brethren, a man of sound sense and sterling piety; and there were few men on the Conference floor heard with greater deference than he. Most of the preachers had been brought up in what was called 'The Church of England;' and, all agreeing that the plan of general superintendence, which had been adopted, was a species of Episcopacy, the motion on Mr. Dickens' suggestion was carried without, I think, a dissenting voice. There was not, to my recollection, the least agitation on the question. Had the Conference indulged a suspicion that the name they adopted would be, in the least degree, offensive to the views or feelings of Mr. Wesley, they would have abandoned it at once; for the name of Mr. Wesley was inexpressibly dear to the Christmas Conference, and especially to Mr. Asbury and Dr. Coke."

A number of preachers were elected to elders' orders at this Conference and received ordination. Methodists could now receive the Sacraments at their own altars, and at the hands of their own ministers. The advantages resulting from this change in the economy of Methodism must have been exceedingly great.   It was inconvenient to members of the societies to be compelled to go to the Episcopal Church to receive the sacraments; and it was not a little repugnant to their feelings to partake of the emblems of the Saviour's passion, when administered, as was too often the case, by men who were known to be deficient, not only in religion, but in morals.   The fact of their being in orders must have added, likewise, to the dignity and influence of the ministry, and to the general harmony and efficiency of the Church.

The preachers elected to the order of elders, of whom there were thirteen, were expected to visit the Quarterly meetings and administer the ordinances, which arrangement was finally substituted by the regular Presiding Eldership, an office necessary, probably, to the complete and successful working of the grand and powerful machinery of Methodism.

Of the preachers appointed to labor in New Jersey this year, the name of SAMUEL DUDLEY stands first. His first appointment in the minutes was to Fluvanna, Va., in 1781.   In 1782 he was appointed to Sussex circuit, Va., with Pedicord; in 1783, Guilford, N. C.; 1784, East Jersey; 1785, Dover, Delaware; 1786, Dorchester, Md., with Joseph Everett as a colleague; 1787, Philadelphia.   In 1788 he retired into the local ranks in consequence of family affairs. Very little is known respecting his personal history, except that he was a good and successful laborer in the vineyard, and endured, during his period of effective service, his due share of the toils and sacrifices of a pioneer itinerant life.

WILLIAM PHOEBUS was born in Somerset county, Md., August, 1754. He entered the Conference on trial in 1783, and was appointed to Frederick circuit, Md. In 1784 he was appointed to East Jersey; 1785, West Jersey. The minutes do not designate his appointment for 1786. In 1787 he was appointed to Redstone; 1788, Rockingham; 1789, Long Island; 1790, New Rochelle; 1791, Long Island, with Benjamin Abbott. In 1792 he located. It cannot but be observed by the reader, how frequently the word "located" occurs. The greater portion of the preachers in the first period of our history retired sooner or later from the itinerant ranks. There must have been strong reasons for this, as many of those who located manifested an ardent and abiding attachment to the work. One of those reasons was, the work required that the preachers should travel extensively, and consequently those who had families must either abandon it or else be almost perpetually from home. Another reason was, the severity of the labor, often taxing the strength beyond what it could bear, and hence many were compelled to retire on account of failing health, there not being at that time any Supernumeraries.   Another, and perhaps the chief reason, was inadequate temporal support.   The people were poor, they were contemned by the world and by many of other sects; they were compelled to build churches in order to meet the exigencies of the cause, and consequently they were straitened in their pecuniary resources; and in many instances in consequence of their poverty, and the various pressing demands made upon them by the Church, they were not able to provide liberally for their preachers.   Still, in numerous instances there can be no doubt that they might have given a better support to those who ministered to them in holy things, had they earnestly and faithfully endeavored to do so, and a more liberal course on the part of the Church would probably have saved to the ministry many, the value of whose services would have been beyond human computation. The last difficulty named had its influence in leading Phoebus to a location.

He continued to labor in the local sphere, practicing medicine at the same time, until 1806, when he again entered the regular work in the New York Conference, and was appointed to the city of Albany.   In 1808 he was removed to Charleston, S. C., and in 1811 he was appointed to the city of New York.   He continued to fill various appointments until 1821, when he became a

Supernumerary.   In 1824, he took a superannuated relation to the Conference, which he continued to sustain until his death, which occurred November 9, 1831, at his residence in the city of New York.

In the early part of his ministry, it is said, he was an earnest and searching preacher, proclaiming the truth often very fluently and successfully.   In his later years his preaching was not of a very popular character, but this arose more from the dryness of his manner, than from a want of solidity and depth of matter.   He was quite eccentric.   He fancied things that bore the stamp of antiquity.   The sayings and opinions of the old divines and philosophers had a great influence with him. He particularly admired Baxter.   He could not pardon Dr. Clarke for his opinions concerning the Sonship of Christ, and his speculation about the serpent.   He sometimes expressed himself enigmatically.   In speaking to the Conference on one occasion, he remarked "that the lease of his house had expired, and therefore he could not tell how soon he might be called to remove, as he was not certain that he could procure a renewal of his lease for any particular length of time; hence he could not pledge himself for any special service in the ministry."   An old minister afterward said to Dr. Bangs, "I thought the doctor owned the house in which he lives; but it seems I was under a mistake, as he says

21

that the time of his lease is run out." The doctor replied, "You do not understand him. He speaks in parables. He is now *three score years and ten*, the common age God has allotted to man, and therefore cannot calculate on living much longer at most." This he afterward explained to be his meaning.

He was a man of sterling integrity, and of deep devotion to the Church and the work of the ministry. He well understood human nature and was skillful in adjusting Church difficulties. He possessed a large fund of varied knowledge, and his discourses were richly evangelical—the character and redemptive work and offices of Jesus being prominently presented in them. He maintained a lofty dignity of deportment becoming the ambassador of God.

Having attained the age of seventy-seven years, he came to the closing scene with a mind clear as the cloudless day. He spoke of the merits of his Redeemer, and of his prospect through him of an endless and glorious life. " A short time before he died he quoted the words of St. James, 'Let patience have its perfect work, that ye may be perfect and entire, lacking nothing,' and commented upon them with much apparent pleasure, and with great clearness of expression, exhibiting, at the same time, a lively exposition of the meaning of those expressive words in his struggles with his last enemy."*

The name of WILLIAM PARTRIDGE first appears on the minutes in 1780, and he was appointed to Pittsylvania, Va.; 1781, Berkeley, Va.; 1782, Lancaster, Pa.; 1783, Somerset, Md.; 1784, West Jersey; 1785, Camden; 1786, New Hope, N. C.; 1787, Yadkin; 1788, Broad River. In 1789 the minutes report him as under a partial location, on account of family affairs, but subject to the order of the Conference. He was a native of Sussex county, Va., and was born in 1754. He was converted when about twenty-one years of age. He re-entered the itinerancy in 1814, and in 1817 he died in Sparta, Ga. One wrote of him as follows: " I have lived a near neighbor to brother Partridge for upward of twenty years, and can with satisfaction say that he was the greatest example of piety that I have ever been acquainted with." He was a constant student of the Bible, but read other authors but little. He ceased nearly at once to labor and to live. He preached his last sermon from the words, " Walk in wisdom towards them that are without." The same evening he was taken ill. " His colleague asked him whether he was ready for the final summons. He said, ' Yes, for me to

* Bangs' History of M. E. Church, vol. iv., p. 134.

die is gain.' His speech left him, and on Saturday night after he was taken he breathed his last.''*

JOHN FIDLER was admitted on trial at the Conference of 1784 and appointed to West Jersey. In 1785 he was appointed to Redstone; 1786, Fairfax, Va. According to Lee he located in 1787.

JOHN HAGERTY was born in Prince George's county, Md., February 18, 1747. He had religious impressions at an early age, and his heart would melt as he read the story of the Saviour's sufferings, but he did not experience religion until he was about twenty-four years of age.

He was converted by means of the ministry of John King. Mr. King visited the town where he resided. He heard him, and liked the sermon tolerably well. The next time he heard him he was better pleased, and the third time the veil was swept from his mind, so that he saw his exceeding sinfulness and his exposure to wrath, and the necessity of obtaining the righteousness which is of faith. The depths of his heart were stirred, and he resolved " on the spot to flee from the wrath to come." After some months of distress and prayer, he obtained a sense of pardon. In 1772 Mr. King formed a society in the town, consisting of Mr. Hagerty and

* Minutes, 1818.

thirteen others, of which Hagerty afterwards became the leader.

Soon after his conversion he began to exhort, and under his second exhortation a man was deeply convicted of sin. This encouraged him to go forward in the work, and his hortatory exercises soon assumed the dignity of sermons. He labored as a local preacher for several years, giving much time to his ministerial labors, and sometimes "he would be away from home on his preaching excursions for many weeks together." His heart was so much engaged in the business of saving souls that he could feel contented only when he was employed in it.

He entered the itinerancy in 1779, and was sent to Berkeley circuit, Va., to which he returned in 1780. In 1781 he was appointed to Baltimore circuit; in 1782 to Calvert; 1783, Chester, Pa.; 1784, he stands on the minutes in connection with Trenton circuit, N. J. At the Christmas Conference he was ordained an elder and was stationed in 1785 in New York. In 1786 and 1787 he acted as Presiding Elder. In 1788 he was stationed in Annapolis; 1789, Baltimore; 1790, Fell's Point; 1791–92, Baltimore. At the end of this year domestic affliction required him to locate. But he did not remain idle. He preached in and about Baltimore with great acceptability. He was ready to meet any call for his ministerial services, whether at night or day. "Distance, weather, or season was no consideration with him when duty called. He has been often known to rise from his bed at midnight and ride for miles into the country to visit a sick or a dying man, and that without fee or reward."*

Mr. Hagerty was of medium size, straight, and well proportioned, "prominent features—a fine retreating forehead, and in profile resembled the best prints we have of Mr. Fletcher."† He was more than an ordinary preacher. It is said he was a close reasoner, and his ministrations were marked by considerable pathos. He had a manly voice, and his enunciation of truth was "clear, pointed, and commanding."

A few days before his death a ministerial friend and brother called to see him, and remarked that he appeared to be drawing nigh to eternity, when he replied, "Yes; and all is straight, the way is clear before me." On the fourth of September, 1823, he entered into rest.

MATTHEW GREENTREE was appointed in 1783, (which is the first he appears on the record,) to Caroline, Md. In 1784 he was appointed to Trenton; 1785, East Jersey; 1786, Little York, Pa.; 1787, Annamessex, Md.;

---

* Memoir, by Rev. Joshua Soule. Meth. Mag., 1824, p. 211.
† Ibid.

1788, Caroline, Md.; 1789, Kent, Md.   In 1790 he located.   Mr. Greentree was, it is said, a native of Talbot county, Md., and was probably the first contribution which Methodism in that county made to the itinerancy.

CHAPTER XVII.

RESULTS AND LABORERS.

THREE Conferences were held in the year 1785, which was the first time that more than one had been held in the same year.   There had, indeed, in several instances, as we have already shown, been two sessions, but they were regarded as but one Conference.   The third Conference this year was held in Baltimore, commencing the first day of June.   We suppose that New Jersey was included in this Conference.   The membership was reported in the aggregate this year, so that we cannot tell what was the number in New Jersey.   There were eighteen thousand members in the entire connection.

The work in New Jersey was supplied with laborers this year as follows: Thomas S. Chew, Elder.   West Jersey, William Phoebus, Thomas Ware, Robert Sparks. East Jersey, Adam Cloud, Matthew Greentree.   Trenton, Robert Cloud, John McClaskey, Jacob Brush.

This was the strongest ministerial force, numerically, with which New Jersey had till that time been favored.

This year was rather barren of incidents, or, if it was not, few have been transmitted to us. Those few, however, indicate the progress of the cause.

It was this year that JOHN WALKER, a name precious to many New Jersey Methodists, united with the Church. He lived until 1849, and was for years a venerated father in our ministry. He joined the society in Mount Holly. As the organization of that society was not permanent till after the period embraced in the present volume, we have made only passing allusions to it. But as it was associated with the earliest days of New Jersey Methodism, and as it contributed two of its first members to the itinerancy, (Ware and Walker,) and two others sustained no insignificant relation to the cause, one being the wife of an itinerant and the other of a most prominent layman, it may be proper that we should here give some of the facts of its early history.

The first Methodist preacher that preached in Mount Holly, so far as our knowledge extends, was George Shadford, one of Mr. Wesley's Missionaries to America. This was probably about 1773. It was sometime after that a small society was formed there. Miss Rebecca Budd, afterward Mrs. James Sterling, joined it in 1779. It is probable that this was about the beginning of the society.   She was the only young unmarried person then in the class, and she was highly gratified when Thomas Ware united with them in 1781, as she thought she would find in him a profitable Christian associate.   Some of the other members of the class were Mrs. Mary Monroe, Mary Lees, afterward the wife of Rev. J. Walker, Mary Morrell, afterward Mrs. Dobbins, the wife of Peter Shiras, Esq., and a colored woman named Drusilla, otherwise called "Old Drusy."

In those days the only place the Methodists could procure for preaching was the Town house, over the Market, which was made the scene of gracious displays of the Divine mercy.   But for some cause the society declined.   Perhaps it was owing, in some degree, to the loss of such noble spirits as Ware and Miss Budd, the former leaving to enter the itinerancy.   For several years there were but two members in Mount Holly, Mrs. Mary Monroe and "Old Drusy."   They were accustomed to go two and a half miles to attend week day preaching, there being no Methodist preaching in the town. In 1794 there appears to have been no society there, as about that time a Mrs. M'Gowan, who was converted under the ministry of Rev. James Rogers, in Dublin, and was a member of the class led by his wife, Mrs. Hester Ann Rogers, became a resident of Mount Holly, and not finding a Methodist society with which she could unite, she joined the Baptist Church, of which she remained a member several years, until the society was reorganized, when she returned to the Church of her birth and of her choice. Mrs. M'Gowan had enjoyed the ministry of Wesley, Fletcher, and Clarke, and she was present when an attempt was made upon the life of Mr. Rogers in the Chapel, while he was in the act of preaching, of which mention is made in Mrs. Rogers' Memoirs. The first Church in Mount Holly was erected about 1810.

As the war was over and quiet restored, Chapels began to spring up in different parts of the State. A Quarterly meeting was held in November of this year at Goodluck, in what is now Ocean county, and on the Sabbath James Sterling and Rebecca Budd were united in holy matrimony in the Church, in the presence of the congregation. There must, therefore, have been a meeting-house there at that time, and of course a society, which must have been formed at a period somewhat earlier. This Church, doubtless, was attended by the Methodists of that entire region.

Bishop Asbury attended a Quarterly meeting on Saturday and Sunday, Sept. 17 and 18, 1785, at Maurice river, in Cumberland county, and on Saturday he says, "Our house was not quite covered, and it was falling weather; the people, nevertheless, stayed to hear me preach." From the remark, "Our house was not quite covered," it appears that it was a Chapel which they had erected but had not finished. That this is not a mere conjecture is shown by the fact that Asbury was at Maurice river the following year, when he preached in the Church. There is scarcely any doubt that it was located in the village of Port Elizabeth. There was in 1785 a good society there. This we infer from the fact that in the love-feast on Sunday the people spoke freely of the dealings of God with their souls. It was, according to Asbury, "a great time."

One of the first Methodists in that part of West Jersey, and probably a member of this same society at the time this Quarterly meeting was held, was Eli Budd. He became a member of the society about 1775, which indicates that it must have been formed about that time. He died at Port Elizabeth early in the year 1830. During most of this time he was a class leader, and a steward of the circuit. When on his death bed he exclaimed, "Fifty-five years ago God converted my soul and I united myself to the Methodist Episcopal Church. Fifty-three years since I was appointed a class leader, and forty-seven years ago God sanctified my soul; since which time I have lived in the precious enjoyment of his perfect love, and now I go to live with and enjoy him forever !"

In the West Jersey circuit, which included about the whole of the State south of Burlington, Methodism had to contend with high toned Calvinism and Mysticism. The rides of the preachers were very long, and many of them very dreary. Yet their labors were, in a degree, successful, a number being converted during the year. Mr. Ware was favored with seeing several of his relatives brought to God through the agency of Methodism this year.

Bishop Asbury visited Stow Creek and Salem this year, and preached at each place "with some consolation."

At Salem he baptized two persons by immersion in the creek. "This unusual baptismal ceremony," he says, "might have made our congregation larger than it would otherwise have been." He was also in Monmouth, and speaks of hearing Mr. Woodhull, the successor of Wm. Tennent, at the Tennent Church, preach a funeral sermon on "Lord, thou hast made my days as an handbreadth." "In my judgment," he says, "he spoke well." He preached with liberty to the people at Monmouth, on Josh. xxiv. 17. The society at Monmouth must have been formed at an early period, probably about 1780, as in that year Job Throckmorton of Freehold was converted under the ministry of Rev. Richard Garrettson, and became a member of the society. He was one of the first members in that region.

The Methodists were much persecuted there at that time. His house was a home for the preachers, and very likely Asbury was entertained in his dwelling during this visit to Freehold. Everett, F. Garrettson, Cooper, Ware, and others were accustomed to stop at his house. He was accustomed to relate incidents illustrative of Abbott's powerful ministry, one of which was as follows:

On one occasion meeting was held in the woods, and after F. Garrettson had preached, Abbott rose and looked around over the congregation very significantly, and exclaimed, "Lord, begin the work! Lord begin the work *now!* Lord, begin the work just *there!*" pointing, at the same time, towards a man who was standing beside a tree, and the man fell as suddenly as if he had been shot, and cried aloud for mercy.

An incident very similar to this, is related by Mr. Amos Opdyke, Sen., a venerable New Jersey Methodist, which is thus given by his son, the Rev. S. H. Opdyke, A. M. "Many years since he became acquainted with an old Methodist lady, who in her childhood had been a member of a family which Abbott visited. On one occasion the family heard the sainted man, after he had retired to his room, earnestly praying for the conversion of one soul at his next day appointment. Next morning whilst praying in the family circle, he offered the same petition—'Lord, give me one soul to-day.' He went to his appointment and in his opening prayer he still called on God to give him one soul. He commenced his discourse, and after having spoken most solemnly for some time, he fixed his eye upon a gentleman standing near the door, and pointing in that direction, cried out, ' Lord, let that be the soul,' and the man fell under the power of God as if pierced by a rifle ball."

In East Jersey the borders were enlarged, so as to include Staten Island. Robert Cloud went thither in the fall, and commenced laboring and a great revival followed. The labor being too great for him, Thomas Morrell was induced to go to his aid. Mr. Morrell remained there until 1788, (twenty months,) when he was ordained Deacon and appointed to Trenton. It was about this period that the first Methodist society was organized on the Island. Asbury, as we have seen, had previously preached there, but little permanent effects seem to have followed his labors. Israel Disosway was, it is believed, the leader of its first class, and an important man in the society. " The first Quarterly meeting was held in his barn ; and the timbers of the first Methodist Church built on Staten Island, were cut from his trees." This Church was built about 1790 or 1791. Some of the other members of this society were Ann Doughty, subsequently Mrs. Disosway, Abraham Çole, Hannah Cole,

Peter Woglam, John Slaught, John Marshall, and Peter Winant.

Bishop Asbury visited Elizabethtown this year and was the guest of Mr. Ogden. He preached in an unfinished church belonging to the Presbyterians.

Of the preachers in New Jersey this year THOMAS S. CHEW, the elder, stands first. He was a man of superior gifts as a preacher, and appears to have been devoted, popular, and useful. While traveling in Maryland during the war, he was asked by a Mr. Downs, the sheriff of the county, if he were "a minister of the gospel." He replied in the affirmative, when Mr. Downs requested him to take the oath of allegiance, but he declined on account of conscientious scruples. Mr. Downs then told him that he was bound by his oath of office to enforce the law upon him and send him to prison. Mr. Chew calmly replied that he did not wish him to perjure himself, that he was ready to submit to the execution of the law. Mr. Downs answered, "You are a strange man, and I cannot bear to punish you, I will, therefore, make my house your prison." He accordingly consigned him under his own hand and seal to his own house as a prisoner, where he kindly entertained him for about three months, during which time both himself and his lady were awakened under Mr. Chew's exhortations and prayers, and the lady was converted. They both became Methodists, and, assisted by others, built the first Methodist meeting-house in that county, called "Tuckey-hoe Chapel," and it was from that place, or its vicinity, that Ezekiel Cooper, Thomas Neall, and others went forth to the battles of the itinerancy.

Mr. Chew appears to have made a strong impression in favor of the cause as elder this year in Jersey. Mr. Ware says "The Presiding Elder appointed to attend the Quarterly meetings in Jersey was an exceedingly popular man, and his presence gave a consequence to these meetings which left no doubt on our minds of the advantage of having men in holy orders among us; and we praised God for the providence which had brought about this new order of things, and established us as a branch of his militant Church."

Mr. Chew continued to serve the Church in the office of elder in different parts of the country until his downfall in 1787 or 1788. His fall occurred in Sussex Co., Delaware. He professed to be restored to the Divine favor, but had to retire from the ministry. He appears as desisting from traveling on the minutes of 1788, but was considered as expelled on the ground of immorality.

THOMAS WARE is understood to have ranked among the strong men of his day with respect to preaching ability and usefulness. The following incident is illustrative of his character and of his devotion to the work

22

of doing good.   He was once overtaken in a severe snow storm and compelled to stop at an inn, where he was detained a week by the storm. He spoke to the landlady about her soul and she seemed affected.   Being a good singer, he sang them some spiritual songs with which they seemed delighted.   One evening as they were seated around the cheerful fire, and the snow and hail were pelting furiously against the windows, Ware observed that his host and hostess seemed pensive.   He sung one of his favorite pieces, and they appeared much affected. He bowed in prayer, and for the first time they kneeled. After prayer he retired, leaving them in tears.   The landlord afterward tried, during Mr. Ware's stay, to resume his former gayety, but the attempt was vain. More than thirty years afterward he visited Mr. Ware and said, "Father Ware, I am happy to see you once more.   Have you forgotten the snow storm which *brought you and salvation to my house?*"

Mr. Ware spent the last years of his life in Salem, New Jersey.   His memory is blessed.

ROBERT SPARKS was admitted this year on trial.   The following year he was appointed to Trenton circuit with Robert Cann.   His appointments embraced an extensive territory, and in 1829 he withdrew from the Church.

ADAM CLOUD was admitted in 1781 and expelled in 1788.   His conduct, it is said, did not give general satisfaction to the Methodists and he left them, and the Conference disowned him and considered him expelled. It has been said that he afterwards joined the Episcopal Church, and became settled as a minister in one of the West India Islands.

ROBERT CLOUD'S early life was spent in New Castle county, Delaware. He must have traveled in 1778, as in 1779 the minutes return him as desisting from traveling. He re-entered the itinerancy in 1785, and was appointed to East Jersey, and was as we have seen, an important laborer in the revival that occurred on Staten Island this year. He was Thomas Morrell's first colleague, and the latter made honorable mention of him. In 1786 he was on the Newark circuit, N. J.; 1787, Elizabethtown; 1788, Long Island; 1789–90, New York; 1791, elder over a district which included the city of New York. In 1792 his district included, among other appointments, the Flanders, Elizabethtown, and Staten Island circuits. He located in 1812. He is said to have been an excellent preacher, but he at length unfortunately departed from the narrow path. A short time previous to the death of Rev. Thomas Morrell, he received a letter from Mr. Cloud in which he stated that he was restored to the Church, and intended to remain within its inclosure till his death. This is the last we know concerning him.

JOHN M'CLASKEY was a native of Ireland. He was born in 1756, emigrated to this country when about sixteen years of age, and settled in Salem county, New Jersey. He was a prisoner in New York for a year in the time of the Revolutionary war, and when peace was proclaimed, he "went begging his way home to New Jersey, and found his wife had died during his absence." He was, as we have seen, one of the first members of the class at Quinton's Bridge. He was brother-in-law to John Ffirth, the compiler of the Life of Abbott. He entered the itinerancy in 1785, and was appointed to Trenton circuit. The first five years of his itinerancy were spent in New Jersey. In 1790 he was appointed to Wilmington; 1791, Chester. In 1792 he was elder, his district comprising Philadelphia, Chester, Wilmington, and Bristol. In 1793 he was appointed to Baltimore with John Haggerty. He remained in Baltimore in 1794 as preacher in charge, having Robert Sparks, Christopher Spry, and George Cannon, as colleagues. In 1795 he was stationed alone in Baltimore for six months. In 1796 he was elder in New Jersey, his district embracing Delaware and Newburg, Herkimer, and Albany in the state of New York. He remained on this district three years. In 1799, 1800, and 1801 he was stationed in New York; 1802, Philadelphia; 1803–4, Chestertown, Md.; 1805, Talbot, Md. In 1806 he was appointed to Salem, but through indisposition failed to go. In 1807 he was stationed in Wilmington. In 1808 he was appointed to Kent, Md., where he remained in 1809. His appointment in 1810 was Talbot. In 1811 he was appointed Missionary; 1812–13–14, Presiding Elder in the Chesapeake district. In this last year he finished his labors and departed in peace.

Prior to his conversion he "was rather a wild young man, much addicted to the common vices of the period," such as drinking, gambling, &c. Attracted by curiosity he went to hear the Methodist preachers when they came into his neighborhood, and at length became concerned for his salvation. He earnestly sought the Lord, and obtained through faith the great salvation, and almost immediately began to warn sinners to repent, which he continued to do until he was thrust into the itinerant field. When he was Presiding Elder in New Jersey in the latter part of the last century, he attended a Quarterly meeting at Clonmell, in the Salem circuit. "There lived in the neighborhood," says one who remembers the occasion, "a man by the name of Patrick Field, who had formerly been acquainted with Mr. M'Claskey; indeed, they were both old countrymen: however, they were old cronies in crime, playing cards, gambling, drinking, &c. But M'Claskey had become religious—a preacher; and now came to see his old comrade and invited him to the meeting. Patrick was a Roman Catholic, and had felt no serious impressions at the Saturday meetings. On Sunday morning when invited to breakfast, Mr. M'Claskey spoke to him on the subject of religion; and when he offered to pray for him, Patrick was convicted. He thought, and expressed it, 'Why, how is it that the preacher felt such a desire for my salvation, and I am so indifferent on the subject myself?' His convictions became more deep and painful until the hour of preaching came; the house could not hold the people, and the meeting was held in the adjoining woods. This was a day of the Lord's power. Many fell to the ground and cried aloud for mercy; young men climbed the trees in order to see into the midst of the congregation; while the greatest excitement prevailed. During the service or preaching an awful thunder storm arose; a peal of thunder rolled over the assembly. The very earth trembled; those in the trees attempted to slide down; many fell; others ran in every direction; that terrific day I shall never forget. In the mean time Patrick Field had obtained a blessing; and, in the midst of the confusion and crowd, was shouting in so boisterous a manner that Mr. M'Claskey stopped preaching for some time, and told the people that Patrick Field was out-preaching him. One young woman cried aloud for mercy as she fell to the ground; and her brother, a large, strong man, rushed into the crowd and carried her away. Many were converted, and it was a time of refreshing to the Lord's people."*

M'Claskey, it is said, was a splendid looking man, large, with fine flowing locks, and his presence in the pulpit was very commanding. "An aged minister," says Rev. J. B. Wakely, "who is hovering between two worlds, gave me an account of a sermon Mr. M'Claskey preached in old John street, about the year 1810, before the Conference on a fast day. His theme was, 'Weeping between the porch and the altar.' He said it was a most masterly effort. The baptism of tears took place as the preacher showed why ministers should weep, the causes for deep feeling, for melting sympathy, for flowing tears."

His brethren have recorded the following tribute to his worth: "As a Christian, he was deeply experienced in the grace of God. As a minister, he was mighty in the Scriptures, orthodox in his sentiments, systematic in his preaching, zealous in his labors; the blessed effects of which were witnessed by thousands, many of whom are gone before him, while others are left to unite with us in deploring the loss of their venerable father in Christ. In the latter part of his life he was greatly afflicted, and suffered much; in all of which he manifested

* Reminiscences of Methodism.

great patience and confidence in God. He preached his last sermon at the Quarterly meeting at Church Hill, on Queen Ann's circuit, from Isaiah lxi. 1, 2, 3. It was observed that he was peculiarly energetic, his own soul was much blessed and drawn out in the cause of God, while a deep solemnity rested upon the audience. He was taken with his last illness at his dwelling in Chestertown, in the State of Maryland, on the 21st day of August, in which he desired to depart and to be with Christ, and was often heard to sing,—

> Surely Thou wilt not long delay,
> I hear the Spirit cry,
> ' Arise, my love, make haste away,
> Go, get thee up and die.'

On Friday morning, the ninth day of his illness, about four o'clock, he closed his eyes in peace, and without a a sigh or groan departed this life, Sept. 2, 1814."

JACOB BRUSH was a native of Long Island. He entered the itinerancy in 1785, and was appointed to Trenton circuit. In 1786 he was sent to West Jersey. In 1787–8–9 he was on circuits in Delaware and Maryland. In 1790 he was appointed to New Rochelle, with William Phoebus and M. Swaim. It appears that he labored in New York a part of this year. He was reappointed to New Rochelle in 1791. About the middle of July he took charge of a district "which included Long Island, other portions of New York, and the State of Connecticut as far east as the Connecticut river, and as far north as the city of Hartford, sharing with Lee (who was Presiding Elder, the same year, of Boston district) the entire Presiding Eldership of New England." In 1793 he was elder over a district all of which lay in the State of New York except Elizabethtown and Flanders circuits, in New Jersey. In 1794 he was Supernumerary in the city of New York. He died in New York of the epidemical fever in September, 1795. He was an active, laborious minister, and "a great friend to order and union." He was afflicted with an inflammatory sore throat, which interfered to some extent with his usefulness. His last illness was so severe that little could be known concerning the state of his mind, but "just before he died, a preacher who was present took him by the hand, and asked him if he was happy. Not being able to speak, he gave his hand an affectionate squeeze, with an expression in his appearance of a calm resignation to God. We entertain no doubt but he rests in Abraham's bosom."*

* Minutes, 1796.

CHAPTER XVIII.

PROSPECTS, RESULTS, AND LABORERS.

IN 1786, a little over a year after the organization of the Church, New Jersey reported its membership as follows: West Jersey, 492; Trenton, 352; East Jersey, 365; Newark, 50; making an aggregate of 1259 members in the State, including Staten Island. This was the result of more than fifteen years' labor. Truly the progress of the work was not remarkably flattering. And yet who will say that twelve hundred and fifty-nine souls, gathered into the Church, and rejoicing, as most of them, no doubt, were, in the salvation of the gospel, were not an abundant, a glorious compensation for all that sacrifice and toil? And then the prospects were brightening. The annual increase was becoming greater. Prejudices were being overcome, strong societies were rising up, churches were being built, and in every way the aspects of the cause were more encouraging and the future was radiant with brighter visions of success than ever before.

We have already noticed, with more or less of detail, the more important points in which Methodism had been established during this period. In the West Jersey circuit there were two societies at Pittsgrove, one at Salem, Maurice river, Quinton's Bridge, Penn's Neck, Pleasant Mills, Goodluck, and Greenwich. Trenton circuit probably included the societies of New Mills, Trenton, Mount Holly, Burlington, and Monmouth. Newark circuit included Elizabethtown and Staten Island. East Jersey embraced the societies of New Germantown, Asbury, and Flanders. In various other localities' there were classes, no doubt, and in several of the above named places the societies had gained such strength that they had erected Chapels. This was certainly true of Trenton, New Mills, Greenwich, Salem, Maurice river, Pleasant Mills, Goodluck, Pittsgrove,* and possibly of

*It is probable that there were two Chapels in Pittsgrove at this time. I am not able to give the precise date of the erection of either Church, but I have good authority for the assertion that the Broad Neck Chapel was built as early as 1785 or 1786; and as Murphy's or Friendship was the first society, and as the Church there was rebuilt more than twenty years before that at Broad Neck, it is entirely probable that it was built first. This accords, too, with the tradition of the place. The Broad Neck society *must have been formed very soon after that at Murphy's*, and as Abbott lived only a few miles from

Flanders. When it is remembered that during this period there had been a deeply exciting and desolating seven years' war, the effects of which were seriously felt in New Jersey; that the Church had only the most slender resources, except those which were Divine; that it was without a regular organization, and its ministry without orders; its condition at this period of its history with a considerable number of societies, and several churches erected, was certainly evidence of no mean success. Equipped for her career of trial and conflict, and panting for wider and grander scenes of battle and conquest, the Methodism of New Jersey rushed forward to the sublime arena before her; while the splendors of her future triumphs, like the rays of light which gleam amid the darkness long before the sun appears, beamed, from afar, upon her path.

The appointments in 1786 were as follows: Thomas Vasey being elder in West Jersey, and John Tunnell elder in East Jersey. Trenton, Robert Sparks, Robert Cann. West Jersey, Jacob Brush, John Simmons, Ja-

there he probably formed it very shortly after he began his ministry. I am strongly inclined to the opinion that this was the society, the origin of which is given on page 108. It would be quite natural for the profane to substitute *Hell Neck* for Broad Neck, the former name being designed merely to correspond with the morals of the place.

cob Lurton.   East Jersey, John M'Claskey, Ezekiel Cooper.   Newark, Robert Cloud.

While laboring this year on Staten Island, which formed a part of the Newark (or Elizabethtown) circuit, Mr. Cloud had a public rencounter with a Baptist clergyman in which he triumphantly vindicated Methodism. An account of it has been kindly furnished for these pages by Rev. Francis A. Morrell, of the New Jersey Conference.   It is as follows :—

" The Baptist challenged Mr. Cloud to a public discussion of the points of difference between Calvinists and Methodists.   The challenge was accepted and a day fixed upon for the discussion.   A minister of the Baptist Church and my father, the colleague of Mr Cloud, were elected to preside at the meeting that no undue advantage might be taken on either side.   On the way to the place of meeting, the Baptist polemic called at the house of one of his friends and said, 'I pity the Methodist, (Mr. Cloud,) for I shall easily overthrow his positions, and utterly demolish him.'   He seemed not aware of the strength of the positions of his antagonist, and of his ability to defend them.   A multitude assembled to hear the debate.   The meeting being organized, the discussion commenced with a speech from Mr. Cloud, in which he gave so clear an exposition of Methodist theology, its agreement with the word of God, and of the

inconsistencies and absurdities of Calvinism, that his
antagonist was scarcely able to make any reply, speaking only about half the time allotted to each speaker,
and sat down.   Mr. Cloud arose and spoke for a few
minutes, observing that his arguments were unrefuted,
and as his antagonist had given him but little, if anything, to reply to, he would take his seat.   No rejoinder
being given, after a pause, my father arose and said,
' As the discussion appears to be closed, I put it to the
audience to decide whether Mr. Cloud or his opponent
has triumphed.'   A rising vote was taken, and Mr.
Cloud declared the victor by an almost unanimous vote.

"Methodism, which was at that time feeble on the
Island, began to take root.   The people flocked to hear
the 'circuit preachers,' received the truth gladly, and
' the word of God grew and multiplied.' "

Some time during 1785 Adam Cloud and Matthew
Greentree, who then traveled East Jersey circuit, visited
Hightstown, and established preaching in a tavern kept
by one Adam Shaw.   They received, however, but little
encouragement.   John M'Claskey and Ezekiel Cooper,
who succeeded them on the circuit this year, did not regard the appointment with much favor, and it is not certain that Cooper preached there.   M'Claskey preached
there once or twice, "and then publicly informed the
congregation that he would preach there once more, and

then if a more suitable place for holding meeting could not be found he should cease to preach for them.   Robert Hutchinson, a young man of about twenty-one years of age, was present; and, being pleased with the preacher, was unwilling to be deprived of the privilege of hearing him.   He, therefore, persuaded his uncle, Joseph Hutchinson, to go and hear M'Claskey, and invite him to preach at his house.   The invitation was given and accepted, and thus, early in the year 1786, the preaching was transferred from Hightstown to Milford, about two and a half miles from the former place. Joseph Hutchinson's was quite a rendezvous for the weary itinerants, and being near the line between 'East' and 'West Jersey,' the preachers on the two charges would sometimes meet here.   Robert Hutchinson, with three brothers, Ezekiel, Sylvester, and Aaron, all four of whom afterward became preachers, went over to uncle Joseph's to 'have the small-pox,' as they were accustomed to call it in 'olden time.'   While there they met with a number of traveling preachers.   On one occasion there were several together.   Ezekiel Cooper, J. M'Claskey from 'East Jersey,' and Robert Sparks from 'West Jersey,' among the number.   They became wonderfully attached to them; and their preaching and conversation made impressions which resulted in their conversion. During the year a class was organized; and, among the number of its members were Joseph Hutchinson and wife. This brother was very zealous and enterprising, and soon after the organization of the class, he erected at Milford, almost entirely at his own expense, a house of worship for the despised band. The location was unfavorable however, and from this or other causes the society never became large. It continued to be used as a place of worship down to about 1835, when a church was built at Hightstown, after which it was sold. The old church was the scene of stirring times, and many have there fallen under the power of God, and many passed from death unto life. Among the number converted here were four sons of William Hutchinson, brother of Joseph, named respectively, Ezekiel, Robert, Sylvester, and Aaron, who all became ministers of the M. E. Church."*

Asbury, the indefatigable servant and the wise overseer of the Church, urged his way heroically through the sands of West Jersey this year, to minister to the spiritual necessities of the scattered flock. "Since this day week," he says, "we have ridden about one hundred and fifty miles over dead sands, and among a dead people, and a long space between meals." The ensuing day, the 29th of September, he says he "preached in a close hot place, and administered the sacrament. I was

* Communication of REV. HENRY B. BEEGLE to the writer.

almost ready to faint.   I feel fatigued and much dispir-
ited." This was, probably, the Pleasant Mills' Chapel,
as he says he lodged with Freedom Lucas, near Batsto,
which place is only about a mile from Pleasant Mills.
Asbury knew the tendency of worldly prosperity to improperly exalt the mind and divest the Christian of his
simplicity.   Hence he said of Lucas, "We shall see
whether he will continue to be the same simple-hearted
Christian he now is, when he gets possession of the estate which, it is said, has fallen to him in England."
He was at Cape May, and other places in that region,
but the impressions he received of the religious condition of the societies were not of a sanguine character.
Of the Cape he says: "I find there is a great dearth of
religion in these parts." He was also at P. Cresey's
where he "had a few cold hearers—the glory," he
writes, "is strangely departed. There are a few pious
souls at Gough's; but here also there is an evident declension.   My soul is under deep exercise on account of
the deadness of the people, and my own want of fervor
and holiness of heart." On Friday, the sixth of October, he preached a warm and close sermon to a people
who were attentive to the word at the Maurice river
Church.   His text was, "Lord, are there few that be
saved?" On Sabbath he preached at New Englandtown.   He says: "We had a small house and large con-

23

gregation. I had liberty in preaching on, 'By grace are ye saved through faith.' Thence I proceeded to M——'s, where I had poor times." At Murphy's, he says, "We had many dull, prayerless people. We came to the widow Ayars's; the mother and daughters are serious, and the son thoughtful." Mrs. Susannah Ayars, of whom Asbury here speaks, was one of the first Methodists in Pittsgrove. She first received "the Lord's prophets" in that place. She died in peace about 1807.

He preached at Bethel, on 1 Peter iii. 18. "Three times," he says, "have I been here, and always straitened in spirit." He also visited Sandtown. The weather was very warm and the people dull. He administered the sacrament. There must have been a society there, or else it does not appear probable he would have held a sacramental service. He rode to Cooper's ferry, and crossed to the city, where he spent the Sabbath. On Monday he rode to Mount Holly, where he preached on "Come, ye blessed of my father," &c.; and at New Mills he addressed them on "Suffering affliction with the people of God." He preached also at Burlington on "Neither is there salvation in any other," &c.; "these," he says, "are not a zealous people for religion." The bishop's impressions of the spiritual condition of the people appear to have been unfavorable in most of the societies he visited in New Jersey at this time. At Monmouth he preached at Leonard's and the people, he said, appeared very lifeless. At the Potter's Church he had many to hear, "but the people," he says, "were insensible and unfeeling."

The society in Penn's Neck, through the characteristic zeal and energy of Abbott, were favored with a Chapel about this year. "I had often urged on the people," says Abbott, ".the necessity of building a meeting-house, for the space of about four years, in Lower Penn's Neck, during which period we had frequently held our meetings under the trees when the weather admitted. One day meeting with a carpenter, I agreed with him to build one. He came at the time appointed. I told him that we had got no timber for the building, and therefore I must go a begging. Accordingly we set out and went to a neighbor, and told him we were going to build a house for God, and asked him what he would give us toward it; he answered, two sticks of timber for sills. We then went to the widow M'C's, a professing Quaker, and she gave us two more, and sent her team to haul them to the place. We then went to Mr. Wm. Philpot, and he gave us sufficient for the house, though not even a professor with us; may the Lord reward him accordingly. I then went among our friends, and told them that they must come and help to get the timber; they did so, and we began on Tuesday morning, and by Friday night we had all the timber at the place. Brother Henry Ffirth, a steward of the circuit, and myself, were appointed managers to carry on the building. The Friday week following, we raised our house, and in the afternoon preached on the foundation. In six weeks the carpenter had done his work, and I begged the money and paid him. This proved a great blessing to the neighborhood, the greater part of which became Methodized, and many were moralized and Christianized, while the enemies of truth daily lost ground, and bigotry gradually declined."

A Quarterly meeting was held in Penn's Neck during the present decade, in Joseph Cassner's barn. B. Abbott, a local preacher named Stratton, and many others, attended. It was a time of power. The people lay prostrate over the barn floor, many obtained religion and joined the Methodists.

Notwithstanding the deadness of the people in West Jersey, of which Asbury complained, the work progressed; and an increase of sixty-five was reported of the West Jersey, and twenty of the Trenton circuit, making an addition of eighty-five to the membership in West Jersey. In addition to this the work had extended to the people of color, and eight colored members were reported in West Jersey this year.

Though the mission of Methodism has been more especially to the lower classes, and its greatest moral achievements have been chiefly among them, yet has it also shown its adaptation to meet the spiritual necessities of the more wealthy, cultivated, and influential. Thousands of such have borne cheerful and emphatic testimony to its power as a redemptive agency, and have rejoiced to number themselves among its trophies.

One such trophy was gained to the cause this year in Warren county. It was COL. WILLIAM M'CULLOUGH. He was, at this time, about twenty-seven years of age. He witnessed the Revolutionary struggle, and bore a part in it in favor of the colonies. He now became the standard bearer of Methodism in Asbury, and about ten years afterward erected a Chapel there almost entirely by his own means. This was the first Methodist Church in Warren and Sussex counties. He was among the most prominent Methodists in the State, and his influence was strongly felt in the region where he resided, and especially upon his own family. By his godly example and counsels they were prepared to receive the truth from the pulpit, and his children and children's children became consecrated offerings to Methodism. He was a man of a progressive spirit, and exercised his influence to promote internal improvements. He occupied important and responsible civil positions, filling some of the most respectable offices of his county, and for more than thirty years acted as an associate judge in the courts of Sussex and Warren. He was also frequently elected to a seat in the legislative council of the State. He was a steward of the circuit, and in his pleasant dwelling the preachers found a congenial home. Bishop Asbury, when traveling in that region, was accustomed to enjoy the pleasures of his hospitality. He lived to a good old age, and, as he passed down the vale of years, religion shed its serene and benignant light upon his path. Having passed beyond the period of three-score and ten, he waited in cheerful confidence and hope for his change. His last illness was mild and brief, and his final hour was distinguished by the calmness of Christian peace, and the triumphs of Christian faith. After the power of speech had failed, a relative asked him if his confidence in Christ was still unshaken, and if so, to raise his right hand. He immediately raised both, one after the other, and attempted to elevate his whole body, thus evincing how powerful was the grace he had professed for over half a century to sustain him as he stood amidst the swellings of Jordan. He died at his residence at Asbury on the 9th of February, 1840, in the eighty-second year of his age. Asbury appears to have been one of the first localities in East Jersey into which Methodism was introduced, but the precise time and manner of its introduction are now un-

known. The Rev. Jacob P. Daily, the present pastor
of the Church there, in a letter to the writer says :

"Unfortunately for the historic interests of this place,
there are no local records of Methodism here for the
period embraced in your work. I doubt very much
whether there ever were any such records, beyond a
class book, until 1795. From conversation with some
very old members of our Church some time since, I conclude that Methodism was introduced into this region
prior to the Revolution. Dr. Coke once passed this
way and called on some Methodist families. . Our oldest
living member, aged ninety-six, remembers Joseph Everett as 'the first Methodist minister she ever heard
preach.' There were some Methodists before that day.
She describes Everett as a fine sized, fine looking man,
wearing a Quaker hat, and a suit of drab colored 'home-
spun.'" Mr. Daily further says that there are no incidents of Methodism during the period of this volume
to be gathered in Asbury, as no data of that sort now
exist. Nearly all the first members of the first societies
have passed away, and much of our history has departed
with them. The wonder is not that so little now remains, but it is rather a marvel, considering the indifference of the Church and ministry generally to this subject, that we are able to obtain so many reminiscences
of the past. Had the attempt which we are now making

been faithfully made twenty years ago, much might have been rescued which is now irrecoverably lost. And yet we should be thankful for what has been done. Sufficient historical material has been preserved to enable us to trace, with a good degree of distinctness, the beginnings, struggles, and successes of Methodism in our State.

There was a handsome addition made to the membership in East Jersey this year. The largest increase was on the Newark (it is reported Elizabethtown at the end of the year) circuit, which was largely, and, perhaps, chiefly, owing to the revival which had taken place on Staten Island. There was reported an increase on this circuit of 190 members. In the East Jersey circuit just one hundred were added to the membership, making an addition of 290 for the Northern part of the work.

Of the ten preachers that labored in New Jersey this year, five had previously labored in the State, and notices of them have already been given. To those who appear for the first time in our pathway our attention will now be turned.

THOMAS VASEY came to America with Dr. Coke and Richard Whatcoat, in 1784, just before the organization of the Church. He was one of the first Methodist preachers that was ordained. In process of time he obtained reordination by a bishop of the Protestant Episcopal Church, and sometime afterward returned to England; but it is believed he was never recognized there as a minister of the Church of England.

ROBERT CANN entered the itinerancy in 1785, and was appointed to Annamessex, Md. In 1786 he appears as remaining on trial, and was appointed to Trenton, N. J. In 1787 he was sent to travel the West Jersey circuit, but his name stands connected also with Clarksburg circuit; in 1788 he was appointed to Chester, Pa.; 1789, Bristol, Pa.; 1790, Bethel, N. J.; 1791, Trenton, N. J.; in 1792 he again traveled Bethel circuit, N. J. In 1793 he was appointed to Burlington. He located in 1794. He continued in the itinerancy longer after he was married than the preachers of that day appear to have been accustomed to do. He was married in 1788, and did not locate till six years afterward. The slight notices of him we have been able to obtain represent him as an earnest, zealous, and effective preacher, declaring the word in demonstration of the Spirit, and of power. He died in 1796, leaving a widow and two small children.

JOHN SIMMONS was admitted on trial in 1786, and appointed to West Jersey. In 1787 he was appointed to Alleghany. He labored in various places in Maryland, Virginia, South Carolina, and elsewhere. In 1807 he located.

JACOB LURTON was also admitted this year, and appointed to West Jersey. The following year he was sent to Berkeley, Va. He continued to labor in Virginia and elsewhere until 1795, when he located, and disappeared from our view.

EZEKIEL COOPER was born in Caroline Co., Md., Feb. 22, 1763. When he was about thirteen years of age Rev. Freeborn Garrettson visited the neighborhood and preached. While preaching he noticed a boy of thoughtful aspect leaning upon a gate, and giving, apparently, close attention to the sermon. That boy was Ezekiel Cooper, afterward so prominent a character in the history of the Church.

It was the privilege of Cooper to be present at the memorable meeting of Coke and Asbury, at Barrett's Chapel, Md., on the 14th of November, 1784. He thus describes the scene: "While Dr. Coke was preaching, Mr. Asbury came into the congregation. A solemn pause and deep silence took place at the close of the sermon, as an interval for introduction and salutation. Asbury and Coke, with great solemnity, and much dignified sensibility, and with full hearts of brotherly love, approached, embraced, and saluted each other. The other preachers, at the same time, participating in the tender sensibilities of the affectionate salutations, were melted into sweet sympathy and tears. The congregation also caught the glowing emotion, and the whole assembly, as if Divinely struck with a shock of heavenly electricity, burst into a flood of tears. Every heart appeared as if filled and overflowing with love, unity, and fellowship; and a kind of ecstasy, or rapture of joy and gladness, ensued."

It was on this occasion that Cooper first received the sacrament of the Lord's Supper. It was administered by Dr. Coke and Mr. Whatcoat. It was on this occasion also that he was induced to enter the itinerancy. Asbury, discerning, no doubt, elements of success in the young man, persuaded him to go forth as a laborer into the field which was ripe for the harvest. Some of the other preachers seconded his advice, and though he had never publicly preached a sermon, nor made application to travel, nor even contemplated it, he consented to enter the work. Of this important event of his life, he says, "It was unsought, and when I went to that meeting, perfectly unexpected. With much diffidence, and great reluctance, I yielded to go; though pressed to it by my greatly beloved and much esteemed brother Asbury, and encouraged and urged to it by some of the other preachers. Old brother W. Thomas held up both his hands toward me, and in a loving and alarming manner, addressed me, 'I warn you, in the name of God, not to refuse! I do not know but your salvation depends upon it! God has a work for you to do, and he has called you to it; and wo be unto you if you preach not the gospel!' That address thrilled through me like thunder; my heart filled, I could say no more. They had some knowledge of my deep exercises about preaching, and they believed that I was 'verily called to the work.' They having heard me in conversation, and in the close of meetings, a few times, exhort and pray, they supposed I had 'a talent to be improved.'"

Cooper was admitted on trial in 1785, and appointed to Long Island. In 1786 he traveled East Jersey circuit. In 1787 he rode Trenton circuit, N. J. In 1788 he was sent to Baltimore. In 1789–90 he was stationed at Annapolis, Md. He continued to fill important positions in the Church for a series of years, when he located, in which position he continued eight years, when he re-entered the itinerant ranks, but was soon after placed on the supernumerary list in the Philadelphia Conference.

He was one of the most powerful logicians in the Church in his day, and his logic was impassioned. It was not that sort of cold dry reasoning which wearied without profiting the hearer, but while it enlightened the understanding it also stirred the emotions. One of the fruits of his ministry in New Mills, New Jersey, more than seventy years ago, is still living at Camden, at the advanced age of ninety years. After he became super-annuated he labored extensively, preaching with zeal and power at Camp meetings, Quarterly meetings, &c.   His last sickness was brief and marked by the serenity of Christian peace.   He also, at times, greatly triumphed in Christ.   On one occasion, having been engaged in prayer, he broke forth into praise, and shouted aloud about a dozen times, "Hallelujah!   Hallelujah!"

On Sunday the 21st of February, 1847, he peacefully terminated his pilgrimage, at the advanced age of eighty-four years and in the sixty-second of his ministry.   At the time of his death he was the oldest member of any Methodist Conference in America.

The following brief portraiture of Mr. Cooper is from the pen of Rev. Dr. A. Stevens:

"Mr. Cooper's personal appearance embodied the finest idea of age, intelligence, and piety combined. His frame was tall and slight, his locks white with years, his forehead high and prominent, and his features expressive at once of benignity, subtlety, and serenity. A wen had been enlarging on his neck from his childhood, but without detracting from the peculiarly elevated and characteristic expression of his face.   He was considered by his ministerial associates, a 'living Encyclopedia,' in respect not only to theology, but most other departments of knowledge, and his large and accurate information was only surpassed by the range and soundness of his judgment.   He sustained a prominent position in the annals of the Church, during both its adversity and its prosperity; the delineation of his remarkable character should devolve upon an able hand, and will form an important feature in the history of our cause."

CHAPTER XIX.

LABORS AND LABORERS—1787.

IN 1787 New Jersey comprised one district, including New York city, New Rochelle, and Long Island, of which Thomas Foster was elder. The other preachers that were appointed to labor in New Jersey were stationed as follows : Elizabethtown, Robert Cloud, Thomas Morrell. West Jersey, Robert Cann, John M'Claskey, John Milburn. Trenton, Ezekiel Cooper, Nathaniel B. Mills. East Jersey, Simon Pyle, Cornelius Cook.

Bishop Asbury made a brief incursion into New Jersey very soon after the Conference. It adjourned at Baltimore on the sixth of May, and before the middle of the same month ne was at Trenton, but found the people there very lifeless. Methodism seems to have prospered most during this early period in New Jersey in the less densely populated communities. In the larger towns its progress was slow, and in several of them, as New Brunswick and Newark, for example, it did not become established until after the period embraced in the present work. Being itinerant in its spirit, and aiming to preach the gospel to the poor, the early Methodism of New Jersey went into the highways and hedges, and sought to bring the maimed, the blind, and the outcast to the banquet table of heavenly mercy.

We have seen that, when Methodism was introduced into Elizabethtown, the Episcopal clergyman there welcomed it, and co-operated with it, and we find this year another evidence of the cordial feeling with which the movement was regarded by that Church. Dr. Coke and Bishop Asbury visiting the town this year, the doctor preached a lively sermon in the Episcopal Church, "and we had," says Asbury, "a good time."

He made an excursion in July through the northern end of the State. The people there appear to have been awake to the subject of Methodism. At Warwick, he says, "I suppose not less than a thousand people were collected. I was very low, both in body and spirit, but felt stirred up at the sight of such a congregation, and was moved and quickened while I enlarged on Gal. i. 4. I baptized some, and administered the sacrament to many communicants."

At B——'s a multitude attended in a barn. This was probably Banghart's—the father of Rev. G. Banghart of the Newark Conference. Mr. B.'s was one of the earliest preaching places in Warren county. The work of religion had already been going on among the people there, for Asbury says, "Here God hath wrought a great work for a poor, blind, ignorant people.' He was also at Sweezy's, where they were blest with a good time, and where there appears to have been a society, or, at least, Methodists, as he administered the sacrament. On Sunday he preached to a multitude in the woods. There were nearly a thousand people to listen to the word. He felt rather depressed, both mentally and physically, but "had some gracious feelings in the sacrament. Others also felt the quickening power of God." He baptized a number of adults and infants, both by sprinkling and immersion.

THOMAS FOSTER, the elder in New Jersey this year, entered the itinerant connection in 1780. His labors were confined chiefly to Virginia and Maryland until 1792, when his name disappears from the minutes. He was esteemed a man of genuine piety and sound talent. He was, it is said, a fair example of the first race of Methodist preachers.

THOMAS MORRELL is a distinguished name in American Methodist history. He was born in the city of New York, November 22nd, 1747. His mother was a member of the first class formed by Philip Embury in the year 1766. The family removed to Elizabethtown, N. J.

24

in 1772, and there being no Methodists there the parents united with the Presbyterian Church. Soon after the first struggle of the Revolutionary conflict at Lexington, a company of volunteers was raised chiefly by a patriotic address which he delivered to a body of Jersey militia, and he marched at their head to New York to join Gen. Washington's army. He was dangerously wounded in the battle on Long Island, and performed valiant service for his country as a military officer in the war of Independence. Under the first sermon of Rev. John Hagerty, as we have seen, in Elizabethtown, he was awakened, and early in the year 1785 was converted. He soon after abandoned a lucrative business and entered the itinerancy. His first field of labor was· Staten Island, in which he was continued in 1787, it forming a part of Elizabethtown circuit. This year he was admitted on trial. In 1788 he was ordained a deacon and traveled Trenton circuit. In 1789 he was stationed in New York where he was continued five years. In 1791, at Bishop Asbury's request, he left New York and accompanied him to Charleston, S. C., where he labored a few months, it being a time of secession from the Church in that city. In 1794–5 he was stationed in Philadelphia. Here he was taken sick and did not fully recover until 1799. He was then stationed two years in Baltimore, and in 1802–3 he was stationed again in New York two

years. This was his last appointment out of Elizabethtown, as failing health compelled him to retire, but he
continued for sixteen years to preach as often as when
he traveled more extensively; and, until a few years before his death he preached once each Sabbath in Elizabethtown.

Mr. Morrell lived to the very advanced age of ninety.
He closed his eventful and useful life on the morning of
the 9th of August, 1838. The following brief portraiture was written at the request of the writer, by Rev.
John Lee, who knew him well and enjoyed his confidence
and friendship:

"In person, Thomas Morrell was below the medium
height, with a square built, well knit frame, indicative
of great muscular strength and capability of endurance;
qualities almost essential in a pioneer of Methodism.
He had a noble physiognomy, a dark piercing eye—the
index of an intelligent mind; and a countenance on
which the most casual observer might read decision and
firmness, in combination with great kindness of heart,
giving him a beautifully symmetrical, intellectual, and
moral character, which, in connection with a strong clear
voice of which he had complete control, admirably fitted
him to become a useful and influential man, and under
the teachings of the Holy Spirit, an acceptable and suc-

cessful preacher of the word of God—eminently a polished shaft in the quiver of the Almighty.

"The air of authority, promptness of decision, and firmness in adhering to his purpose when deliberately formed, might sometimes appear to a stranger like sternness and dogmatism; but to those intimately acquainted with him this was well understood, and attributed, doubtless, to its proper cause—the habit of command—acquired while a field officer (major) in the army of the Revolution, and not likely to be diminished by the highly responsible positions he was called to occupy during his early ministerial career, and which adhered to him, in some degree, during the remainder of his life.

"As a preacher, Thomas Morrell must unquestionably take rank with the first class of Methodist ministers in his day. His appearance and manner in the pulpit was grave and dignified, befitting the ambassador of God. His sermons were characterized by strong sense and sound theology; his deductions were logical, his analysis clear, and his application forcible, discriminating, and faithful; and not unfrequently his preaching was attended with an unction that affected his own heart, causing the tears, unbidden, to trickle down his cheeks, and being communicated to his hearers, a large part of his audience would be melted down in humility, reverence, and love."

His son, Rev. Francis A. Morrell, speaks of him, and his last moments as follows:

"In his life he was the friend of the indigent—his house the home of the way-worn itinerant, and his attachment to the Church of his choice strengthened as years multiplied upon him; as a husband and father he was affectionate and kind.

"In his last illness, which was protracted; he suffered much from soreness of the throat, accompanied with an asthmatic affection, yet he uttered no complaint—not a murmur was heard; and, though he desired the hour of deliverance to arrive, yet was perfectly resigned to the will of God. On Monday morning previous to his death he repeated audibly three times, 'Though I walk through the valley of the shadow of death I will fear no evil, for the Lord is with me.' To our deeply afflicted mother he said, 'Why do you weep? I am going to glory.' On the 8th inst., at his request, the 23d psalm was read and the 'Christian's home' was sung, in which he made an effort to join, and said, 'I shall soon be there.' Being asked if death was a terror to him, he replied in the negative, and said, 'I have gotten the victory.' He retained his consciousness to the last, and faintly uttered, a few minutes before his death, 'All is well.'"

Of JOHN MILBURN we are able to obtain no information other than that he joined the traveling connection in 1787, and was appointed respectively to West Jersey, Chester, Pa., Talbot, Somerset, Caroline, Northampton, in Md., Dover, Del., Prince George's, Somerset, and Dorchester, Md. In 1798 his name does not stand connected with any appointment on the minutes. In 1799 he located.

NATHANIEL B. MILLS was born in New Castle, Del., the 23d of February, 1766. Until the fifteenth year of his age he indulged in the usual follies and vices of youth, though not without frequent reproaches of conscience. At this early age he was led, chiefly through the instrumentality of Methodism, to a discovery of his perilous condition as a sinner, and his need of a saving interest in the atonement of Christ. Under the influence of these convictions he "became an habitually serious seeker of salvation." It was two years, however, before he became consciously reconciled to God. Not long after he was convinced of his need of a deeper work of grace, and he began to seek the entire sanctification of his nature, "which," he says, "I trust, I found in some degree, at least, about the twentieth year of my age." Soon after his conversion, he felt desires to warn his fellow men to flee from the wrath to come, and he began to exhort them accordingly, first in his own neighborhood, and then at a distance as Providence opened the way. After much deliberation and prayer, that he might not be deceived in a matter of so great importance to himself and others, he offered himself to the Baltimore Conference in May, 1787, and was received and appointed to Trenton, N. J.   The following year he was on Salem circuit, and in 1789 he was appointed to Newburg, N. Y. The next year he appears as one of the coadjutors of Lee in the land of the Puritans, and was appointed to Hartford, Conn., and in 1791 to Fairfield, Conn.   The following year he was appointed to Dorchester, Md.; in 1793 he was sent to Bristol, Pa.; 1794, Caroline, Md.; 1795, Lancaster, Pa.; 1796, Federal, Md.   "In 1797–8 we find his appointment bearing the significant designation, ' *Ohio ;*' it, doubtless, verged on, if it did not penetrate, the wilderness which since, under the same name, has become the noblest State of the West."   In 1799 he was in Maryland, on Prince George's circuit; "in 1800 he was colleague of the veteran James Quinn, at Pittsburg, under the Presiding Eldership of Daniel Hitt, an illustrious companionship.   During twenty-four years we find him pursuing his ministerial career in the Baltimore Conference, moving to and fro, from its eastern circuits to Ohio, and from the interior of Pennsylvania to that of Virginia, until 1824, when he appears in the list of the 'superannuated and worn out preachers' of that Conference, in company with Nelson Reed, Joshua Wells, and other distinguished veterans.

But it is hard for a hero to retire from the field while the clarion is still sounding, or the shout of battle is on the air; and even the old war horse 'saith among the trumpets, Aha! aha! and smells the battle afar off, the thunder of the captains and the shouting.' Though he had passed nearly forty years in the ministry, we find the hoary headed Mills, at the next Conference, leaving the ranks of the superannuated, and entering again the effective lists, where he continued till 1829, when, after a laborious ministry of forty-two years, he took his place among the supernumeraries of the Conference. He continued, however, to preach regularly, being appointed that year to Rockingham; in 1830, to Great Falls; 1831, Loudon and Fairfax; 1832, Baltimore circuit; 1833, Liberty; and in 1834, Frederick. In 1835 he was compelled to retire again to the ranks of the superannuated, where he continued till his death. The ministry of the word was, however, 'a ruling passion' with him, and it was strong even till death. He continued to labor with untiring constancy, as he had strength and opportunity; and the last public act of his protracted ministry was performed on the last Sabbath of his life. On the morning of that day he preached his last sermon. The selection of his final text was characteristic of the veteran soldier of Christ, it was from Judges v. 31: 'So let all thine enemies be scattered, O Lord; but let them that love him be as the sun when he goeth forth in his might.' "*

On the Thursday morning following, the day on which he died, he led the devotions of the family. "He was," say his brethren, "a holy man of God, and though we are not permitted to claim for him entire exemption from the ordinary infirmities and weaknesses inseparable from humanity, we are, at least, warranted in saying that these infirmities are seldom found associated with greater purity of purpose and innocency of life. He was also a sound, good, and practical preacher, of the primitive school of Methodist ministers. He was, indeed, one of the last of that highly interesting class of men, to whom, under God, the Church and the world are so deeply indebted. His death may, to some extent, be regarded as the severance of the last link—so far, at least, as the ministry of this Conference is concerned—by which the past and the present have heretofore been united. 'Mark the perfect man, and behold the upright; for the end of that man is peace.' "

SIMON PYLE was born in or near Westchester, Chester county, Pa., in the year 1759. He was received on trial in 1784, and appointed to Juniata, Pa. In 1785 he was sent to Fairfax, Va.; 1786, Sussex, Va. The remaining years of his itinerancy were spent in New Jersey,

* Stevens's Memorials.

on the following circuits respectively: East Jersey, 1787; Elizabethtown, 1788; Salem, 1789; Trenton, 1790; Burlington, 1791. This is the last year his name appears on the minutes. He married in 1792 and retired from the itinerant ranks, and settled upon a farm in Monmouth county, New Jersey, about three miles east of Freehold. His wife was a Miss Leonard, who, although her parents were Episcopalians at Shrewsbury, Monmouth county, had embraced religion and joined the M. E. Church. In 1812 she and his eldest daughter died, and in 1817 he married the widow of Benjamin Tharp, whose maiden name was Abigal Lippencott. She still survives him in the 78th year of her age, and the 63d or 64th of her membership in the Church. For sixty years she maintained a remarkably punctual attendance upon the ordinances of the Church.

Mr. Pyle died in 1822, and very little information can now be gathered concerning his ministerial character and labors. We are indebted for the following brief sketch to Rev. Garner R. Snyder, of the New Jersey Conference, the present pastor of the M. E. Church at Freehold, N. J.:

"Simon Pyle lived in this community for thirty years, but was known rather as a farmer and local preacher than as a regular minister; and having been dead nearly 38 years it is not strange that he is nearly forgotten.

But to the extent he is remembered his memory is respected. He seems to have borne an unblemished Christian character, and for many years to have swayed a wide and wholesome influence as a Christian and local preacher. He solemnized many marriages, went far and near to visit the sick and bury the dead, and generally preached once or more on the Sabbath. I gather that he was a clear, sound, instructive preacher, but comparatively unimpassioned, and hence of limited popularity; and being chiefly occupied in other pursuits, as a matter of course he became less and less attractive as years and infirmities increased. He was not a sensation preacher, and, indeed, labored under the disadvantage of a poor delivery, and so never drew crowds to hear him, and never occasioned any special excitement. But his consistent piety, his uniform course, his marked punctuality, his strong sense and clear insight into the plan of salvation, together with his self-sacrificing responses to calls on behalf of the sick and dead, and to supply the lack of ministerial service in those destitute times, rendered him a usefully influential man.''

CURNELIUS COOK was a native of Great Britain, but was converted and called to preach in this country. He entered the itinerancy in 1787, and was appointed to East Jersey. In 1788 he was appointed to Dutchess, N. Y., and in 1789 to Schenectady, N. Y. He was a very feeble man physically, and his career was brief but useful. During his last illness he was visited by Asbury and Garrettson, both of whom found him happy in the faith and hope of the gospel he had preached. "He was a faithful laborer and patient sufferer," says the brief obituary notice in the minutes, "while he was employed in the Church for three years; and departed in peace and confidence, in the month of August, 1789."

CHAPTER XX.

THE ECCLESIASTICAL YEAR 1788.

THE labors of the past year resulted in an increase of nearly four hundred members in New Jersey, making at the beginning of the ecclesiastical year, 1788, a membership of 2046, white and colored. Twelve preachers were appointed to labor in the State this year, as follows:—James O. Cromwell, *elder*.

Salem, Joseph Cromwell, Nathaniel B. Mills, John Cooper.

Trenton, John Merrick, Thomas Morrell, Jethro Johnson.

Elizabethtown, John M'Claskey, Simon Pile.

Flanders, Jesse Lee, Aaron Hutchinson, John Lee.

It will be observed that the West Jersey circuit appears, for the first time this year, under the new name of Salem. There was a small decrease in the membership of this circuit the present year.

It was about this year that the first Methodist house of worship was erected in Burlington.

Burlington enjoys the signal honor of being the first place in New Jersey in which Methodism was established. The progress of the cause was slow during the first years of its history there, yet it has always been a prominent society, and was from the beginning favored with the presence and labors of such men as Capt. Webb, its founder, Francis Asbury, Richard Boardman, and John King. Indeed, Asbury acted the part of a pastor over the Burlington and Trenton societies in the time of their early infancy. In his Journal, May 22, 1791, he says: "Eighteen years ago I often slipped away from Philadelphia to Burlington one week, and to Trenton another, to keep a few souls alive: I had then no Conferences to take up my time and occupy my thoughts; and now— what hath God wrought!"

During the Revolutionary struggle, like most of the societies in New Jersey, it suffered reverses. The preaching was held, during the first years of its history, in the Court house; the courts being then held in Burlington, but since removed to Mount Holly, about six miles distant. The following account of the building of the first Church in Burlington is from the pen of Rev. Dr. Porter of the Newark Conference, and was published in the Christian Advocate and Journal in the year 1840:

"Soon after the war of the Revolution the Court

house was taken down, and the Methodists were compelled, from the necessity of the case, to meet in a small private house, occupied by Mr. George Smith, who was himself a Methodist. While things were thus, it was sometime about the year 1787 or 1788, that General Joseph-Bloomfield (who was for some time governor of this State) asked Mr. James Sterling, who was then a member of the M. E. Church, why they did not have a house of prayer 'where they might meet for public worship and the preaching of the word.' The answer of Mr. Sterling was, 'We are too poor; we have no ground to build it on, and nothing to build it with.' The general generously replied, 'I will give a lot of ground if you will put up the house.' Mr. Sterling at once resolved to make an effort, and said to Mr. Smith, at whose house the meetings were held, 'If you will beg the money to pay the workmen, I will find all the materials.' This Mr. Smith did, and thus they obtained their first house of prayer, which, for the time, was considered quite respectable. In the month of September, 1790, there was a Conference held here. Bishop Asbury remarks in his Journal: 'On Tuesday night we had a shout; then came the bulls of Bashan and broke our windows. It was well my head escaped the violence of these wicked sinners.' "

Methodism has ever demonstrated its power as a purifying and elevating agency in society, by its beneficent effects upon the masses. For that reason it has always commended itself to the good sense and hearty sympathy of many persons of intelligence and influence outside of its ecclesiastical enclosure, who have evinced their appreciation of it by generous efforts to promote its influence. Gen. Bloomfield believed, no doubt, that a Methodist Church in Burlington would be a blessing to the inhabitants, and, accordingly, he presented to the society the ground on which they might rear their temple of worship. This noble expression of sympathy and good will should ever be held in grateful remembrance by Burlington Methodists.

Soon after this church was erected, Bishop Asbury visited Burlington, and October 6, 1789, he writes in his Journal, "After twenty years preaching they have built a very beautiful meeting-house at Burlington, but it is low times there in religion."

Methodism has since been steadily advancing in Burlington. In 1821 larger church accommodations were found to be necessary, and accordingly the present Broad Street Church was erected. It stands upon the ground which was occupied by the old Court house, which, in connection with the Market house, was the scene of the first labors and triumphs of the cause in the city. During the two years in which Dr. Porter was pastor of the Church, (1838–39,) the membership was almost doubled, and for several years there have been two Methodist Churches in the city, each supporting its own pastor. For an account of the introduction of Methodism into Burlington, and also into Trenton, and of its first struggles in those cities, the reader is referred to the first chapters of this work.

When Jesse Lee entered upon his work in the Flanders circuit, which lay partly in New Jersey and partly in New York, he found there were formidable difficulties to contend with in the prosecution of his labors. The population was very heterogeneous, being composed of people of various nations, and their religious creeds were as different as the places of their nativity. But the predominant creed was that of Calvin. It was maintained in all its rigor. There was no softening down of its distinctive features of unconditional election and reprobation in its presentation from the pulpit, the Churches generally were in a lukewarm state, and what zeal they did manifest was more for doctrines than for graces. Mr. Lee could not be satisfied without attempting to counteract this state of things. He was the herald of what he regarded as a purer faith, and he exhibited it clearly and boldly. Sometimes, too, he publicly attacked Calvinism, "and opposed it with all the energy and skill he could command. On one occasion he spoke

25

'freely and fully against unconditional election and reprobation;' and he 'found great liberty in speaking, and the power of God attended the word. Many of the people wept, and some cried aloud.'" He became so bold in his utterances that at length he asserted "that God had taken his oath against Calvinism, because he had declared, by the mouth of the prophet: 'As I live, saith the Lord God, I have no pleasure in the death of the wicked, but that the wicked turn from his way and live.' On uttering these words," he says, "I felt so much of the power of God, that it appeared to me as if the truth of the doctrine was sealed to the hearts of the hearers."

The following incident which, it is said, probably occurred on this circuit, affords a good illustration of the spirit and manner of Mr. Lee in combating Calvinism. He went to hear a Calvinistic minister preach, and seated himself in the congregation, in front of the pulpit. The minister announced his text, Psa. cx. 3. "Thy people shall be *made* willing in the day of thy power." Mr. Lee did not feel quite comfortable. The minister slowly and solemnly repeated it. Lee rose upon his feet, and respectfully addressing the minister, said:

"My dear sir, have you not mistaken the text?"

The minister, somewhat astonished, replied, he had not.

"Will you please read it again?" said Mr. Lee.

He read it again, but in the same way.

"Are you quite sure you read it *right?*" asked Lee.

"Quite certain of it," replied the minister.

"Well, that's very singular; it don't read so in my Bible," said the earnest advocate of free will, at the same time holding up a small pocket Bible towards the pulpit, with the request, "Will you be good enough to read once more, and see if the word *made* is in the text?"

The minister commenced reading, slowly, "Thy—people—shall—be—" he paused, gazed earnestly at the words, and again read,—"Thy people shall be willing in the day of thy power." "True enough, there's no such word in the text." Lee resumed his seat. Notwithstanding, the minister did not see how the people could be willing unless they were made so, and he preached the doctrine, though the congregation perceived the force of Lee's commentary.

"The obstacles this *forcing* theory of Christianity was constantly opposing to the success of Mr. Lee," remarks his biographer, "had no inconsiderable influence, it is likely, in leading him so publicly and earnestly to seek to expose its unscripturalness. But perhaps his zeal for truth was more commendable than his mode of pursuing it, at least, in the instance above related."

The condition of the work on this circuit during the former part of the year was not encouraging. Several months passed before any fruit appeared to cheer the hearts of the laborers. At length, in January, 1789, signs of promise began to be visible. The congregations increased in number, and were more solemn. The classes were better attended, and all the religious meetings were more interesting and spiritual. At a watch night service Lee preached on 1 Cor. xvi. 13:—" *Watch ye.*" "I found," he says, "great liberty in speaking from these words, and was blessed in my own soul. I spoke very long and loud, the power of God came down among the people, and many of them wept greatly; many groaned and wept aloud. O my soul, praise the Lord, and let the remembrance of this meeting make me ever thankful. I spoke with tears in my eyes and comfort in my soul. If I may judge from my own feelings, or the looks of the people, I should conclude that a revival of religion is about to take place in the neighborhood. I have not seen so melting a time among them before. I knew not how to give over speaking, and continued for an hour and three quarters."

The work began to prosper, and the revival influence vouchsafed to the circuit continued until the time for the preachers to take their departure to Conference. Still, the minutes show a decrease of 274 white members on

Flanders circuit this year, and one colored member. The cause of this large decrease we have no means of ascertaining. Whether it was caused by wholesale backsliding, or removals, or members joining other churches, or all of these combined, we cannot tell, but surely the declension was a just reason for painful inquiry and sorrow.

While on the Flanders circuit Mr. Lee received an account of the conversion of an Indian woman, which he recorded in his Journal. It is a singular illustration of the truth, that

"Prayer is the soul's sincere desire,
Uttered or unexpressed;"

and of the Scripture declaration, that God looketh at the heart. It is given by Lee as follows:

"An Indian squaw, who was awakened some years past, when there was a great work among the Presbyterians in this part of the world, concluded that God would not hear her because she could not pray in English; but in the depth of her distress she recollected that she could say January and February; and she immediately began to pray, 'January, February; January, February,' and repeated the words till her soul was happily converted."*

The decrease in the entire white membership of the

* Life and Times of the Rev. Jesse Lee.

several circuits in New Jersey this year was three hundred and one, while there was an increase of six in the colored membership, making the total decrease two hundred and ninety-five.

We turn now from the work to the laborers.

JESSE LEE is the most distinguished name in the list the present year. He was born in Prince George Co., Va., on the 12th of March, 1758. His parents were moral and respectable, but plain. At an early age he was taught the catechism "out of the prayer book." These lessons produced a saltuary effect upon him. "In a thousand instances," he says, "when I felt an inclination to act or speak amiss, I have been stopped by the recollection of my catechism, some parts of which I did not understand; yet it was good, upon the whole, that I learned it."

His early life was unstained by flagrant offences, "except," he says, "one night, being in company with some wicked young people, I uttered some kind of oath for which I felt ashamed and sorry all the next day : and when alone, I felt that God was displeased with me for my bad conduct. I believe I never did anything in my youth that the people called wicked. I used, however, to indulge bad tempers, and use some vain words." When he was about fourteen years of age his father was made the subject of renewing grace through the labors of Rev. Devereux Jarrett, a zealous and useful Episcopal clergyman, who rendered important service to early Methodism in Virginia. A remark made by his father about this time was the means of his conversion. In conversing with a pious relative on the subject of experimental religion, the elder Mr. Lee said that "if a man's sins *were* forgiven him he would *know* it." That sentence "took hold," he says, "of my mind, and I pondered it in my heart." He asked himself the question, "Are *my* sins forgiven?" He felt conscious they were not. A sense of his guilt and exposure to the retributive justice of the Almighty filled his heart with sadness. In his distress he cried unto the Lord. "I would frequently get by myself," he says, "and with many tears pray to God to have mercy upon my poor soul and forgive my sins. Sometimes in the open fields I would fall on my knees, and pray and weep till my heart was ready to break. At other times my heart was so hard that I could not shed a tear. It would occur to my mind, 'Your day of grace is past, and God will never forgive your sins.' It appeared to me that of all sinners in the world I was the greatest; my sins appeared to me greater in magnitude and multitude than the sins of any other person."

Thus he continued for about four weeks, "in which time," he says, "I never, for an hour, lost sight of my wretched condition. The cry of my soul was, 'How shall I escape the misery of hell?' I cared little about the sufferings of this life, if I could but escape eternal misery. I read 'that some asked and received not, because they asked amiss;' the remembrance of this made me, for a season, afraid to use many words in prayer, for fear I should pray improperly, and, therefore, ask amiss."

One morning being in deep distress, and fearing, momentarily, that he would fall into hell, he cried earnestly for mercy and his soul was delivered of its burden, and received the peace of God. He felt an indescribable pleasure, which lasted about three days, but he did not communicate to any one his new and delightful experience. "I anxiously wished for some one to talk to me on the subject," he says, "but no one did. I then began to doubt my conversion and to fear that I was deceived. I finally concluded that if I were not converted I would never rest without the blessing, and began to pray to the Lord to show me my lost condition, and let me feel my danger as I had previously done; but, as I could not feel the burden of my sins, the enemy of my soul suggested to my mind that the Lord had forsaken me, and that I had sinned away my conviction, and deceived my own soul. Thus I was a prey to those doubts and perplexities for about six months before I could as-

suredly believe that I was in the favor of God.   One
evening, traveling in company with a religious neighbor,
he asked me if I were ever converted.   I told him I believed I had been.   He asked me several questions relative to the circumstances of the change, which I endeavored to answer.   He then said, 'You are surely converted.'   I was much strengthened by that conversation,
and so much encouraged as to tell other people, when
they asked me what the Lord had done for my soul."

It was not long before his misgivings were entirely
removed by clearer evidences of the Divine favor, and
he was enabled to say, "I know in whom I have believed."

No Methodist preacher had entered the neighborhood,
but when, in 1774, a Methodist society was formed, he,
being then sixteen years of age, united with it, and from
that time he was an ardent advocate of the doctrines of
Methodism, and illustrated in his life their excellence
and power.

He commenced his ministry in the manner usual in
those days, by exhorting in prayer-meetings, &c., and
laboring as he had opportunity for the salvation of souls,
in which work his heart was deeply enlisted.   He did
not, however, indulge the thought of rising to a more
prominent position in the Church.   But God had evi-

dently designed him for more public and extended labors, and was now leading him towards his ultimate destiny.

After he became a local preacher he was drafted into the army, but he refused to bear arms though he took his place in the military ranks. While detained in the army —a period of nearly four months—he did not forget that he was a soldier of the cross, and he fought bravely for the Lord.

For more than a year after he was released from the army, he zealously proclaimed the word of life in his native neighborhood. He was frequently impressed, meanwhile, with the conviction that he ought to enter the itinerancy, but a sense of the responsibility of the sacred office led him to hesitate. While the matter was thus resting upon his mind, he attended the Conference at Ellis's preaching-house, in Virginia, in 1782. The spectacle of the devoted and self-sacrificing laborers there assembled moved his heart. He says, "The union and brotherly love which I saw among the preachers, exceeded everything I had seen before, and caused me to wish that I was worthy to have a place among them. When they took leave of each other, I observed that they embraced each other in their arms, and wept as though they never expected to meet again. Had heathens been there, they might have well said, 'See how these Christians love one another!' By reason of what I saw and heard during the four days that the Conference sat, I found my heart truly humbled in the dust, and my desires greatly increased to love and serve God more perfectly than I had ever done before. At the close of the Conference, Mr. Asbury came to me and asked me if I was willing to take a circuit. I told him that I could not well do it, but signified I was at a loss to know what was best for me to do. I was afraid of hurting the cause which I wished to promote; for I was very sensible of my own weakness. At last he called to some of the preachers a little way off, and said, ' I am going to enlist brother Lee.' One of them replied, ' What bounty do you give?' He answered, ' Grace here and glory hereafter will be given if he is faithful.' Some of the preachers then talked to me, and persuaded me to go, but I trembled at the thought, and shuddered at the cross, and did not at that time consent."

It was not long, however, before he entered upon the arduous and responsible work to which his life was to be consecrated. "Before the end of the year," says Rev. A. Stevens, in his Memorials of Methodism, "he was on his way, with a colleague, to North Carolina, to form a new and extensive circuit. The next year he was appointed to labor regularly in that State, and being now fully in the sphere of his duty, he was largely blest with the comforts of the Divine favor, and went through the

extensive rounds of his circuit 'like a flame of fire.'
His word was accompanied with the authority and power
of the Holy Ghost.   Stout hearted men were smitten
down under it, large congregations were often melted
into tears by irrepressible emotions, and his eloquent
voice was not unfrequently lost amidst the sobs and
ejaculations of his audience.   Often, his own deep sym-
pathies, while in the pulpit, could find relief only in
tears."

After Mr. Lee left Flanders circuit he offered himself
for New England, and was appointed to that field, where
he succeeded in laying the foundation of Methodism.
The Rev. Thomas Ware speaks of Mr. Lee in this connection, in an article in the Christian Advocate and
Journal, as follows:—"Jesse Lee, styled, by some, the
Apostle of New England, was persuaded Methodism
could live where men can breathe.   He therefore in
1789 offered himself a missionary for the land of the
Pilgrims.

"For this mission Mr. Lee was singularly qualified.
He possessed colloquial powers fascinating in a high degree to the people of the East.   His readiness at repartee
delighted his friends, and taught those who might wish
to be witty with him it was safest to be civil.

"He knew he would have to contend with a learned
clergy, venerable for their outward deportment, and with

a shrewd adventurous people who would not hesitate to tell him to his face he preached damnable heresies. At the same time he knew such was their thirst for knowledge, and their independence of spirit, that they would hear for themselves; and the truth that had made him free, and that God had commissioned him to preach with a power sinners could not resist, he felt assured, would cut its way and open in that land a wide field of action. He was, in a word, a man of courage. He feared not the face of man, and was no ordinary preacher. He preached with the greatest ease of any man I have known, and was, I think, the best every day preacher in the Methodist connection. He states in his history that on the 17th of June, 1789, he visited Norwalk, and not being able to obtain a house to preach in, he took his stand in the street. In 1793, the district of which I had charge took in a part of Connecticut, and I found the people full of anecdotes of elder Lee.

" 'When,' said an inhabitant of Norwalk, 'he stood up in the open air and began to sing, I knew not what to make of it. I, however, drew near to listen, and thought the prayer was the best I had ever heard, but rather short. He then read his text, and began in sententious sentences, brought home to every heart, and compelled, I thought, all who were present to say to himself, I am glad I am here. All the time the people were gathering, he continued this mode of address, in which time he held up to our view such a variety of beautiful images that I began to think he must have been at infinite pains to crowd so many pretty things into his memory.   But when he entered upon the subject matter of his text, it was in such a tone of voice, and in an easy, natural flow of thought and expression, that I soon began to weep, as did many ; and when he was done we conferred together, and our conclusion was, that such a man had not visited New England since the days of Whitefield.   I heard him again, and thought I could follow him to the ends of the earth.' "

At the General Conference held in Baltimore in the year 1800, Mr. Lee came within one vote of being elected a bishop in the Methodist Episcopal Church. On the first ballot the votes were scattering, and there was no election.   On the second ballot the tellers reported a tie between Mr Lee and Richard Whatcoat. Had the former received only one more vote at this balloting he would have been bishop, but on the third ballot Mr. Whatcoat "was declared to be duly elected by a majority of four votes."

Mr. Lee's public labors extended over most of the Union.   In 1783 he traveled Caswell circuit, N. C.; 1784, Salisbury: 1785, Caroline, Md. ; 1786, Kent; 1787, Baltimore ; 1788, Flanders; 1789, Stamford, Ct.;

1790–1–2, elder in Connecticut; 1793, province of Maine and Lynn; 1794–5–6, Presiding Elder in New England. In 1797–8–9, he traveled with Bishop Asbury. In 1800 he was stationed in the city of New York; 1801–2–3, Norfolk district; 1804, Petersburg, Va.; 1805, Mecklenburg; 1806, Amelia; 1807, Sparta; 1808, Cumberland; 1809, Brunswick; 1810, Meherrin district; 1811, Amelia; 1812, Richmond; 1813, Brunswick; 1814, Cumberland and Manchester; 1815, Fredericksburg; 1816, Annapolis. During this year he ceased "to work and live."

The Rev. and venerated Henry Boehm of the Newark Conference, was privileged to be with him in his last hours. He thus describes the good man's end :—

"Through the first part of his illness his mind was much weighed down, so that he spake but little. On Tuesday night, September 10th, he broke out in ecstasies of joy. Also on Wednesday, 11th, about nine o'clock, A.M., he delivered himself in words like these : 'Glory ! glory ! glory ! Hallelujah ! Jesus reigns.' On the same evening he spoke nearly twenty minutes, deliberately and distinctly ; among other things he directed me to write to his brother Ned, and let him know he died happy in the Lord.

"'Give my respects to Bishop M'Kendree,' said he, 'and tell him that I die in love with all the preachers ;

that I love him, and that he lives in my heart.' Then he took his leave of all present, six or seven in number, and requested us to pray. This solemn night will never be forgotten by me. After this he spake but little. Thursday, the 12th, in the early part of the day, he lost his speech, but appeared to retain his reason. Thus he continued to linger till the same evening, about half past seven o'clock, when, without a sigh or groan, he expired, with his eyes seemingly fixed on the prize." *

AARON HUTCHINSON was born at Milford, Mercer county, N. J. the 17th of May 1767. He was converted to God about the year 1786, and though the youngest of the four brothers who became preachers, he was the first to enter the itinerant field. " When converted to God," says Rev. H. B. Beegle, to whom I am indebted for the following notice of him—" When converted to God he gave evidence of such gifts, and promise of so much usefulness to the Church, that brother M'Claskey immediately took him along with him around the circuit requiring him to exercise his gifts in prayer and exhortation. When they came came back to Joseph Hutchinson's, brother M'Claskey said he must preach there. It was a great cross to the youthful soldier. But a few months since he was converted; and no opportunities for study, for they had been on the wing from the time they

* Minutes.

left until they returned.   And then to open his commission among his own kindred too.   But he lifted his cross and stood up, and preached from Isa. ii. 3.   They were all astonished at the marvelous manner in which God assisted the stripling.   His mother, especially, wept profusely through the whole service.   He was immediately called out as a supply on some of the large circuits. Whether he labored with M'Claskey and Cooper on 'East Jersey' or went elsewhere we know not, but it is settled that ,he labored somewhere during most of the year 1786.   At the Conference of 1787 he was admitted as a traveling preacher, and appointed to Dover, Del. ; in 1788 and '89 he was on Flanders circuit ; in 1790 he was appointed to Trenton, where he ended his labors.

" The General Minutes, in noting his death, contain an estimate of him by his brethren of the Conference. They say he was 'a man of clear understanding ; gospel simplicity ; blameless in his life ; acceptable as a preacher ; fruitful in his labors, which ended in the short space of four years.   He was patient, resigned, and confident in his last moments.'

" He was married some time during his ministry to a lady by the name of Jaques.   He frequently tried his hand at poetry.   On meeting with Mrs. Hannah Salter, a daughter of Aaron Hutchinson, she informed me of her father's poetic tendencies, and of the many effusions
26

of his she had stored away. She was away from home
at the time, but with one she was so familiar that she
could repeat it, and as she did so I penned it as follows:

THE GOOD SAMARITAN.

The road that leads to Jericho,
That bloody way that sinners go :
They fall among the thieves of hell,
Eternally with them to dwell.
I never shall forget the day
When on that road I bleeding lay ;
Was stript, and wounded—left half dead,
And not a friend to raise my head.
A priest came there, but he passed by ;
He never stopped to hear my cry :
A Levite looked upon my wound
But no relief from him I found.
Samaritans I did despise,
Yet one drew near and heard my cries ;
He gently raised me from the ground,
Poured oil and wine into my wound.
He kindly took me to an Inn,
A place where I had never been ;
He watched, and fed, and clothed me there—
Made me the object of his care.
And when my friend departed thence
He called the host and gave two pence ;
Saying, "If more on him he spent,
I will repay ; it's only lent."

I will repay thee when I come
To take my ransomed people home,
Where sickness, sorrow, death, nor pain
Shall never trouble them again.
What rapturous awe will fill my soul
When I see Him who made me whole;
Throughout eternal, boundless days
This GOOD SAMARITAN I'll praise!

"Brother Hutchinson departed this life at Milford, July 30, 1791, and his remains lie in the old burial ground there."

JOHN LEE was a brother of Jesse, and was admitted on trial the present year and appointed to Flanders circuit. The ensuing year he was appointed to Long Island with Wm. Phoebus. In 1790 he went to New England and labored on the New Haven circuit. He located in 1791 in consequence of ill health.

He was but about eighteen years of age when he traveled Flanders circuit, but he was devoted and useful. He was emphatically a man of prayer, "rising, often, in the midst of wintry nights, while all others around were wrapped in sleep, and struggling, like Jacob, in supplications for himself, the Church, and the world." The Rev. Enoch Mudge gave the following sketch of Mr. Lee, which we extract from Stevens's Memorials of Methodism in New England: "He was a lively, animated preacher, had a strong, clear, musical voice, and was affectionate in his address. As he had drunk deep of the cup of bitterness, of wormwood and gall, for his own sins, he had a sympathizing heart for those who were in distress. He was the instrument, in God's hand, of ministering the balm of comfort to my sin-sick soul. He was emphatically a son of consolation. He had a pleasant and profitable gift of exhortation, which he often improved after his brother Jesse and others had preached. He had the happy faculty of bringing religious truth home to the minds and hearts of his hearers, in an easy, familiar way, and of carrying their feelings with him into the pleasant paths of practical piety. - He was of a consumptive habit, frequently spitting blood, which was increased by often speaking in public."

The circumstances of Mr. Lee's death were quite remarkable. In the summer of 1801 he left his home in Petersburg, Va., and took a tour through the mountainous parts of the State with the view of recruiting his feeble health. During this journey his mind was in a very devout frame, and in one of his letters he wrote, "I thank God that I delight in resigning myself to him, and wish with all my heart

'His pleasure to fulfill.'

I long to be like him, and to suffer with him, that I may

reign with him." Late in the day on which he died he stopped at the residence of a pious widow in Wilkes county, North Carolina, and he had been there but a short time when he informed the family that he expected to die during the night. They were greatly surprised at this, as he was then walking about the room. He then went out to his servant, who was feeding the horses, and requested him to take good care of them as he should never see them fed again. He asked his servant to sit down beside him on a log, when he told him that the ulcer on his lungs had broke, and he should die that night. He placed some valuable papers in his hands directing him what to do with them; he also instructed him about getting home, and continued his conversation with the utmost composure until nearly dark, when he arose and walked to the house. He desired some water, with which he bathed his feet, and remarked, "I am sure I am about to die." He inquired of some of the family if they could sing, and on being answered, "Not well," he asked if any of them would engage in prayer. No response being given, he kneeled down and prayed aloud for some time, requesting the Lord to give him patience and take him to heaven. He rose and said to his servant, "Give my love to everybody, and tell my friends not to mourn or grieve after me, for I am happy and sure of heaven." After a time he again bowed in prayer, then arose, walked about and told the family he was then about to die. He knelt the third time and prayed until his servant, perceiving that his voice was failing, lifted him up and placed him on a chair. Being in a profuse sweat, he requested his servant to wipe his face, which he did, and then took him in his arms and laid him on a bed. He stretched himself, and then "died in Jesus without a struggle or a groan."

JETHRO JOHNSON was appointed to four different circuits in New Jersey during his itinerancy,—Trenton, Salem, Elizabethtown, and Flanders. He entered the traveling connection in 1788, and withdrew in 1794.

JOHN MERRICK was received on trial in 1786, and appointed to Somerset, Md.; 1787, Kent; 1788, Trenton; 1789, New York, for four months; 1790, Burlington. In 1791 he was elder of the New Jersey district. In 1792 his district did not extend any farther than the Trenton circuit in Jersey, but embraced the city of New York. In 1794 New York appears on another district, and Mr. Merrick's district embraced only Freehold, Salem, Bethel, Trenton, and Burlington,—Staten Island, Elizabethtown, and Flanders being in the same district as New York. In 1794 he remained on the same district. In 1795 his district remained the same, so far as New Jersey was concerned, but was extended from Wilmington in the south to Canada in the north, embracing Wilmington, Chester, Bristol, Philadelphia, Niagara, Bay Quinte, and Oswegotchie. It does not seem possible that one man should be able to perform the labor which such a district would require. We cannot learn his appointment for 1796. In 1797 he is returned among the located. Mr. Merrick was, it is said, a superior preacher, and a man much beloved by those who knew him. As an evidence of the esteem in which he was held, many families named children after him.

One day, as he was riding along the road somewhere in West Jersey, he was accosted by an old Friend in the following manner :—" Is thee not a public speaker ?"

He replied he was a person who " endeavored to instruct people when he had an opportunity."

" Is thee not a Methodist ?"

" I belong to that denomination."

" Well, I have heard the Episcopalians, Presbyterians, Baptists, and several others, but I never heard any like the Methodists."

" Why so ? In what do they differ from others ?"

" Why they get right into the heart, and there they stick until they tear it all to pieces."

There were two JOHN COOPERS in the work this year, one of whom appears in the ranks for the first time. We presume it was he that was appointed to Salem circuit this year. He went to Nova Scotia and finally located.

CHAPTER XXI.

THE WORK AND THE LABORERS IN 1789.

THE Conference for the district of New Jersey was held at Trenton, beginning on Saturday, May 23, 1789. "It was opened," says Asbury, "in great peace. We labored for a manifestation of the Lord's power, and it was not altogether in vain." The session appears to have been remarkably brief, as Asbury speaks of riding to Elizabethtown through a heavy rain on Monday, and the ensuing day he arrived at New York. Annual Conferences in those days, however, had fewer members and far less business to transact than now.

At this Conference Benjamin Abbott, among others, was admitted on trial. By his earnest and untiring labors for fifteen years as a local preacher, he had greatly promoted the work of God in West Jersey, and made an impression upon the rising Methodism of that portion of the State which can never be effaced. He now felt that Providence directed him to a more extended sphere of labor, and though well advanced in life he heroically entered upon the work of a regular itinerant preacher in Dutchess circuit, N. Y., and continued to toil in the various fields assigned him until his vigorous constitution sunk beneath the pressure of years and labor, and his mighty spirit, radiant in the lustre of heavenly virtues, ascended triumphantly to its immortal rest. The delineation of his noble character will fall within the scope of a subsequent volume should it ever be prepared.

The appointments for the ensuing year were as follows:—

James O. Cromwell, *Presiding Elder.* Salem; Simon Pile, Jethro Johnson, Sylvester Hutchinson. Trenton; Joseph Cromwell, Richard Swain. Burlington; John M'Claskey, William Jackson. Flanders; Aaron Hutchinson, Daniel Combs. Elizabethtown; John Merrick, John Cooper.

On the 26th of June Asbury appears in the northern end of the State, "and the power of God," he says, "came down among the people at B's, and there was a great melting. After meeting we rode through the heat fifteen miles to Pepper Cotton." The next day he rode to the Stone Church, and Mr. (afterward Bishop) Whatcoat, who accompanied him in this journey, preached for him there. This seems to have been a Church in which the Methodists preached by sufferance, as he says, "The

Methodists ought to preach only in their own houses; I have done with the houses of other people." "When I see the stupidity of the people," he continues, "and the contentiousness of their spirit, I pity and grieve over them. I have hard labor in traveling amongst the rocks and hills." On Sabbath he "spoke a few words at Sweezey's, to insensible people," and then drove to Axford's, where he enjoyed life and liberty among his hearers. On Monday Mr. Whatcoat preached at C.'s, "while some of the audience slept." Thence they went to Col. M'Cullough's, where Asbury was annoyed by Adam Cloud, who had been disowned by the Conference. "He had," says Asbury, "in some instances fallen short of his quarterage during his ministry, and now insisted on my paying him his deficiencies: I did not conceive that in justice or conscience this was required of me; nevertheless, to get rid of him, I gave him £14."

Though there was a declension in the membership of 295 during the past year, the work greatly prospered in the several circuits in the State this year, and when the preachers went to Conference at the end of the year they had very encouraging reports to bear from their fields of labor. Salem circuit was favored with wonderful effusions of the Spirit, and within the bounds of the present county of Salem hundreds were converted to God.

Sylvester Hutchinson, who was one of the preachers on this circuit the present year, was one day made the object of sport by two young women, in the house where he was temporarily lodging. "They began to banter him upon his size and insignificant appearance; when, suddenly lifting his head from its reclining posture, he repeated in slow, solemn tones, a verse of a hymn:—

> 'My thoughts on awful subjects roll:
> Damnation and the dead;
> What horrors seize a guilty soul
> Upon a dying bed!'

"The time, the place, the words, and manner of recitation, all combined to produce pungent and lasting conviction; the young women both immediately fled from the room, weeping, and were without rest or peace until their hearts were given to the Lord. Both ladies, for such they were, joined the then 'poor, despised' Methodists.

"On a certain day a man on horseback overtook the young preacher riding along the road, and, no doubt, thought to have some fun.

"'How do you do? Which way are you traveling?'

"'I do the Lord's work; you do the devil's. I am on the way to heaven; you are going to hell, where fire and brimstone are the fuel, and the smoke of torment ascendeth for ever and ever.'

"The alarmed man put spurs to his horse and rode away, but was found at the next meeting, weeping among the seekers of religion.   He became an eminent servant of God."*

During this year Mr. Hutchinson received an invitation from Rev. Ethan Osborne, the pastor of the Presbyterian Church in Fairfield, Cumberland county, to occupy his pulpit when he came to preach in Fairfield, which invitation was accepted, and, as the result numbers were added to the Church.   But they were not added to the *Methodist* Church.   They became members of Mr. Osborne's Church, and perceiving this Mr. Hutchinson declined preaching there any more, but henceforth confined his labors to his legitimate sphere as a minister of the Methodist Episcopal Church.

There was also, Asbury informs us, "a most genuine work" in Flanders, Trenton, Burlington, and Bethel circuits.   At the Conference of 1790, Salem reported 933 white members and 21 colored; Burlington, 353 white and 12 colored; Trenton, 429 white and 33 colored; Elizabethtown, 237 white and 16 colored; Flanders, 322 white and 7 colored.   The increase this year of white members was 570, and of colored members 42, making the total increase 612.   The entire membership,

* Raybold's Methodism in West Jersey.

white and colored, in the five circuits in New Jersey at the close of the present ecclesiastical year was 2363.

The most distinguished name in the ministry the present year is that of SYLVESTER HUTCHINSON. He was the third of four brothers, all of whom, as we have seen, became preachers, and three of them itinerants. Sylvester was born at Milford, Mercer Co. N. J., April 20, 1765. The Rev. H. B. Beegle of the New Jersey Conference, in a sketch of him, which he kindly furnished the writer, the material for which he derived mainly from his surviving widow and son, Mr. Daniel P. Hutchinson, of Hightstown, N. J., says:

" Of his early life but little is known beyond the fact that he was quite correct in his habits, and was what would be called a steady and moral young man. He was not regarded in his early days as giving as much promise as his brothers. He was by no means as forward as Aaron; and Thomas Baldwin, his old school teacher, now a resident of Cranberry, Middlesex county, once asked him why he did not learn as fast as his brother Aaron. He replied, ' Because they keep me at home to work and send Aaron to school.' "

He was awakened about the year 1786. " But he was a long time," continues Mr. Beegle, "in obtaining a satisfactory evidence of his acceptance with God. He wept and prayed, read the Scriptures, sought advice from

Christians, and used all the means likely to advance his soul's interests. The Baptist minister at Hightstown, learning of his seriousness, visited him at his father's house, and tried to persuade him to join their communion and become a *preacher* among them. He expressed a decided preference for the Methodists, and said ' If the Methodists are not the people of God, I think he has no people upon earth.' While he was under exercise of mind, he was in the habit of reading the Bible and praying much every day all alone in his bed room. One day, while he was meditating upon his condition, a figure appeared at the foot of his bed which he believed to be the figure of Christ. This at once satisfied him and he no more doubted. He went on his way rejoicing. He fully expected when he reached heaven he should see and know the same figure which appeared to him on earth.

"He entered the ministry and joined the Conference in 1789, and was appointed to Salem circuit. In 1790 he was appointed to Chester; 1791, to Fell's point; 1792, at Wilmington; 1793–4, Croton; 1795, Long Island; and from 1796 to 1800 he was Presiding Elder. But we cannot follow him through all his ministerial life. Dr. Clarke, in his Life and Times of Hedding, gives us a very interesting description of this eminent man and his labors. He says: ' The district was of gigantic proportions and the Presiding Eldership no sinecure in those

days.   It embraced New York city, the whole of Long
Island, and extended northward, embracing the whole
territory, having the Connecticut river on the east and
Hudson river and Lake Champlain on the west, and
stretching far into Canada.   It embraced nearly the
whole territory now included in three Annual Conferences.   This immense district was then traveled by Sylvester Hutchinson.   He was a man of burning zeal and
of indomitable energy.   Mounted upon his favorite horse,
he would ride through the entire extent of his district
once each three months, visiting each circuit, and inva-
riably filling all his appointments.   His voice rung like
a trumpet's blast; and, with words of fire, and in powerful demonstration of the Spirit, he preached Christ
Jesus.'

"His travels were indeed extensive, and his labors
herculean.   He often stated to his son and wife (now
widow) that he rode from fifty to sixty miles per day, and
preached from one to three times per day, except Saturday, when he seldom preached more than once.   His allowance, he said, was thirty dollars per annum, and often
he did not get that.   He was not accustomed to think
what he *wanted*, but what he could not possibly *do without*.   At one time he started for home, a distance of some
three hundred miles.   He had but little money and that
was soon gone.   Riding along he saw a house a short

distance from the road, and concluded to ride up and seek for entertainment for the night. The gentleman of the house was not at home, but he was assured by the good lady that he would be soon, and was invited to stay. The gentleman proved to be a member of the legislature, and a very agreeable and benevolent man, for the next morning when he left he voluntarily placed in his hands money enough to carry him home. Thus God provided, sometimes, for his faithful and needy servants.

"In 1806 his name appears on the Minutes in the list of those located. It is impossible to get all the facts at this late day which would give a true history of this location. The widow and son, however, are very distinct in their recollection of having heard Sylvester say over and over again that Mr. Asbury was to blame for his leaving the Church. He said that he was in the good graces of Mr. Asbury until the difficulty occurred about his marriage. He was to marry a young lady belonging to an influential family, and the friends, especially one brother, made such desperate opposition that it was broken off on the day the wedding was to have taken place. That Mr. Asbury reprimanded him severely for not marrying the girl at all hazards, as he was engaged to her; that both of them being of good metal they had a warm time; and that Sylvester came home on a visit, and that Mr. Asbury had his name left off the Minutes of the Conference. There would seem to be truth in this from the fact that in the year 1804 his name appears in the list of elders, but he has no appointment given him; while in 1805 his name is not to be found in the Minutes anywhere. But in 1806 he is set down as located. He was deeply moved at the omission of his name from the Minutes, he says, without the consent of the Conference too, and he could not get over it."

We must here interrupt the flow of brother Beegle's graceful narrative to record a fact which illustrates this matter more fully. It is given upon the authority of Mr. Daniel P. Hutchinson. He says: "Finding, on his return from his visit home, that his name was dropped from the Minutes, he remonstrated with Mr. Asbury for having done it, and offered to continue in the ministry. Mr. Asbury finally offered him a circuit, but it was one in which he was not acceptable to the people. There was also another preacher who was not very acceptable where he had been sent, and Mr. H. and he proposed to Mr. A. that they should be exchanged; but this was refused, and turning to Mr. H. he said, 'Go there or go home,' to which Mr. H. answered, 'Then I must go home,' and thus ended his connection with the M. E. Church."

He joined the Methodist Protestant Church some time afterward, and preached more or less among them

27

for several years.   The last station he filled was Kensington, Philadelphia.   "Before he died," continues Mr. Beegle, "his wife asked him if he had not better come back to the old Church.   He expressed himself perfectly willing, but his death occurring soon after, it was never consumated.   He felt an ardent attachment to the ministers of the M. E. Church, and felt at home in their society, and delighted to entertain them.   In view of what he had suffered for the Church, and his remarkable labors in her behalf, we can account readily for this, even while he belonged to another branch of the Methodist family.

"Brother Wakeley, in his 'Lost Chapters,' gives some account of Sylvester Hutchinson, but has fallen into some errors and also casts a dark reflection upon him. He was not born in Burlington county as he asserts, but in Mercer county, and he never was engaged in a land agency in the West as he says.   He also says, page 532, that 'His history after his location shows the exceeding danger of ministers leaving their legitimate calling,' &c. Now one would infer from this that he lost his piety, became immoral, or suffered some terrible calamity, which would make him an example of warning to others.   But if anything more is intended than the fact that he joined another branch of the Methodist family (for which he thought he had good reason) it is utterly unfounded.

He was the same in spirit from the first sermon he preached until the last.   Many will testify to that.

"About the last time the son heard his father speak in love-feast or class meeting, which was a short time before his death, he said, 'I feel that my work is done.   I am ready to go but not impatient to depart; willing to wait till the Master calls.' "

We have seen that he abounded in labors and endured his full share of hardships in the itinerancy.   At one time, his son informs us, while he was traveling in the North he was attacked with the winter fever, but he persisted in traveling and rode all day, taking ten grains of calomel every two hours, until he had swallowed eighty grains.   At another time he took calomel and rode all day in the rain.   He could not enjoy a day's rest, for if he stopped he would fall so far behind his appointments that he could not overtake them.   He was accustomed to rise at four o'clock and ride twenty miles before eating breakfast, sometimes arriving at his place of breakfast before the people had risen from their beds.   He traveled through forests, in storms, over mountains, and across rivers, sometimes on snow drifts from 20 to 30 feet deep, at other times almost buried in them.

Mr. Hutchinson was married on the 10th of May, 1808, to a very estimable lady by the name of Phebe Phillips, who still survives him.   For two years previous

to his death he was afflicted with disease of the heart.
The last day of his life he was as well as usual, and after
retiring for the night, Mrs. H. supposed him going into
a sound sleep, but soon discovered it was death.   He
died Nov. 11th, 1840, and his remains lie in the cemetery
of the Borough of Hightstown, whither they were removed a few years since by a devoted son.   The following is the inscription upon his tombstone:

SACRED

TO THE

Memory of

REV. SYLVESTER HUTCHINSON,

WHO DEPARTED THIS LIFE

Nov. 11, 1840,

AGED 75 YEARS

AND SIX MOS.

From infancy to hoary hairs
He all my griefs and burdens bears;
Supports me in his arms of love,
And hides my ransomed life above.

"The family from whom these Hutchinsons sprung is
a very remarkable one for longevity.   Ann Hutchinson,
wife of William Hutchinson, and grandmother of the
four brothers who were ministers, has this remarkable
inscription on her headstone:

"'Sacred to the memory of Ann Hutchinson, relict of
Wm. Hutchinson, Esq., departed this life, Jan 4, 1801.

Aged 101 years 9 months and seven days. She was mother of 13 children, and grandmother, and great-grandmother, and great-great-grandmother of 375 persons.'

"She retained her faculties to the last, and could see to thread a needle, and read without spectacles, when in her 101st year."*

DANIEL COMBS entered the traveling connection in 1787, but was never received into full connection in the Conference.

WILLIAM JACKSON entered the traveling connection in 1789, and was appointed to Burlington. In 1790 he was sent to Bethel circuit; we do not learn his appointment for 1791; in 1792 he located.

RICHARD SWAIN was a native of New Jersey, and entered the itinerant ministry in 1789. He traveled the following circuits respectively: 1789, Trenton; 1790–91, Flanders; 1792, Middletown, Connecticut; 1793, New London; 1794, Salem, New Jersey; 1795, Burlington; 1796, Freehold; 1797, Trenton; 1798, Freehold; 1799–1800, Salem; 1801, Bethel; 1802, Cape May; 1803, Salem. From 1804 to 1808 he was a supernumerary. On the 17th of January of the latter year he died "in confident peace, triumphant faith, and smiles of a present God."

* Communication from Rev. H. B. Beegle.

He was endowed by nature with quick and solid parts, and sometimes gave evidence of possessing wit, which gleamed out pleasantly in his preaching and conversation.   He maintained an unexceptionable character as a minister, and his labors were productive of good.   "He traveled," say his brethren, "in the extreme parts of the work before things were made ready to his hands, and bore a part of the burden and heat of the day.

"We trust that he was made perfect through suffering, and triumphant in death.   And possibly it requires more faith and fortitude to wear out in a confirmed affliction, and a state of dependence, than to go through the most extreme labor and sufferings in the field of action.   It must be exceedingly painful for a person accustomed to extensive traveling to be bound and fettered by affliction, as a prisoner of Divine Providence; and, in a great degree, cut off from the service of God, his worship, and all Christian fellowship; not only as a minister, but as a member of society.   Thus some souls are tried in the furnace of affliction.   Deep calleth unto deep!   The raging billows go over them: but they will soon reach the peaceful shore; gain their haven, the rest of the weary and afflicted, the palace of angels and God, where, with new powers, they will see the rising glory, and sing forever the praise of Jesus, their Lord!

"Oh! what are all my sufferings here,
   If, Lord, thou count me meet
With that enraptured host t' appear,
   And worship at thy feet!"*

Kind and patient reader, my task is done.   May it be fraught with as much blessing to thee as it has been with toil, and care, and pleasure to me.   May the examples of Christian fidelity and zeal, and of ministerial heroism, herein so imperfectly portrayed, incite thee to an intenser devotion, and to more abundant and successful labors for God and humanity; and then shall my labor not be in vain.

* Minutes, 1808.

In Preparation, and to appear from the Press of Perkinpine & Higgins,
No. 56 North Fourth Street, Philadelphia.

JOHN ALBERT BENGEL'S

GNOMON

OF

THE NEW TESTAMENT.

POINTING OUT

FROM THE NATURAL FORCE

OF THE

WORDS, THE SIMPLICITY, DEPTH, HARMONY,

AND

SAVING POWER OF ITS DIVINE THOUGHTS.

A NEW TRANSLATION

BY

CHARLTON T. LEWIS, A. M.

Prof. of Pure Mathematics in Troy University.

In two Vols. 8vo. of at least 800 pages each. Price $5 00. Vol. I. will
be ready in June, 1860. Vol. II. in a few months thereafter.

The following are but a few of many commendatory opinions of the original work :—

"I once designed to write down barely what occurred to my own mind, consulting none but the inspired writers. But no sooner was I acquainted with that great light of the Christian world, lately gone to his reward, BENGELIUS, than I entirely changed my design, being thoroughly convinced it might be of more service to the cause of religion, were I barely to translate his GNOMON NOVI TESTAMENTI, than to write many volumes upon it."—JOHN WESLEY, *Explanatory Notes*, p. 4, Preface.

"The persons whose concurrence I should have most highly prized are precisely those in whom the exposition of Bengel, to which also I owe more than to any other for the explanation of particular passages, has taken deepest root; insomuch that an attack on it, which has made the Revelation dear and precious to them, will scarcely be regarded by them in any other light than as an attack on the Revelation itself."—HENGSTENBERG, *Revelation*, Preface.

"Bengel, in one of the pregnant notes in his invaluable GNOMON—a work which manifests the most intimate and profoundest knowledge of Scripture, and which, if we examine it with care, will often be found to condense more matter into a line, than can be extracted from pages of other writers, says," &c. * * * "In this microscopic nicety of observation, which, as we have seen, will often detect important fibres of thought, no commentator that I know comes near Bengel."—ARCHDEACON HARE, *Mission of the Comforter*, vol. ii. p. 403.

"Bengel was endowed with a remarkable depth of insight and breadth of mental view, together with a marvelous conciseness and felicity of expression. He makes every word of the Bible utter some truth you never thought was in it, and leaves you wondering why you had not seen it before. Under the touch of his magic pen, even the genealogical tables of the Evangelists, which we have been accustomed to pass by as dry and marrowless bones, are set before us full of fatness."—*Methodist Quarterly Review*, 1859, p. 665.

The Publishers have no doubt, that all lovers of choice religious and theological literature will appreciate the work, the mechanical execution of which they promise shall be in the best style. *Early orders are solicited.*

METHODIST BOOK STORE

AND

Sunday School Depository.

PERKINPINE & HIGGINS,

No. 56 North Fourth St., Philadelphia.

Have constantly on hand the Publications of the

METHODIST BOOK CONCERN

in large quantities, which they offer wholesale and retail at New York prices: together with an extensive collection of

THEOLOGICAL, HISTORICAL, SCIENTIFIC, AND MISCELLANEOUS BOOKS.

SABBATH-SCHOOL LIBRARIES, REWARDS, AND REQUISITES!

They would respectfully call attention to their large, varied, and select assortment of

BOOKS, CERTIFICATES, CARDS, PICTURES, ETC.,

calculated to make the Sabbath-school attractive and interesting.

THE MORAL AND RELIGIOUS CHARACTER OF EVERY BOOK IS GUARANTEED,

their miscellaneous selections being made with great care, and with special reference to adaptation to Methodist schools.

With hearty thanks to their numerous regular customers for past favors, they trust by careful and prompt attention, to merit the continuance of their patronage. Sabbath-school Committees and Superintendents will find it to their interest to call and examine for themselves, before purchasing elsewhere.

A BOOK FOR EVERY CHRISTIAN!!!

REMARKABLE PROVIDENCES,

ILLUSTRATING THE DIVINE GOVERNMENT,

Collected and arranged by Rev. S. HIGGINS and Rev. W. H. BRISBANE. With an Introductory Essay on Providence, by Rev. JOS. CASTLE, D.D. 12mo., 425 pp. Price $1.

Many a child of God will find in it needed consolation and guidance. It cannot fail to do much good.—*N. Y. Chris. Ad.*

The providences related show in the clearest light God's care over his people, and his terrible judgments against sin, and can scarcely fail to affect the heart, make a lasting impression on the memory, and exert a salutary influence over the life.—*Western Christian Advocate.*

The volume may be read with much profit.—*Cecil Democrat.*

It is the most intensely interesting book we ever read.—*Brownsville Times.*

No minister should be without it; the array of facts adduced to support the doctrine of a special Providence appears complete.—*Eastern Star.*

A highly interesting volume for the general reader; and especially interesting for youth.—*Cecil Whig.*

It will do much to correct the prevalent lukewarm notions about Providence. Here are soul-cheering facts.—*Baltimore Christian Advocate.*

The record of such providences confirms the view of God's special superintendence and care over all His creatures, given in His Word. His providences, like His other works, are wonderful.—*Christian Observer.*

Its illustrations should not fail to convince the reader that there is a God of Providence, and that the events of time are not the result of blind chance.—*Presbyterian.*

The contents of the volume are well selected and well arranged.—*Allentown Democrat.*

Buy it the first opportunity. It may be worth, under God, a thousand times its price to you.—*Rev. John F. Wright of Cincinnati Conference.*

Sent, post-paid, on receipt of retail price. A liberal discount to wholesale purchasers.

VALUABLE WORKS

RECENTLY ISSUED.

A Voice from the Pious Dead of the Medical Profession ;

Or, Memoirs of Eminent Physicians who have fallen asleep in Jesus; with a Preliminary Dissertation on the Cross as the Key to all Knowledge. By HENRY J. BROWN, A. M., M. D.   Price, 90 cts.

NOTICES.

From Thomas E. Bond, M. D., Editor Christian Advocate & Journal, New York. — * * * * We hail with joy the work before us. The author has done good service by showing examples of Christian belief and practice among the most eminent of the faculty, both in Europe and America. We especially recommend this work to our brethren of the Medical Profession. They will find, especially in the dissertations which precede the Memoirs, a fair exhibition of the peculiar difficulties which the study and practice of medicine and surgery present to the theory of Christianity; and are able and satisfactory solutions of these difficulties.

From G. C. M. Roberts, M.D., Baltimore. — After having carefully read the book, and re-read portions of it, with increased interest, I take great pleasure in returning you my sincere thanks for affording me the opportunity, through you, of commending it most earnestly to the community at large, and to the members of the Medical Profession in particular. At this particular juncture, when strenuous efforts are in progress for the purpose of elevating the standard of medical education throughout the land, this excellent Memoir of some among the most distinguished physicians, who have died in Christ, appears most opportunely. I trust you will be successful in placing a copy of it in the library of every medical man in our country; where it will not only prove the means of spiritual benefit to preceptors, but likewise to those who may be under their supervision.

From the Boston Medical & Surgical Journal. — This volume is written with a view "to refute a charge of incompatibility between the Christian religion and science, sometimes made by wicked and ignorant persons." It contains three short Dissertations on the subjects of The Cross in the Life-Union, The Cross in Nature, and The Cross in Medicine; which are followed by Memoirs of Wm. Hey, Dr. Hope, Dr. Good, Dr. Bateman, Dr. Godman, Dr. Gordon, Dr. Broughton, and Dr. Capadose. The Dissertations are intended "as an incentive to inquiry suggestive of a form." The Memoirs are interesting; and fully prove, what hardly requires proof, that there is nothing in science which tends to lessen men's faith in the Divine doctrines of the Christian Revelation, or deter them from fulfilling all its obligations. Dr. Brown's book will doubtless be read with interest by many who are not members of the profession, as well as by physicians.

From the Christian Observer, Philadelphia. — It affords us pleasure to call attention to this interesting volume. It contains an impressive argument for the truth and excellence of the Gospel, drawn from the lives of scientific men. It shows that faith in the teaching of the Scriptures is not merely a persuasion, but a power, stronger than the innate passions of our nature—a Divine power manifested in the development of all that is pure and lovely and of good report in real life. The memorials of these excellent men show conclusively, that science and religion are not, as a few sciolists have imagined, incompatible with each other. The Preliminary Dissertation is rich in thought, suggestive, adapted to awaken inquiry on the most important subject.

From the Western Christian Advocate, Cincinnati. — No book of a similar character is before the American public, and we trust it will find a good sale, not among physicians merely, but among all lovers of healthy, religious biography.

2

From the Pittsburg Christian Advocate.
—The narrative of the closing scenes in the life of Dr. Gordon, of Hull, is of itself worth double the price of the book. Medical men, whose time is necessarily engrossed with professional engagements, will appreciate the aim of the author in collecting and condensing more extended memoirs of their worthy brothers in similar toils; and when they would not take up a long and laboured production, they can find in this volume that which will refresh and strengthen in the midst of their unceasing labours. Ministers and others, who sometimes wish to testify their high appreciation of the faithful services of the physician, will recognise in this volume a testimonial which cannot but be regarded as beautiful, appropriate, and valuable.

From the Christian Chronicle, Philadelphia.—The object of these pages is to show that there is a harmony between religion and science. It is decidedly a religious book, abounding with the most useful lessons from the highest authority. The Dissertation that precedes is a valuable production, much enhancing the value of the work.

From the National Magazine. New York and Cincinnati.—We commend the volume to the general reader; while, in the language of the preface, "To medical men of every class, these Memoirs come with singular force, involving, as they do, the modes of thought, the associations, and the difficulties common to the medical profession. Their testimony is as the united voice of brethren of the same toils, proclaiming a heavenly rest to the weary pilgrim. It comes, too, unembarrassed with any considerations of interest, or mere purpose of sect or calling."

From Rev. J. F. Berg, D. D.—The selection of a number of Memoirs of Physicians eminent for their piety, who have adorned their profession in our own country and in other lands, as examples of the living power of piety, is itself a happy thought; and the primary Dissertation on the Cross as the Key to all Knowledge will suggest valuable reflections to the mind of the thoughtful reader. It is an able presentation of the great theme of the Cross of Christ as the foundation of all genuine science.

The Bible Defended against the Objections of Infidelity.

Being an Examination of the Scientific, Historical, Chronological, and other Scripture Difficulties. By Rev. Wm. H. BRISBANE. Price, 50 cts.

NOTICES.

From the Western Christian Advocate.— The work is on a plan somewhat original, and meets a want long felt by Sabbath School Teachers and Scholars, private Christians and others. We can most heartily commend the little manual to all seeking the truth as it is in the Gospel of Christ.

From the Christian Advocate & Journal. —The author, in the body of his work, commencing with the account of the Creation, as given in the book of Genesis, goes through the principal facts recorded in the Old and New Testaments, stating and answering the objections of infidelity cogently and logically, bringing to his aid the result of extensive reading and patient investigation. It is a small book,—so small that none will be deterred from reading it by its size; yet it condenses the most general objections to the Bible, with a clear statement of the refutation of them, by the best authors who have written on the subject.

From the National Magazine.—A small but good review of the chief infidel objections to the Bible has been published by Higgins & Perkinpine. It is by Rev. W. H. Brisbane, and examines the scientific, historical, chronological, and other difficulties alleged against the Scriptures. It is especially adapted to meet the wants of Sunday School and Bible Class Teachers.

From the Easton Star.—The title page indicates the character of this little volume, which has evidently been prepared with great care, by one who appears to have thoroughly investigated the subject, and whose researches well qualify him to elucidate the difficult questions reviewed. The style is chaste, perspicuous, and comprehensive, and the volume replete with original thoughts and pertinent quotations from the first biblical and scientific authors, to support the Divine authority of the Scriptures and refute the objections of sceptics. The book contains in a nut shell most of the points of difference be

34 *

tween infidels and Christians, and should be read by all who experience any difficulty in reconciling those texts of Scripture that are in apparent conflict. but which accord in beautiful harmony when explained by their contexts, and other subjects to which they relate. We take pleasure in commending it to those readers who have not the time to investigate heavier works, as a book that will amply repay a careful perusal.

Lectures on the Doctrine of Election.

By the Rev. A. C. RUTHERFORD, of Greenock, Scotland.

Price, 50 cts.

NOTICES

From the National Magazine.—These Lectures are remarkable for logical acuteness and sagacity, and a comprehensive knowledge of the subject. There is a strong spice of Scottish acerbity, too, in their style. Arminian polemics will receive this volume as among the ablest vindication of their views produced in modern times.

From Rev. Bishop Scott.—I have carefully read through your late publication, entitled "Lectures on the Doctrine of Election, by Alexander C. Rutherford, of Scotland," which you were kind enough to put into my hands. I am very much pleased with it. It is an admirable book. It refutes the Calvinistic theories on this subject with, I must think, unanswerable force of argument, and unfolds and exhibits the true Bible theory with clearness and power. And, unlike many controversial works, it is a very readable book. The author's style is so clear, so natural, so easy and flowing, and withal so animated and forcible, and his manner and illustrations so interesting and striking, that one is led on from page to page, and from chapter to chapter, not only without weariness, but with increasing interest. The spirit of the book, too, I think, is excellent, independent, frank, candid, affectionate, exhibiting a profound regard for the unadulterated teachings of the Bible, and a yearning love for souls. The author, indeed, sometimes uses harsh words, but almost only of theories and systems and dogmas—seldom, indeed, of persons. He treats his opponents with Christian courtesy, occasionally only rebuking them sharply, while he deals with a fearless and unsparing hand with their false and soul-destroying errors. This book ought to be sown broadcast over the land. I could wish that a copy of it should go into every family; especially at this time, when there seems a disposition in certain quarters to force on us again this wretched Calvinistic controversy.

From Zion's Herald.—The author of this work is a Scotch clergyman, who was formerly a Calvinist, but who, by honestly seeking the truth as revealed in God's Word, was led to embrace the more Scriptural tenets of the Arminian school. Having first spread his views before the religious public at Greenock and Glasgow, in a series of lectures delivered in 1847, he afterwards gave them to the world in form of a book, which is now, for the first time, reprinted in America. Bating some few inferior points of doctrine, we think the work to be a sound, strong, and vigorous expose of the Calvinistic theory. It is finely adapted for popular circulation; could it be scattered broadcast, it would doubtless aid in extirpating the stubborn errors of that theory from such portions of the community as are still afflicted by its presence.

The Sunday School Speaker;

Or, Exercises for Anniversaries and Celebrations: Consisting of Addresses, Dialogues, Recitations, Bible Class Lessons, Hymns, &c. Adapted to the various subjects to which Sabbath School Efforts are directed. By Rev. JOHN KENNADAY, D. D. Price, 38 cts.

The Minftrel of Zion.

A Book of Religious Songs, accompanied with Appropriate Music, Chiefly Original. By Rev. WILLIAM HUNTER and Rev. SAMUEL WAKEFIELD. Price, 38 cts.

Select Melodies.

Comprising the Best Hymns and Spiritual Songs in common use, and not generally found in standard Church Hymn Books; as also a number of Original Pieces, and Translations from the German. By Rev. WM. HUNTER. Price, 40 cts.

A Short Poem,

Containing a Descant on the Universal Plan. By JOHN PECK. *Multum in Parvo.* To which is added

Univerfalifm a very Ancient Doctrine;

With some Account of its Author. By LEMUEL HAYNES, A. M. Price, 6 cts.

The Calvinistic Doctrine of Predestination Examined and Refuted;

Being the substance of a series of Discourses delivered in St. George's Methodist Episcopal Church, Philadelphia, by FRANCIS HODGSON, D. D. Price, 35 cts.

Prophecy and the Times;

Or, England and Armageddon: an Application of the Predictions of Daniel and St. John to Current Events. By Rev. JOSEPH F. BERG, D. D

Abaddon and Mahanaim;

Or, Dæmons and Guardian Angels. By Rev. JOSEPH F. BERG, D. D.

A liberal discount made to wholesale purchasers.

5

JUL 18 1933

Check Out More Titles From HardPress Classics Series In this collection we are offering thousands of classic and hard to find books. This series spans a vast array of subjects – so you are bound to find something of interest to enjoy reading and learning about.

Subjects:
Architecture
Art
Biography & Autobiography
Body, Mind &Spirit
Children & Young Adult
Dramas
Education
Fiction
History
Language Arts & Disciplines
Law
Literary Collections
Music
Poetry
Psychology
Science
…and many more.

Visit us at www.hardpress.net

Im The Story

personalised classic books

"Beautiful gift.. lovely finish. My Niece loves it, so precious!"

Helen R Brumfieldon

⭐⭐⭐⭐⭐

UNIQUE GIFT

FOR KIDS, PARTNERS AND FRIENDS

Timeless books such as:

Kids

Alice in Wonderland • The Jungle Book • The Wonderful Wizard of Oz
Peter and Wendy • Robin Hood • The Prince and The Pauper
The Railway Children • Treasure Island • A Christmas Carol

Adults

Romeo and Juliet • Dracula

Highly Customizable **Change** Books Title **Replace** Characters Names with yours **Upload** Photo (For inside page) **Add** Inscriptions

Visit

Im The Story .com

and order yours today!